GERMAN SHEPHERD DOGS
AN OWNER'S COMPANION

Brian H. Wootton

The Crowood Press

First published in 1999 by
The Crowood Press Ltd
Ramsbury, Marlborough
Wiltshire SN8 2HR

British Library Cataloguing-in-Publication Data

A catalogue record for this book is available from the British
Library.

ISBN 1 86126 145 4

Picture Credits

Black and white photographs taken and/or supplied by:
Amos, page 8; Besterman, page 222; Coleridge, pages 104, 107;
Connolly, pages 123, 124, 126; Jones, page 85; Nye, pages 97, 98;
Oliver, pages 4, 37, 53, 56, 58, 115, 116, 119, 122, 125, 128, 133, 137,
139, 156, 161, 162, 165, 167, 212; Sale, pages 80, 86, 180, 189;
Stuttard, pages 22, 25, 26, 28, 36, 42; Sullivan, page 88; Swan,
pages 33, 39, 78, 79, 134, 142, 176, 183, 184, 185; Urma, pages 63,
144, 150, 153; Van Delden, page 214; Vawda, page 111; Vera,
page 146;

Line-drawings by Annette Findlay, except those on pages 46, 57,
59, 60, 61, 64 and 65, which are by the author.

Edited and designed by OutHouse Publishing Services

Printed and bound in Great Britain

Contents

Int. Ch. Rosehurst Chris.

1

History of the Breed

German Origins

As the evening light faded on a summer's day in July 1898, a writer bent over his desk in the growing illumination of an oil-lamp. So deep was his concentration and so quiet the atmosphere in the wood-panelled study of his newly built house in Grafrath, Upper Bavaria, that the man could be forgiven for not noticing the dark grey, wolf-like dog lying at his feet and the attentive way in which the dog's pricked ears responded to the scratching of his pen upon the paper.

The man was Max Friedrich Emil von Stephanitz. Two years earlier he had left military service, in which his work as a cavalry officer

Captain Max von Stephanitz, first president of the SV and architect of the breed.

had developed his already strong interest in animals. He had found time, too, to continue his study of science and particularly those ideas relating to animal breeding. While on manoeuvres with his regiment near Cologne, he had witnessed a shepherd working two dogs with a large flock of sheep. Deeply impressed by the dogs' initiative and intelligence, he knew what he wanted to do when he re-entered civilian life: build a house, marry, and begin breeding German Shepherd Dogs. He had wasted no time in fulfilling all three intentions. He purchased his first German Shepherd for 163 German marks from an unknown shepherd from Hanau, on the river Main. The first pages of the book in which he was writing on that July evening contained details of her appearance and that of her offspring. With typical German thoroughness, von Stephanitz had determined to record such information in a kennel book which would enable him to review his progress in breeding. He named the bitch Freya von Grafrath, the first German Shepherd to carry his kennel name. He had written: 'Colour and markings: brown, tan, short-coated, 52cm tall, head too heavy. Ears tipped and usually carried flat. Weight 23 kg. Pedigree unknown.' His kennel book would go on to record the following about Freya's offspring:

> Ears did not go erect, head too heavy, occasionally one ear would go up beautifully but mostly they flattened loosely. Construction, coat and colour good. Small ears but not erect; ears vary in size and position, not raised. Head rather lacking in expression. Tails are inclined to be curly. Dog 61cm. Bitch 53cm. Dog 59cm. Bitch 58cm.

Horand von Grafrath S.Z.1 (Stud Book No. 1), 'the Adam of the breed'.

Poor Freya had obviously failed to produce two of the essential features von Stephanitz was aiming to perpetuate: erect, wolf-like ear carriage and a low tail carriage. That July evening's entry was to record details of Schwabenmädle, another bitch he had purchased:

> Grey, brown with tan markings; put ears up at 3½ months. Good construction, coat and general appearance. Tail rather too long with tendency to curl (all pups from Freya and Schwabenmädle had curled tails). Beautiful head. Height 52cm, length 58cm. Sire: Fritz von Schwenningen. Dam: Fides von Neckarsprung.

But the entry in the book which gave him most satisfaction was the one giving details of the grey dog that lay watching him as he wrote. He had bought the male on 15 January 1898 from Herr Eiselen from Heidenheim. Bred by Herr Sparwasser from Frankfurt-Sachsenhausen, he had been shown by Eiselen in 1897 at Würzburg, where he won first prize in the open class for sheep dogs, and at Baden-Baden where he was also placed first. Since purchasing him for 222 marks, von Stephanitz had shown him at Stuttgart, where he was the class winner, and at Munich, where he was awarded a special prize for the best German Shepherd Dog in the show. The kennel book entry read 'tawny grey with tan markings. Ears 13cm long. Good in all parts. Height 60/61cm, length 66/67cm. Weight at beginning of 1898 25kg.'

The dog's name was Hektor Linksrhein but Stephanitz renamed him Horand von Grafrath, a name destined to stamp itself upon the annals of the breed for all time. On that summer's evening in the darkening study the man could have had no idea that both he and Horand would play an indispensable part in the creation of the world's most popular breed: the German Shepherd Dog.

While von Stephanitz had been serving his country in the army, the world of dog-breeding in Germany was undergoing rapid development. Influenced by the pattern of affairs in England, breeders began to organize shows for *Luxushunden* or fancy dogs. In 1891 breed clubs were established for several breeds, standards defining a breed's essential characteristics were finalized, and the first illustrated breed books for Dachshunds and Griffons were published. But agreement about what constituted a typical German Shepherd Dog was not easy. Classes for sheep dogs were held at shows but the exhibits were, as often as not, of unknown parentage and, as early photographs show, bore little resemblance to the German Shepherd as we know it today.

A 17th-century wall tapestry in the German castle of Burg Elz,
showing white Shepherd Dog type.

At the end of 1891 a fancier named Max Riechelmann and his associate Klaus Graf Hahn, a Dachshund breeder, founded the Phylax
Society for the breeding of German Shepherd Dogs, but it existed for a
mere five years before fading into oblivion. The flag of the Shepherd
Dog had been kept flying by Riechelmann's dog Phylax von Eulau,
who was shown with considerable, if controversial, success from 1895
to 1897. Controversial, because there was no consensus among
Shepherd enthusiasts that Phylax was the type that embodied the
ideal German Shepherd. At an all-breeds show at Munich in
September 1895 Phylax competed against working sheep dogs from
the Württemberg area of southern Germany. The judge Herr Kull,
himself from the south, was impressed by the sheep dogs, giving
Pollux von Hanau first prize because of his 'pronounced Shepherd
type'. Of Phylax, however, he wrote:

> I could hardly believe that he had won first prize at Apolda, Berlin,
> Efort and Dresden. I regard him as an impressive, beautiful, pure-
> wolf-coloured, long-legged, short-backed very big wolf-cross who,
> with his wild expression, stiff movement and undomesticated
> demeanour would be ten times more suitable to a zoo than working
> usefully behind a flock of sheep.

Clearly some breeders were not averse to introducing wolf blood to attain the features they wanted in a German Shepherd, but these were the 'fancy dog' breeders, interested only in external appearance, and not in the dog's capacity to work. Those who espoused the cause of the genuine sheep-herding dog were highly critical of Phylax, and when he won the supreme prize for the best Luxushund in the show for all breeds at Leipzig in 1897, it served only to highlight his role as a mere show dog with none of the genuine Shepherd Dog qualities. Doubtless von Stephanitz would have been an avid reader of the only magazine devoted to dogs in his day, *Hundesport und Jagd*. In the year he left the army, the paper printed pictures of what it regarded as useful representatives of German Shepherd Dogs: 'Carex' and 'Mores'-Plieningen', Sparwasser's 'Lux' and 'Pluto', 'Fritz von Schwenningen', Fides von Neckarsprung', and a show dog called 'Leo von Habsburg', bred in Basle, Switzerland and a first prize winner there and in Mailand. Leo's tipped ears had been cropped to make them erect but he was to be described by von Otto, who gave him second prize at Heidelberg, as 'the first international German Shepherd Dog'. Significantly, on the opposite page, Phylax von Eulau appeared as a representative of the type that was not desirable. His detractors had already spread rumours that Borzois, Russian wolf-hunting dogs, had reacted fiercely when he had passed their benches at a show in Dresden. His skull, too, they claimed, resembled that of a wolf.

Von Stephanitz began breeding, then, at a time when there was a pressing need for agreement about the way forward. In purchasing Horand he bought a dog that, as far as external appearance was concerned, already fulfilled the aspirations of those trying to define their

Smooth-coated Shepherd Dog (Germany, 1880).

9

ideal German Shepherd. Much later, in his famous book *The German Shepherd Dog in Word and Picture* (1923), he wrote, 'for the Luxushund enthusiasts of that time Horand embodied the fulfilment of their fondest dreams'. The image of a medium-sized, strong dog with a natural, unspoiled, distinctively wolf-like appearance was not von Stephanitz's concept. It existed in the minds of enthusiasts before his involvement with the breed. But von Stephanitz's greatest contribution to the breed's development was to provide a controlled and directing influence upon early breeding programmes and to insist that the breed's original working ability must be maintained at all costs. Breeding for external features such as ear and tail carriage, coat and heads was essential if a standard type was to be perpetuated, but never at the expense of Shepherd character. Like most young men of his class and military background in a recently united Germany, von Stephanitz was a staunch patriot. The fact that the English Collie was so popular as a show dog must have been something of a reproach. He had doubtless heard stories of the efforts to use imported collies to herd sheep and of how ineffectual they had been – they had little idea of running up and down the furrow all day to keep sheep from unfenced crops, and they lacked the courage to confront a hungry flock determined to graze on some forbidden strip. Some dogs had even been trampled underfoot. He and men of like mind would strive to fashion a national breed, the German Shepherd Dog, which would undoubtedly be strikingly handsome but which, first and foremost, would be a sheep dog.

In the spring of 1899 *Hundesport und Jagd* advertised the forthcoming all-breeds show to be held at Karlsruhe in April. A notice printed in the same edition announced the intention of forming a new society for the German Shepherd at the show. Von Stephanitz had already engaged in enthusiastic contact with other fanciers and had intimated he would be prepared to take up office in any new club. He entered Horand and Schwabenmädle at the show where both won first prizes, Horand being declared best German Shepherd Dog. The group of enthusiasts met and the Verein für Deutsche Schäferhunde (German Shepherd Dog Club), known throughout the world as the SV, was founded on 22 April 1899. Arthur Meyer from Stuttgart had been largely instrumental in promoting the idea and he undertook the role of secretary and administrator of the first stud book, in which dogs declared useful for breeding were officially registered. Von Stephanitz had already inspired groups of working shepherd men with his theoretical knowledge of breeding and they readily proposed and accepted him as the society's first president. His beloved Horand was to be the first dog officially registered as a German Shepherd by the society. 'Horand von Grafrath S.Z.1 (Stud Book No. 1)' became on that day the Adam of the breed, from whom all future pure-bred German Shepherds would trace their descent. The founding members of the society included Berlin architect A. Besser, local mayor Herr Barth, the hotel-owner Eiselen (Horand's previous owner), two factory-owners from Switzerland and Austria called Fehr and Kammerer, a hotel-owner called Schlenker, a lawyer named Ohler, and three shepherd men Arnold Ristell, Gaumann and Weber. They unanimously submitted to the authority of von Stephanitz, the once Prussian cavalry captain, and his single-mindedness and discipline directed the society's affairs from the beginning.

Von Stephanitz had purchased the bitch Marie von der Krone, winner of the first prize at a Munich show the year before. She was descended from southern working dogs. He mated her to Horand, thus beginning his breeding programme based on combining the wiry, athletic, spirited, and distinctively prick-eared dogs from Thüringia, with the larger, working animals from Württemberg in the south. The aim was to shape a breed combining the best qualities of both. At the outset the society insisted there must be only one type: that laid down in the Standard for the breed formulated by the society's executive committee and published in *Hundesport* in August 1899. It was necessary to be insistent, for there were still those who preferred one type to the other. Herr Ruth of Wandsbek, owner of a well-known, winning Horand son, Baron von der Krone, wrote a pamphlet entitled 'An address to all interested parties' in which he argued for the official recognition of two types: the Thüringian, with his rather wolf-like appearance, firm erect ears, curled tail and dew-claws, and the larger Württemberger dog, with his beautifully carried tail, hanging ears, large tough pads and strong feet that never went lame on rough terrain. He went on to describe the difference in character of the two types:

> While the Thüringian strikes one with his cunning wolf-like expression and beautiful head, the other is distinguished by his powerful majestic appearance with a shrewd, more good-natured expression, and a cool reserve that warrants respect. The Thüringian is easily provoked and will bite at the slightest opportunity while the Württemberger is more discriminating and will only bite when it is necessary but then with conviction and without apology.

11

The suggestion of recognizing two types was immediately rejected by the SV committee. Arthur Meyer, stud book director, was particularly resistant to special pleading for the so-called Thüringian. In *Hundesport und Jagd* No. 35, he wrote:

>...this Thüringian type – in short, any sheep dog that resembles a wolf – must be ruthlessly eradicated. If there are people who choose to have wolf-dogs or crosses as pets, then they should be given exactly what they want but such animals must never be described as German Shepherd Dogs.

The term 'Luxushund', in general use for all breeds apart from hunting dogs, should be frowned upon to describe the new breed. Priority in breeding had to be given to head and expression, strength and nobility of character rather than external cosmetic features. Thus by the end of 1899 the foundations of the breed had been firmly established.

Horand was to produce fifty-three litters in von Stephanitz's ownership and much inbreeding on him took place. The captain even mated Horand to Horand's own daughter, Grete von Grafrath. Significantly, however, von Stephanitz always balanced the inbreeding on Horand with lines from the working sheep dogs of Württemberg. Regarding the bitches used for breeding, it is interesting to note that Godrun Mari, Lotte von Klostermansfeld, Hascherl, Bissola, Mira, Eva, and Greta all descended from unknown sheepherding dogs. In February 1902, fearing that there was developing too high a concentration of Horand blood, von Stephanitz purchased Audifax von Grafrath, a male bred from two generations of working dogs. Audifax himself carried the sheep-herding qualification H.G.H (working sheep dog) and was the 368th German Shepherd to be registered since Horand. He was shown at Salzburg and Worms in November 1902 and at Berlin and Fürth in the following year, winning first prize on each occasion. When Audifax died in 1906 the Captain bought back his litter-brother, Adalo, to continue his programme of line-breeding to Horand with strong, unrelated working lines as an outcross.

But Horand's greatest success as a sire was destined to occur in hands other than the captain's. He was mated to a Württemberg herding bitch, 'Mores Plieningen', and produced Hektor von Schwaben, who was Sieger (Grand Champion) at the SV speciality show in 1900 and 1901. Another son, Peter von Pritschen, won the title in 1902.

Hektor was mated to his half-sister Thekla I von der Krone and this resulted in the influential dog Beowulf, who was closely inbred to Horand. Registered under Arthur Meyer's prefix as Beowulf-Sonnenberg 1, Beowulf was soon to prove a prepotent stud force, being widely used in the Württemberg area of the country. He was a dark-grey brindle with an excellent character, living as a house-dog, not in a kennel; and, according to Ernst von Otto, one of the earliest chroniclers of the breed's development, he should rightly be regarded as 'the originator of the present day Shepherd dog'. He produced very many good bitches that were successfully to perpetuate a desired type.

A Beowulf grandson, the all-black Roland von Starkenburg, gained the Sieger title in 1906–7. He was the product of a half-brother to half-sister mating, both sire and dam sharing the same mother, Lucie von Starkenburg, a daughter of Horand's grandsire, Pollux. In addition he was line-bred to Horand himself. In subsequent years early German breeders were to concentrate Roland blood through intensive line-breeding especially through descendants of the 1909 Sieger Hettel Uckermark. Soon warning voices were raised about the increasing size of the breed. The judge's comments on Hettel when he was made Sieger in Hamburg read 'Hettel reaches the limits allowable in size and heaviness of bone for an effortlessly moving working dog'. The conflict between show-breeders who want a big, impressive German Shepherd and the working fraternity who demand a more utilitarian animal within the parameters of the size set down in the Standard, existed then as it exists today.

The Kriminalpolizei kennel achieved considerable success with large dogs in the show ring. Tell von der Kriminalpolizei took the

Beowulf (1899).

13

Sieger title in 1910 and the bitch Hella won the Siegerin (Bitch Champion) title in 1911 and 1912 while Gisa became Austrian Siegerin. A study of the breeding of these dogs shows how concentrated the blood of Horand was. Gisa was the dam of the famous Nores von der Kriminalpolizei, a widely used sire of his time producing 180 litters and 877 progeny. A very tall, imposing, silver-sable dog, Nores was much admired by the show fraternity and was subsequently sold to America, where interest in the new breed was developing rapidly. Probably most German breeders would not regret Nores' departure for the New World: his genetic legacy had not been positive. Oversize, colour paling, incorrect proportion, short tails and questionable temperaments were all attributed to Nores, whether with justification or not.

In the first twenty years of its existence the breed enjoyed rapidly rising popularity. In 1919 thirty-eight shows were held for the breed in Germany with a total entry of 2,410 dogs. In 1920 this was to show a dramatic increase to eighty-one shows and 7,414 entries. The show craze seemed unstoppable and much breeding was done from

Nores von der Kriminalpolizei (1915).

14

unsuitable animals. Germany had experienced four years of war, with its deprivations and turbulence. The most resilient of the breed had found themselves in service with the military, carrying messages or medical supplies across the battlefield. Many litters had been poorly reared at a time of national shortages. At the end of the war, the SV realized the importance of more rigorous control of breeding activities if the German Shepherd was not to fall prey to those who cared little for its future. In 1921, in the town of Halle, von Stephanitz assembled a body of men who were to become the first breed survey-ors. In various pre-selected towns and villages, breeders would bring their dogs to be assessed and the information about their construc-tion, movement, height, weight and character as well as recommendations for breeding would be published in an annual sur-vey book. The aim was to select animals suitable for breeding and discourage the use of inferior dogs. The system has survived into the present day and is an indispensable part of German Shepherd breed-ing, not only in the dog's homeland but in many other countries in Europe and beyond.

The early years of the survey system enabled von Stephanitz to gauge more accurately how the German Shepherd was developing. It became clear that many dogs were too big and leggy and even the best of them, such as the Siegers Erich von Grafenwerth (1920), Harras von dem Jüch (1921), Cito von Bergerslust (1922 and 1923) and Donar von Overstolzen (1924), were showing a departure from the medium-sized German Shepherd of the Standard. At the Frankfurt Sieger Show in 1925 Stephanitz decided he must indicate a new direction. The previ-ous year's Sieger, Donar, a practically all-black dog measuring 27 inches (67cm), was relegated to fourth position, while at the head of the class was a small, dark-grey dog just 24 inches (60cm) high, a veri-table pygmy amongst the giants. This was Klodo von Boxberg, who had been Czechoslovakian Sieger in 1923. He was to set in motion the process towards a deeper-bodied, lower-stationed German Shepherd. The crowning of Klodo was a watershed in the breed's development, fashioning what would be recognized as a more 'modern' type. Klodo proved an excellent sire, siring the show star Erich von Glockenbrink (who won the Sieger titles in Germany, Austria and Holland in 1926 and the German title again in 1928), and the famous Utz vom Haus Schütting, Sieger in 1929. Though both were sired by Klodo, it was Utz that von Stephanitz preferred. He was the dog who would perpetuate the smaller, more angulated type demonstrated by Klodo. Dr Werner Funk, later president of the SV and owner of the influential vom Haus

15

Donar von Overstolzen, Sieger 1924.

Schütting kennel, was to practise intensive line-breeding to Utz, producing many important winning animals of the time. Utz, like most of the top show dogs of the time, was exported to the United States, leaving behind him an influence not entirely for good. Both von Stephanitz and Dr Funk were forced to defend him against those who blamed him for a host of faults such as whites, missing teeth and poor temperament. And there were still many breeders whose eyes could not get accustomed to the lower, longer type that Utz embodied. In his foreword to the report of the 1930 Sieger Show in Wiesbaden, von Stephanitz wrote:

> We have in Utz and Erich two significantly differing German Shepherds as far as external appearance is concerned. That both dogs could become Sieger under the same judge is neither here nor there; in the ring one has to put up the best present. If Utz and Erich had been presented in competition together before me, I would certainly have preferred Utz, as the one who embodied my idea of a working dog.

The emphasis on working ability is evident. The fashionable, tall, over-elegant type that had dominated the 1920s was to be replaced by a dog that embodied von Stephanitz's dictum that to breed German Shepherd Dogs was to breed working dogs. Much intensive line-breeding to Utz was to be practised in the 1930s and inevitably the genetic failings in his make-up would surface. The recurring conflicts between the 'show' fraternity and those committed to the working dog were evident in calls by some breeders to develop alternative bloodlines from old herding lines. It became more and more common to read advertisements for German Shepherds free from Utz blood. Nevertheless, Utz had stamped his influence indelibly upon the breed, not only in Germany but abroad. Like Erich and Klodo before him, in 1929 he was sold to the United States where the breed had experienced a phenomenal growth in popularity during the 1920s. Perhaps the greatest sire the breed has known in that country, Pfeffer von Bern, imported from Germany in 1936 and the producer of hundreds of champions and winning dogs, was line-bred to Utz. The other great show dog of that time was Odin von Busecker Schloss, who also carried Utz blood. British breeding, too, was to be shaped by the influence of Utz's son Voss von Bern, imported by Gwen Barrington of the famous Brittas kennel. But before we look at the development of the breed in Britain in recent years, a look back at its early establishment there is called for.

Early Establishment in Britain

On the evening of 12 October 1917, local police descended upon a country cottage near St Ives in Cornwall, searched it thoroughly and issued orders expelling the residents from the county. Their offence? They had entertained themselves by singing Hebridean folk songs in Gaelic which local people had taken to be German. Besides, one of the residents was herself German, wife of the famous novelist D. H. Lawrence. Both were ostracized by local people and compelled to leave – such was the strength of anti-German feeling during and immediately after the First World War. However, serving British Army officers had witnessed at first hand, and admired, the courage and fidelity of dogs used by the enemy in trench warfare, and their admiration was not at all diminished by the fact that the breed was of German origin. They had seen dogs move across the battlefield, in the face of fearful explosions and fire, carrying medical supplies for

17

the wounded strapped to their backs, or running with communications cables to facilitate contact across the trenches. It is impossible to say how many lives were saved or how much suffering was alleviated by the work of such dogs. The war left many blinded, and the same German Shepherd Dog that had shared the horrors of warfare was later trained to guide the sightless in Germany, America and subsequently in the UK.

On returning from the war, however, the army officers and others who wanted to establish the breed in Britain could not be indifferent to anti-German sentiment. They realized that the name German Shepherd would be an obstacle to its acceptance by both the Kennel Club and the general public. So the Alsatian Wolf-dog Club was formed, and officially recognized on 6 August 1919. Its founder members included Colonel Moore-Brabazon and Major James Baldwin, whose famous 'Picardy' kennel was founded in 1917, together with Mrs Thornton (of the Southdown prefix) and Mr H. Robbins. The name Alsatian Wolf-dog, which deliberately obscured

Eng. Ch. Teut von Haff (1924). Owner, Rex Walker.

the breed's German origin, was chosen because serving soldiers had seen the breed in the disputed territory of Alsace-Lorraine, and because the distinctive appearance of the breed and its natural unfawning nobility led to its association with the wolf. Soon, however, the term 'Wolf-dog' was dropped. It had created a negative impression of the breed in the public mind and provided its detractors with dubious grounds for attacking it as savage and unreliable. In 1924 the Wolf-dog Club and the Alsatian League amalgamated to form the Alsatian League and Club of Great Britain, now the GSD League of Great Britain. In 1920 the Kennel Club awarded Challenge Certificates at championship shows for the breed, which meant that 'Alsatians' could now become show champions. On 23 June 1920 Southwold Wisdom became the first British champion male and at the same show the bitch, Fearless of Mattesdon, was crowned with her title. How appropriate that their names should emphasize the breed's essential qualities: sagacity and courage.

The 1920s saw a rapid increase in the breed's popularity so that by 1926 it had risen to top position in the list of Kennel Club registrations with over 8,000 dogs recorded. Many Shepherds were imported from Germany at that time. Of the 104 dogs winning Challenge Certificates during the decade, no fewer than fifty-one came from abroad. But it was a home-bred dog who became the first top show dog of the time. Ch. Allahson of If won his first CC at Crufts in 1922, going on to collect twelve more. He was a popular stud-dog, siring six champions. Allahson was a flashy, well-coated black and bright-fawn dog who must have stood out amongst the prevailing rather drab, short-coated dogs of the time. His success in the ring was soon to be eclipsed by Ch. Caro of Welham, who had been bred in Germany and registered under the name of Caro von Blasienberg. Caro won a total of twenty-two Challenge Certificates, equalling the record held by the top dog of the period, Ch. Cillahson of Picardy. The Welham kennel, owned by F. N. Pickett, was an important one during these years, if only because its owner was an active and contentious apologist for the tall, leggy Shepherds that were going out of favour in Germany. He imported Donar von Overstolzen in 1926 after the dog had won the Sieger title in Germany, Czechoslovakia, France, Belgium and Holland and became the USA Grand Victor in the year of his importation. In 1925 Donar had been relegated to fourth place in the Open Dog class at the German Sieger Show when von Stephanitz deliberately chose Klodo von Boxberg for the title.

Head study of Klodo von Boxberg, Sieger 1925.

The scope of this book does not allow reference to all the important dogs of this time. They are, after all, of historical importance only, being many generations away from the German Shepherds we keep and breed from today. Anyone absorbed in the study of past animals could do no better than refer to the books of Dr Malcolm Willis, which are full of historical detail. Nevertheless, no review of the pre-war development of the breed would be satisfactory without reference to outstanding figures such as Major Baldwin of the Picardy kennel, already mentioned as a founder member of the first club for the breed. The kennel distinguished itself in the early 1930s through the success of its 'J' litter. Janitor, Jade and Jocose all gained Champion titles whilst Jasmine became an Irish champion. Their dam, Beda von Anderton of Picardy, was a daughter of Utz von Haus Schutting. Benign of Picardy is still the only British-bred German Shepherd to hold the titles of Working Trials Champion and Show Champion.

Miss Jean Workman of Hayling Island achieved renown with her Ceara kennel. A personal friend of Herta von Stephanitz, the

20

Utz vom Haus Schütting (1920).

Ch. Donna vom Allerheiligentor (1929), left, carrying the lost brindle colouring. Owners Mrs and Miss Workman.

captain's daughter, Miss Workman imported several excellent dogs from Germany and was a keen enthusiast of the working German Shepherd. In 1927 she imported Armin Ernaslieb who carried the German working qualification P.H. (Polizei Hund). Miss Workman also bred successfully from the bitch Ch. Seffe von Blasienberg, a daughter of Caro of Welham. She was the dam of champions Ansa, Karin and Dolf. Armin's most influential son was Ch. Adalo of Ceara who was the sire of seventeen CC-winning progeny, including the outstanding show dog Ch. Roland of Coulmony who was awarded thirty CCs and twenty reserve CCs.

The impact of Utz vom Haus Schütting, however, was to be particularly marked through the influence of his son, Voss von Bern, litter-brother to Vikki von Bern, an outstanding brood-bitch in Germany and grandmother of the 1937 Sieger, Pfeffer von Bern, who was destined to shape the development of the breed in the United States. Voss qualified as a working sheep dog in his homeland before being bought by Mrs Gwen Barrington to live on her farm in

Int. Ch. Gerolf of Brittas (1936), the most widely used sire of the 1930s.

Co. Meath, Ireland. He regularly worked with cattle and gained British Working Trials qualifications for protection work and tracking. Mrs Barrington founded her world-famous Brittas kennels upon Voss and his offspring. In the years after the Second World War there were few German Shepherds that did not have the name 'Brittas' somewhere in their pedigrees. In 1934 the grey sable bitch, Daga, was the first Brittas animal to gain a title, establishing a line of sables that was to produce many excellent German Shepherds both immediately before and after the war. The Voss son, Gerolf, was the first dog in the breed's history to gain titles in Ireland and Britain, qualifying as an International Champion. Mrs Barrington was to breed twenty champions in all, of whom twelve were to carry the International title. Gerolf was the most-used sire of the 1930s and laid the foundation for the development of the breed in Britain after the war. It is difficult to see how Mrs Barrington's achievements will ever be equalled, let alone surpassed.

Other important prefixes of the 1930s were Southdown, Charavigne and Silverlands, all of whom produced champion German Shepherds.

The rapid rise in the breed's popularity that had characterized the 1920s was to be followed by an equally rapid decline. Over 8,000 German Shepherds were registered with the Kennel Club in 1927 and the number slumped to a mere 1,308 in 1939. Whether the breed was paying the penalty for over-commercialization and irresponsible breeding is hard to say. Certainly the media's tendency to highlight every negative incident involving the breed did not help. Nevertheless, 1934 saw the establishment of the Guide Dogs for the Blind, pioneered by Captain N. Liakhoff, first at Wallaway and then at Leamington Spa. In the same year Frank Riego, a local cinema proprietor, founded the Birmingham and District Alsatian Club, which became the Midland Alsatian Association in 1936. The Association encouraged the 'man-in-the-street' to train his German Shepherd and gave considerable impetus to the growing popularity of obedience training as an absorbing leisure activity. In 1946 the club's successful growth encouraged it to claim national status and it was recognized as the British Alsatian Association. Now known as the British Association for German Shepherd Dogs, it has training branches throughout the country. There is no doubt that the public reputation of the breed was considerably enhanced by the work of the Association's branches. Many a devotee of the breed was first smitten while watching demonstrations by club teams at village fêtes and carnivals where the breed's intelligence and trainability were displayed. Mr Riego directed affairs with a fierce

23

commitment to the breed's welfare, and remained chairman of the Association until he died.. He was particularly proud of the club's annual championship show, where visiting judges from abroad usually officiated. The show enjoyed much civic prestige in Birmingham; the local mayor usually attended with other dignitaries whose goodwill Mr Riego usefully cultivated. He persuaded Pathé News to film the show before the days of TV; cinema audiences throughout the country saw pictures of the event in July 1954 where Int. Ch. and Obed. Ch. Danki of Glenvoca won Best in Show. Among the crowd was a teenage boy who stared in awe at the great dog, and began a long involvement with the breed which culminated in the writing of this book.

The Post-war Years

The foundations laid by Gwen Barrington and her Brittas dogs proved a solid basis for breed development during these years. The first two British post-war champions, Yvo of Ravenscar and Karaste Karenina av Hvitsand, were sired by champions Gerolf and Orest of Brittas. Karenina was to prove the foundation of the famous Vikkas av Huitsand kennels, owned by Percy and Nem Elliot. From her came Ch. Vikkas Delsa av Hvitsand who in turn produced Ch. Vikkas Donna av Hvitsand.

But while Delsa was by a Brittas sire, Ch. Vagabond, Donna was sired by a young dog of different breeding destined to become the most influential sire of the post-war period. Ch. Avon Prince of Alumvale gained his title in 1950 and went on to win twenty-eight CCs, taking Best of Breed at championship shows on no fewer than twenty-two occasions. He was the first German Shepherd Dog to win Best in Show All Breeds at a general championship show at Blackpool. Widely used at stud, he produced seventeen champions, most of whom were immediately recognizable as his offspring. Avon Prince had great charisma and ring presence. Mr Carver, his breeder and owner, was a showman himself. One flick of a long show lead and Avon Prince would assume a dramatic pose, head held alert and high on an elegant neck, with sweeping hindquarters stretched behind him, a long tail brushing the ground. Carver would stand apart, allowing this dream of a show dog to draw all eyes to him. Then, at a signal, off he would move, gaiting around the ring with great rhythm and fluency on a loose lead. Avon Prince initiated the craze for

24

Ch. Avon Prince of Alumvale (1950), an outstanding show dog and sire of his time.

extreme hind-angulation which was often to be taken to excess by some breeders in subsequent years. Most of the winning kennels of the time owed their success to Avon Prince and his progeny.

In 1947 Major Scott, who had served in the British Army in northern Germany imported a very dark, masculine dog who also played a very important part in breeding at this time. Ch. Danko von Menkenmoor of Hardwick won his title in 1949 and gained ten CCs. He sired 192 litters and thirteen champions. Many winning dogs in subsequent years were the outcome of a combination of Avon Prince and Danko lines. Interestingly, though of completely differing type and general appearance, both dogs were related to each other, being descendants of the top German sire, Ingo von Piastendamm. Perhaps this in part explains the success of such a combination.

Danko's first champion offspring were the bitches Anna Karenina Vitalis and her litter-sister Vitalis Amazon, together with the jet-black Sabre Sectetainerie. The latter was subsequently mated to Danko's first champion son, the dark bi-colour Dual Ch. Terrie of

25

Glenvoca. The result of this half-brother to half-sister mating was Triple Ch. Dankie of Glenvoca C.D. Both were bred, owned and trained by George Crook, a natural trainer whose record in breeding two champions in work and showing is unlikely to be matched. The Johnsons' Combehill kennel produced two fine champion sisters from Danko in Grizel and Gitana, while George Woods of the long-established and successful Novem kennel owned Ch. Rhiot of Rhosincourt who won the CC at Crufts, beating the famous Avon Prince into the Reserve spot. Other Danko champions were Cip of Lynrowe, Southdown Nireus, Lodo of Bucklebury, Dora of Eveley, Cimlan Plainsman and Marquita of Eveley, the last a very good bitch and dam of Ch. Ulele of Silverlands, an outstanding mover who won a CC at ten years of age.

The 1950s saw the emergence of May Tidbold's famous Eveley kennel, which was to prove highly successful over the next decades. Mrs Tidbold's dogs were always very flashy and colourful and immediately caught the eye in the show ring. Avon Prince's first champion, Invader, was Eveley bred and was later sold to the States where he gained his title. A litter-sister, Iona, was also crowned. The Birmingham-based Byenroc kennel also struck gold with Avon Prince, producing the litter-brother and -sister, champions Ransome and Rebecca, the latter inheriting her sire's impressive movement. Nelly Barker, breeder and owner of the outstanding bitch Int. Ch. Fidala of Cranville, holder of the record for bitch CCs (nineteen) from 1947 until 1969, bred the excellent Querida of Cranville. The Aaron's Aronbel prefix was to make itself well known through the achievements of the Avon Prince son, Yokel, whose son Ch. Allegro of Seacroft was to sire Ch. Sparky of Aronbel, line-bred to Avon Prince

Ch. Danko von Menkenmoor of Hardwick (1949), the first influential post-war import.

26

and three times Best of Breed at Crufts. That great enthusiast Marie O'Grady bred the beautiful bitch Chiquita of Kelowna, and her litter-brother Vaqueel, from a mating of Avon Prince to Helium of Kelowna. Marie owned and handled Chiquita to her breed title and Vaqueel to his Obedience Champion title – a remarkable achievement.

The Mason brothers, whose Shralycar kennel was based in the Potteries region of North Staffordshire, bred the sisters, Duchess, Diane and Fiona, three very typical Avon Prince champions. From the same area emerged Avon Prince's top-winning son, Celebrity of Jackfield, who was out of a Danko daughter. Celebrity won an impressive total of twenty-one CCs during his long show career and was admired by foreign judges as well as British experts for his masculinity, correct proportions, and stolid temperament. He had none of the showy exaggerations of his sire but showed with less panache and enthusiasm. He was the grandsire of the excellent Ch. Shootersway Persephone who won a CC under Dr Funk, the then President of the SV, and who was bred by Roy and Clarissa Allen out of their foundation bitch Lucretia, who was from Dorothy Beach's Stranmillis kennel. The Allens went on to produce a further five champions carrying the Shootersway prefix. But Celebrity was not a significant sire and the Avon Prince influence was to be perpetuated through other offspring, notably his daughters, Eveley's Happy and Hella of Charavigne and Vikkas Alda av Hvitsand.

Hella of Charavigne, mated to the import Cent zu deri Fünf Giebeln, produced Ch. Ludwig of Charavigne who inherited his sire's brilliant rich red-tan colouring and the showy deportment of his dam. He gained his title in 1964 and, in the hands of Shirley and Edwin White of the famous Hendrawen prefix, he was widely used at stud. By the time he died in 1972 he had sired 395 litters, from which emerged twenty champions, most of whom carried his striking colour and glamour. Ludwig's influence was to persist throughout the 1970s through his grandson Hendrawen's Charade of Charavigne, a popular sire who produced the famous 'E' litter for Mary Tidbold from which three, Eclipse, Efne and Enchantment, all became champions. Eclipse carried no fewer than ten lines back to Ch. Avon Prince, and sired five champions himself.

Brian and Dorothy Lindsay's Brinton kennel came to the fore in the late 1950s and achieved consistent success in the show ring. With Hella's sister, Happy, they bred Ch. Vasko of Brinton and Vanity, who was the dam of the influential Ch. Archer of Brinton. Archer was by another son of an Avon Prince daughter, Int. Ch. Asoka

27

Cherusker, whose dam was Vikkas Alda. But Cherusker, like Archer, owed little to Avon Prince in general appearance or 'type'. Indeed, he bore little resemblance to either of his parents. His sire, Ch. Crusader of Evesyde, was a top-size, very well-constructed sable dog, with little to criticize in stance. Breeding theorists argued that since Cherusker was not typical of his breeding he would be an unpredictable sire. But Cherusker confounded the pundits: he consistently transmitted his own type to his progeny so that most were instantly recognizable as Cherusker offspring. Cherusker had a dazzling show career, winning thirty-two CCs, thirty Best of Breed awards and gaining Best in Show at all-breed championship shows on five occasions. In the hands of ace professional handler, Eric Gerrard, he was popular with specialist and all-breed judges alike. He produced eleven champions before dying in 1963 at the young age of six years. Very many of the show dogs of this period combined Cherusker and Ludwig lines with considerable line-breeding to Avon Prince of Alumvale. Cherusker's half-brother, the Crusader son Int. Ch. Gorsefield Granit, an outstanding sable dog of a type to please the most exacting of international judges, did not, regrettably, prove a

Int. Ch. Asoka Cherusker, handled by top handler Eric Gerard (1959). The judge is Mrs Jean Beck of Letton fame.

successful stud. He won sixteen CCs in a long and consistent show career, but it was the more flashy and glamorous Cherusker who was to leave his stamp on the breed.

During the 1960s a small band of enthusiasts made annual visits to the great Sieger Show for Shepherds in Germany. Reg and Dorothy Beach of the Stranmillis kennels organized a coach party to the event each year, and fanciers like Nem and Percy Elliot, Mrs Dummett of Charavigne fame, and Gwen Barrington were regular pilgrims. The difference between the British 'Alsatian', as it was then called, and the German Shepherds in their home country was striking, and the enlightened few saw the dangers of a radical departure from the desired type as established by the SV. During the 1970s more and more enthusiasts visited Germany and were impressed by what they saw. Returning home, they dreamed of breeding German Shepherds like the Sieger Show dogs. More importing was done, particularly of prospective stud-dogs, and Shepherd clubs invited a greater number of SV judges than ever before to officiate at their shows. To win an award under a German specialist judge became a much sought-after honour. The two existing national breed clubs, the then British Alsatian Association and the Alsatian League and Club of Great Britain, had regularly invited foreign experts to judge their annual championship shows, but now provincial clubs followed suit. Clearly, there existed a growing number of breeders and exhibitors who welcomed this. Invariably, judges from abroad attracted large entries and the shows where they officiated had a special atmosphere of excited anticipation.

It seemed as if the days of the loose, overlong, exaggerated dogs were numbered until a movement developed in reaction to the growing influence of the Germanophiles. Some breeders were very critical of imported stud-dogs, pointing out their failings rather than considering the potential improvements they might offer. Such disaffection led to the formation of the GSD (Alsatian) Club of the UK by a group of fanciers who wanted to continue to win with dogs that were increasingly regarded by international opinion as deviating in type from the Standard. The 1970s saw a continuing polarization of the breed into two factions: those who were sympathetic to the type of German Shepherd bred in its homeland and those to whom anything German was anathema. There was discord over attempts to effect a change in the breed's name from Alsatian (GSD) to its international nomenclature of German Shepherd Dog. In 1977 the Kennel Club recognized a compromise by accepting its proper name but retaining the misnomer 'Alsatian' in brackets. The GSD (Alsatian) Club of the UK initially attracted a large number of adherents, and with the support of influential members of the Kennel Club it gained championship status. Fired with enthusiasm by its rapid success, it felt confident enough to suggest to its members that the breed should be split into two different breeds; the German Shepherd Dog and the British Alsatian, each with its own Standard. Thankfully such a suggestion was convincingly rejected.

In 1986 the German Shepherd Dog Breed Council was formed. In the following year it was recognized by the Kennel Club as the official forum for clubs to discuss breed affairs. Though membership of the Council is not obligatory, the overwhelming majority of breed clubs joined, representing German Shepherd breeders and owners throughout the United Kingdom. Regrettably the three 'national' clubs for the breed rejected the concept of a KC Council and played little part in its development. The GSD (Alsatian) Club is not a member of the Council even though almost half of championship show judging appointments are taken by people from its list of recommended judges, whose interpretation of the Breed Standard often differs markedly from that of international experts. Probably no other breed has suffered from such wide discrepancies in judging as has the German Shepherd in recent years.

But while the problems of judging the breed are as yet unresolved, the Breed Council has made sound progress with the development of a survey system, the monthly publication of its own magazine, a blood-testing scheme to detect haemophilia, a breeders' charter and a breed database to store computerized information on all aspects of breeding. The Council is undoubtedly an effective vehicle for breed improvement, but only if breeders and the Kennel Club are prepared to co-operate and use it.

In spite of the 'political' turbulence that has accompanied the struggle to establish the 'international type' of German Shepherd in the UK, the last twenty-five years have seen significant progress. The breed has grown in popularity, not simply as a show dog, but as a family companion and guard. In 1972 KC registrations for the breed numbered 15,078. By 1996 the figure had soared to an impressive 25,690. Inevitably many old-established kennels have disappeared and new ones emerged. In the show ring the breed hit the high spot when three dogs took the Best in Show All Breeds award at Crufts, for many the ultimate accolade. Miss Godden's Kentwood kennel, having bred two excellent champions from her Brittas foundation

Ch. Spartacist of Hendrawen (1975), winner of thirty-five CCs.

lines in champions Demetrius and Francesca, took the top award in the 1960s with her Asoka Cherusker son, Ch. Fenton of Kentwood. His success was matched later by Ch. Ramacon Swashbuckler and Ch. Hendrawen's Nibelung of Charavigne, both handled to the top by Edwin White who, with his wife Shirley, enjoyed considerable success with his Hendrawen Shepherds, particularly with the outstanding show dog Ch. Spartacist of Hendrawen, who won his title in 1975 and went on to gain thirty-five CCs. Spartacist was a clean-lined, good-moving dog with extravagant proportions and extreme angulation. Widely used at stud, he sired eight champions. As a son of Swashbuckler, he almost equalled his sire's performance at Crufts, when he was judged best in the Non-Sporting Group. Many of the winning Shepherds of the so-called 'British' type carry several lines back to Spartacist and he was the grandsire of the outstanding Ch. Ariomwood High and Mighty through his daughter Ch. Fascination of Ariom mated to an import. High and Mighty appealed to international experts, winning twenty-one CCs and gaining Best of Breed at the annual two-day National Show for German Shepherds.

Through the 1970s the impact of Ludwig, Spartacist and Ch. Archer of Brinton upon winning animals was very evident and many kennels were concerned to avoid the dangers of an over-exaggerated type of Shepherd that such lines could produce. Some clever breeders, however, were still able to exploit such material and avoid loss of a balanced type. Harry and Rose Emmett's Emmevale kennel produced the excellent champions Venitta and Majestic, the latter winning a gold medal under an SV judge.

31

While Spartacist was the grandson of a German import and Ludwig was also sired by one, it was another dog, judiciously combining home-bred lines with contemporary German breeding, who was subsequently to appeal strongly to breeders aiming at a more balanced, less extravagant German Shepherd. Molly Hunter, of the well-established Yorkshire Rossfort prefix, mated a typical, somewhat short-legged bitch of Archer breeding to a rugged working police-dog of all-German pedigree. This inspired move resulted in the significant Ch. Rossfort Premonition. 'Prem', as he was known to his many admirers, won twenty-seven CCs (including one under Dr Rummel, President of the SV) and sired 276 litters before being exported to New Zealand. Gaining his title in 1972, he was to prove a dominant influence in the following decade, producing fourteen champions here and fourteen more abroad.

Premonition was one of several excellent dogs that made the journey 'down under'. In 1974 the Australian government lifted a ban on the importation of German Shepherd Dogs, persuaded by the view that fears of indiscriminate matings with dingos were groundless. Australian enthusiasts needed new 'blood' from Europe and soon several German dogs on their way to the Southern Hemisphere were quarantined in British quarantine kennels. Malcolm Griffiths' Bedwins kennel played an important part in disseminating the influence of contemporary German bloodlines in Britain by importing dogs for stud use. The kennel possessed its own quarantine facilities, enabling it to send bitches to the Continent for mating, then whelping them on home ground.

For many years imported studs were associated with Percy Elliot and his late wife, Nem, who first owned German males here in the

Int. Ch. Rossfort Premonition, influential sire in Britain, Australia and New Zealand.

32

1960s. Their Vikkas kennel has not been without one or more such dogs ever since. An early import, Ilk von der Eschbacher-Klippen, was the grandsire of Ch. Rossfort Premonition while another dog, Dux von der Braunschweiger Land, sired the foundation bitch of the Delridge kennel, owned by Beryl Budd and Eileen Wilson. This kennel was to produce Ch. Delridge Erhard, himself line-bred to Dux, who won twenty-three CCs and sired nine champions. Erhard and his brother Echo, who won his title in Australia, were impressive males with the type and general appearance that found favour with foreign judges as well as British experts. Both were sons of Delridge Camilla, an outstanding brood-bitch of her time and dam of Ch. Delridge Indigo, Austral. Ch. Delridge Joll and Delridge Jola, a Reserve CC winner. Erhard sired the top-winning Ch. Royvons Red Rum for Roy and Yvonne James. 'Rummie' was a glamorously coated, darkly pigmented showman who appealed strongly to all-rounders and to those who favoured a deeper-bodied, somewhat lower-stationed Shepherd. He won a magnificent total of forty-six CCs and sired six champions. Erhard also appears on the pedigree of Ch. Muscava's Rocky, perhaps the finest moving German Shepherd ever to grace British rings. After a meteoric show career to his title, Rocky was purchased by the late Jack Ogren, a wealthy American enthusiast and international judge. Ch. Muscava's Arnie, Rocky's full brother, and also an outstanding mover, remained here.

Ch. Delridge Erhard winning his first CC under Jayne Swan at Blackpool (1976).

Ch. Royvons Red Rum, winner of forty-six CCs, with owner, breeder Roy James.

The 1970s and 1980s saw a considerable increase in the number of imports of varying quality, from top-winning animals such as Ch. Joll von Bemholt and Youth Sieger Molto von Elbachtal to relatively mediocre specimens. But such was the interest in experimenting with German bloodlines that most of them enjoyed some stud use. Inevitably results were mixed and much indiscriminate breeding took place. One dog, however, was to have a marked influence on the breed during this period. When Paul Bradley of the Vornlante kennel visited the Sieger Show in 1980, his eye was taken by a young dog placed in eighteenth position, which he subsequently purchased. This was Cito von Königsbruch, a son of the excellent stud, Nick von der Wienerau. At his first show in England under Dr Rummel, the then President of the SV, Cito was placed down the line and a despondent Paul must have wondered whether he had a made a wise purchase. Soon, however, the dog's sterling qualities of firmness, correct proportions and enduring gait gained recognition and he won his title in May 1982. But it was as a sire that Cito proved his worth. From the beginning it was evident that he could produce the sought-after 'international' type. He produced seventeen champions and very many top winners and was the most widely used stud in the breed's UK history.

Paul Bradley imported from Germany not only a stud-dog but also a style of handling in the ring. Cito was deliberately trained to pull out on a long lead well in front of his handler, with ears erect, emphasizing his good topline both walking and trotting.

The influence of successful contemporary bloodlines in Germany upon the winning German Shepherds of recent years is clear. Relatively new kennels have emerged which have exploited the value of imports either directly or through good daughters. Audrey Ringwald's Rothick kennel was founded upon imported bitches who produced sons that transmitted excellent qualities. Rothick Ezra, a quarantine-born son of the top German dog Gundo von Klosterbogen sired Ch. Rothick Invictor, who in turn produced Ch. Iolanda Britta and Ch. Kemjon Biene (the dam of the excellent Int. Ch. Kemjon Lex). A repeat mating of the 'I' litter produced Rothick Vinobe who sired Ch. Labrasco Paco and Ch. Deshwar Marshadesh of Nidebed. George Woods' long-established Novem kennel has produced Ch. Novem Volka, whose son, Music Man, sired Ch. Kurtridge Dino. From the imported bitch Xenja von der Baiertalestrasse came Novem Xenia, the dam of Ch. Novem Adagio of Silkenwood, who in turn sired Ch. Copybush Quant and the 1996 Crufts Best of Breed winner Ch. Middross Xaver.

The Middross kennel, owned by David and Wendy Middleton, owes its success to the influence of a good brood-bitch. Kurma of Rosetown was a daughter of Ch. Alf von Quengelbach, a stud imported by the Bedwins kennel who won his three Challenge Certificates to gain a title at three successive shows within a fortnight. Kuma was mother of the grand Ch. Xaver and the dam of Ch. Middross Sonny, whose sister Sassy produced the good CC-winning Middross Vicky and, after being sent to Germany for a mating with the 1990 Youth Sieger Gorbi von Bad-Boll, produced Middross Panto (the sire of the outstanding Ch. Sagaro Goby who was twice top-dog at the National). Panto also produced Ch. Sagenhaft Tamara, who won the bitch Reserve CC at the National in 1996 while her sister bitch Tsarina not only won her class at the 1997 National event but was the dam of the Best Puppy in Show. Kuma was also mated to another of the Bedwins' imports, Ch. Lauser von Hasenborn, which resulted in Ch. Middross Mica, two of whose litter-brothers gained titles abroad.

35

Another kennel to benefit greatly from the influence of Alf von Quengelbach and Lauser von Hasenborn is the Lindanvale establishment of Danny and Linda Wilson. Their first champion, the very good bitch Banya, was by Lauser out of an Alf daughter, Bedwins Uta. Most of the top animals carrying this successful prefix go back to the Alf daughter Malkris Fenya, who was twice mated to Lauser to produce Bedwins Tosca of Lindanvale and Becky of Lindanvale, both significant broods for the Wilsons. Tosca was the dam of Int. Ch. Lindanvale Odessa and her CC-winning brother, Odin, Ir. Ch. Lindanvale Hurricane. Tosca's little sister produced Ch. Vorhanden Aphrodite. Lindanvale Stella, a Tosca daughter, is the dam of the top-winning Ch. Lindanvale Rena. Rena is a daughter, too, of Ch. Lindanvale Vegas who is a son of Becky of Lindanvale and, consequently, a result of line-breeding back to the Wilson's original Alf-daughter. Rena certainly bears a clear resemblance to Alf himself. Vegas has produced many excellent winning progeny, particularly bitches, and stamps a definite type. His top-producing son Jemness Atlas sired the 1997 National Best of Breed winner Ch. Markoy Eiko at Jemness.

While the Lindanvale kennel owes much to its bitch line, it is also indebted to the influence of another outstanding stud of this period. Practically all their winning stock is by Int. Ch. Rosehurst Chris (bred by Annette and Eric Broadhurst) or his son, Ch. Vegas. Chris was

Ch. Lauser von Hasenborn.

36

Ch. Lindanvale Vegas, a top stud-dog.

born in quarantine from a mating of Rosehurst Ramana to the outstanding German sire Uran von Wildsteigerland. Uran, whom
Annette Broadhurst had seen only on a video film, was probably the
most influential sire in the breed's post-war history. His dam, Palme
von Wildsteigerland, was also the mother of the Sieger Quando von
Arminius, so that the combination of Uran and Quando breeding has
intensified Palme's influence on the breed throughout the world.
Annette's gamble in driving to the south of Germany for the mating
paid off. Chris became the outstanding stud force of his generation.
He caused something of a sensation by winning his first CC at the
West Yorkshire GSD Championship Show under an SV judge at the
remarkably early age of ten months, going on to gain his title twelve
months later while still a yearling. Until his death, aged nine and a
half, in February 1996, he had dominated the show ring in the UK
and produced, among many winning progeny, six British and five
Irish champions. Interestingly his dam, Ramona, descended from Ch.
Cito von Königsbruch and the Rothick 'E' litter.

Successful Scottish kennels include Betty and John Young's Jonal
establishment which made up Jonal Basko by Ch. Cito and his son
Xaran of Jonal. The Dunmonaidh kennel, owned by Elizabeth

Moncrieffe, enjoyed considerable success over many years, making up its first champion in 1965 and importing Condor von Schiefen Giebel who made his title in 1967, subsequently becoming an international champion. Miss Moncrieffe went on to win titles with the Condor sons, Rolf and Peregrine, and the good Crufts CC-winner Gytha. The Graloch kennel has bred top-class stock over the years, culminating in the crowning of Ch. Graloch Domingo, while Neil Murray's Cotchee prefix, based largely on contemporary German lines, prefaces the name of Ch. Digger. Jayne Swan's Starhope kennel dates back to the 1960s, making up the English bitch Ch. Starhopes Mireille of Charavigne and breeding the excellent Ch. Starhopes Kassie in 1982. Before moving to Ireland the Fairycross kennel of Anne Adams produced three fine champions in Salina, High Society and the sable Lindy Lu.

A dog on his way from Germany to Australia and spending the statutory time of residence in the UK at the Jonimay kennels of Lily and Terry Hannon, proved influential. Condor von Arminius was to be an important stud down under and, with little use in Britain, produced a daughter whose grandson was Ch. Jonimay Shannon. A Condor son, Gero of Jonimay, sired Ch. Jacnel Nacale, the dam of Ch. Kassieger Tamil of Alatrack who in turn produced Ch. Alatrack Banma.

During the period under review Harry and Isobelle Anderson's kennel in Scotland, now re-established in Belgium, demonstrated the evolution in type evident in the longer-established kennels that were not prepared to be satisfied with the type of animal that Ludwig/Archer breeding was producing for them in the 1970s. Using Premonition lines they bred the outstanding show dog, Ch. Amulree's Heiko, who won forty-seven CCs, a testimony to his wide appeal to judges of all persuasions, whether specialist or all-rounder. With the present 'split' in the breed, it is unlikely that we will ever see dogs follow in the footsteps of Heiko and Red Rum to amass such a dazzling number of Challenge Certificates. From Ch. Rintilloch Havoc of Amulree, Heiko sired Ch. Amulree's Hassan, who owed little to his sire, being very much his dam's type. Introducing Ch. Cito blood into their breeding programme, the Andersons bred a very good grey sable champion bitch in Amulree's Cindy. From the Cito son, Ch. Longvale Octavius, came the excellent Ch. Amulree's Tisn't, who was mated in Germany to Tony von der Wienerau, a son of the twice Sieger Zamb von der Wienerau. The resulting litter produced Amulree's Tulyar sire of Ch. Josalka Barracuda, who won his title in

Ch. Amulrees Heiko, breed record-holder with forty-seven CCs.

1997. Tulyar's sister is the dam of Ch. Markoy Eiko at Jemness, Best of Breed at the National in 1997 and strongly reminiscent of Tulyar in appearance. Tulyar also sired the very good CC-winning bitch, Caddam's Amber.

Miss Pam Meaton's Moonwinds kennel, like so many successful kennels, demonstrated the importance of a good producing bitch line. The bitch Moonwinds Golden Showers was mated to Emmevale Zaroff to produce Ch. Moonwinds Golden Cumulus whose sister, Cloudburst, mated to Ch. Cito, gave champions Golden Harrier and Golden Mirage. Cloudburst's daughter Golden Tempest was the dam of the CC-winning Golden Tigress. Mirage, mated in Germany to the Sieger Eiko von Kirschental, was the dam of champions Golden Emir and Golden Mahdi. The latter produced Ch. Fanta and Ch. Amulree's Aramis C.D.Ex. Sch.H1, the only British-bred champion to gain a Working Trials qualification since Ch. Karenville Ophelia C.D.Ex. in 1972.

Although the Kayards kennel of Mick and Jill Wileman had produced some good animals using contemporary British breeding of the time, it was when they formed a friendship with Albert Platz

Quanto von der Wienerau, a pillar of the breed.

Canto von der Wienerau, an outstanding influence in modern GSD pedigrees.

of the famous Adeloga kennels in Germany that they hit the high spots, with Ch. Kayards Dixie (from a quarantine-bred litter of Adeloga breeding) and Ch. Kayards Babsi, a daughter of Neck von Arminius, imported by the Wilemans. Their third success came with Ch. Kayards Eva, a daughter of the widely used Sieger Uran son, Ch. Bedwins Pirol, bred and owned by Malcolm Griffiths.

Wendy and Graham Stephens began visiting the annual Sieger Show in 1968 and have enjoyed the ownership of several imported German dogs since the early 1970s. After purchasing the Arden Grange quarantine kennels in 1981, they began breeding and exhibiting. The imported Alfa von Steigerhof whelped a litter in quarantine to the Continental sire, Fando von Sudblick, which produced the Stephens' first champion, Ardenburg Fina, crowned in 1992. In the same year they also gained a title with the imported Ch. Laios von Noort and with the outstanding Ch. Quaxie von Haus Gero bred by Rolf Jansen in Germany. Laios was the top-winning male in the year and the most widely used imported stud during the early 1990s. The crest of the wave continued for them in the following year, when another import, Ch. Quant von Kirschental, gained his title, impressing judges and spectators with his superb movement.

Probably the most consistently successful show kennel in recent years has been that of the Gayville's prefix, registered in 1968 by Davy and Joan Hall. Their very first litter, by Ch. Spartacist of Hendrawen, produced the CC-winning brother and sister, Ambition and Allacante. With time they began to shift their perception of good type towards a firmer, more athletic German Shepherd embodied for them at the time by Ch. Cito von Königsbruch. From Cito they bred the outstanding Ch. Gayville's Canto, thought by many to be his best daughter, and the New Zealand Ch. Gayville's Celli. In 1984 the Halls purchased a beautiful rich sable bitch, Trethvane Barbara Anne who, mated to the imported Ch. Meik von der Talquelle, gave Ch. Gayville's Dixie and NZ Ch. Gayville's Dingo. Determined to establish a consistent international type, the Halls imported Cello von Aschera and the excellent bitch Ronnie von der Berghütte. Both carried the cream of contemporary winning German bloodlines and together produced Ch. Gayville's Xera, an outstanding bitch both in the show ring, where she won nineteen CCs and ten Reserve CCs (including the Bitch CC at the National Two-Day Show in 1993 and 1995), and in the breeding kennel. She was the dam, to Ch. Rosehurst Chris, of the top-winning Int. Ch. Gayville's Nilo and Ch. Gayville's Natalie. The latter looks set fair to emulate her brother's success,

Ch. Cito von Königsbruch, the most widely used imported stud.

which would make the Halls the first breeders to produce two British-bred international champions from the same litter.

Another outstanding bitch of her day was Ch. Catja of Vornlante, a quarantine-bred granddaughter of Sieger Uran. Catja won her title in 1990 and went on to win twenty-eight CCs, beating the previous record-holder for a bitch, Ch. Athena of Hatherton, who gained twenty-six certificates. Catja is the grandmother of Ch. Cotchees Digger while Ch. Peterwel Wasp is her great-granddaughter.

The Kurtridge kennel, owned by Beryl Budd (previously of Delridge fame) and Margaret Lee, was lucky enough to purchase the quarantine-born Greenstan Elkie, a Uran granddaughter, and make her into a champion. Her first litter produced Ch. Kurtridge Quando at Videx, owned and campaigned to his title by David and Rhoda Payne. The dam of Elkie was returned to Germany to be mated to the full-brother of Elkie's sire, and a bitch from this litter produced Ch. Kurtridge Dino. The Amondahl kennel owes its success to the

Cito daughter Karikburg Barbel at Amondahl, whose good type was transmitted to Ch. Melissa. Another bitch who has produced consistently and whose type is immediately apparent in many of her descendants is Ch. Shotaans Bianca, a Crufts Best of Breed winner.

A large number of German Shepherds is shown almost exclusively under British judges and non-specialists. They rarely appear at shows judged by international experts and are unlikely to be seen at the two-day annual German Shepherd show, which is the major event for the breed in the show calendar. Successful kennels showing such dogs to a Champion title include Lornaville, Gregrise, Marvick, Bilnetts and Akbir. The Norwulf prefix, owned by Margaret Barron, has bred champion stock over the years, successfully introducing imported bloodlines into its established British bitch line. Dorothy Beach's Stranmillis kennel goes back to the 1950s, when it produced two champion grandchildren of the imported Ch. Danko von Menkenmoor of Hardwick. Some owners decline to enter under 'international' judges because they are aware their dogs will stand little chance of being highly graded, others because they are not enamoured of the method of presentation apparently necessary to win under such judges, with its emphasis upon movement and fitness of both dog and handler!

British breeders aiming at producing German Shepherds embodying the best international type and from top-producing bloodlines have faced the obstruction of the six-months' quarantine imposed upon imported dogs. This has limited access to the best stud-dogs abroad and deterred many from sending bitches to the Continent for mating since, after whelping, they have to complete their full term of incarceration. Quarantine, too, has made it difficult for British dogs to compete at shows abroad, though the Bedwins kennel has successfully shown dogs at the annual German Sieger Show. With changing quarantine regulations, we may face the exciting prospect of the best German Shepherds in Britain competing with the best bred on the Continent, both in breed and in Schutzhund competition.

2

The Breed Standard

Although some writers like to trace the history of the German Shepherd Dog back into the distant past with fanciful stories of wolf-like dogs in the company of man, no breed can really be said to exist until a conscious effort is made to describe and define its essential characteristics and until breeders aim at perpetuating dogs possessing those definitive features. The concept of a sheep-herding dog of a distinctive type began to emerge in Germany during the late decades of the nineteenth century, but it was the newly formed SV, under the leadership of von Stephanitz and Arthur Meyer, which laid down the original Standard for the breed in September 1899 at Frankfurt. With very minor revisions, this remains substantially the same today. The 1976 version of the SV Standard formed the basis of the current British Standard accepted by the KC in 1982 after discussions involving the major breed clubs. The American Standard, similarly, is based upon the German blueprint for the breed. In spite of the fact that the Standard is essentially the same throughout the world, some countries have shaped the breed according to 'show-ring' fashion, resulting in exaggerations which the SV, the acknowledged guarantor of the breed's correct type, can only deplore.

A standard attempts to describe the ideal representative of its breed in character, general appearance, size and anatomical construction. It will be specific about some features such as size, colour and general proportions while acknowledging that there are some areas that will allow a degree of latitude in interpretation. Although the GSD standards have hardly changed for almost a century, our understanding of how a particular dog embodies a standard is constantly evolving. One wonders whether von Stephanitz, in the early years, could ever have imagined such a creature as the modern German Shepherd, so different is that animal from the first specimens of the breed. But whatever changes may have occurred in the breed's general appearance over the years, one essential guiding principle must remain: the German Shepherd is a herding dog, bred for a particular task, and if we forget that fact in our interpretation of the Standard, we can so easily end up with an exaggerated caricature of the breed.

The UK Breed Standard

The following is the Standard drawn up by the British Association for German Shepherd Dogs and the GSD League of Great Britain, and approved by the World Union of German Shepherd Dog Clubs (WUSV, *see* Chapter 11). It was subsequently published as the official KC standard in 1986, in abbreviated form (*see* Appendix 00).

Characteristics

The main characteristics of the GSD are: steadiness of nerves, attentiveness, loyalty, calm self-assurance, alertness and tractability, as well as courage with physical resilience and scenting ability. These characteristics are necessary for a versatile working dog. Nervousness, over-aggressiveness and shyness are very serious faults.

General Appearance

The immediate impression of the GSD is of a dog slightly long in comparison to its height, with a powerful and well-muscled body. The relation between height and length and the position and symmetry of the limbs (angulation) are so inter-related as to enable a far-reaching and enduring gait. The coat should be weatherproof. A beautiful appearance is desirable but this is secondary to his usefulness as a working dog. Sexual characteristics must be well defined – i.e. the masculinity of the male and the femininity of the female must be unmistakable.

A true-to-type GSD gives an impression of innate strength, intelligence and suppleness, with harmonious proportions and nothing either overdone or lacking. His whole manner should make it perfectly clear that he is sound in mind and body, and has the physical and mental attributes to make him always ready for tireless action as a working dog.

With an abundance of vitality, he must be tractable enough to adapt himself to each situation and to carry out his work willingly

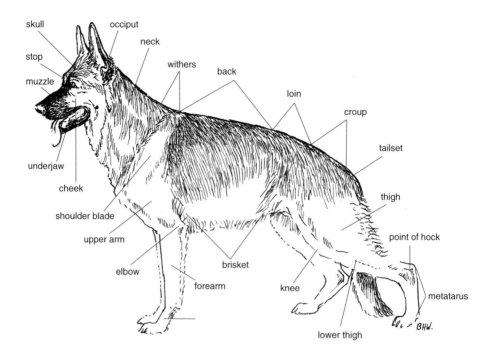

Parts of the German Shepherd.

and with enthusiasm. He must possess the courage and determination to defend himself, his master or his master's possessions, should the need arise. He must be observant, obedient and a pleasant member of the household, quiet in his own environment, especially with children and other animals, and at ease with adults. Overall he should present an harmonious picture of innate nobility, alertness and self-confidence.

Head

The head should be proportionate in size to the body without being coarse, too fine or overlong. The overall appearance should be clean-cut and fairly broad between the ears.

Forehead: should be only very slightly domed, with little or no trace of a centre furrow.

Cheeks: should form a very softly rounded curve and should not protrude.

46

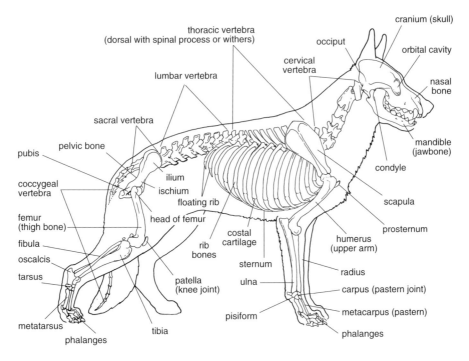

The Points of the skeleton.

Skull: extends from the ears to the bridge of the nose, tapering gradually and evenly, and blending without a too pronounced 'stop' into a wedge-shaped, powerful muzzle. (The skull is approximately 50 per cent of the whole length of the head.) Both top and bottom jaws should be strong and well developed. The width of the skull should correspond approximately to the length. In males the width could be slightly greater and in females slightly less than the length.
Muzzle: should be strong and the lips firm, clean and closing tightly without any flews. The top of the muzzle is straight and almost parallel to the forehead. A muzzle which is too short, blunt, weak, pointed, overlong or lacking in strength is undesirable.

Eyes

The eyes are medium-sized, almond-shaped and not protruding. Dark brown eyes are preferred, but eyes of a lighter shade are acceptable provided that the expression is good and the general harmony of the head is not destroyed. The expression should be lively, intelligent and self-assured.

Ears

Of medium size, firm in texture, broad at the base, set high, they are carried erect (almost parallel and not pulled inwards). They taper to a point and open towards the front. Tipped ears are faulty. Hanging ears are a very serious fault. During movement the ears may be folded back.

Mouth

The jaws must be strongly developed and the teeth healthy, strong and complete. There should be forty-two teeth, twenty in the upper jaw (six incisors, two canines, eight premolars, four molars); and twenty-two in the lower jaw (six incisors, two canines, eight premolars and six molars). The German Shepherd Dog has a scissor bite – i.e. the incisors in the lower jaw are set behind the incisors in the upper jaw and thus meet in a scissor grip in which part of the surface of the upper teeth meet and engage part of the surface of the lower teeth.

Neck

The neck should be fairly long, strong with well-developed muscles, free from throatiness (excessive folds of skin at the throat) and carried at an angle of 45 degrees to the horizontal; it is raised when excited and lowered at a fast trot.

Forequarters

The shoulder blade should be long, set obliquely (45 degrees) and laid flat to the body. The upper arm should be strong and well muscled and joined to the shoulder blade at a near right-angle. The forelegs, from the pasterns to the elbows, should be straight viewed from any angle and the bones should be oval rather than round. The pasterns should be firm and supple and angulated at approximately 20–23 degrees. Elbows neither tucked in nor turned out. Length of the forelegs should exceed the depth of the chest at a ratio of approximately 55 per cent to 45 per cent.

Body

The length of the body should exceed the height at the wither, the correct proportions being as 10 to 9 or 8.5. The length is measured from the point of the breast-bone to the rear of the pelvis. Over- or under-sized dogs, stunted growth, high-legged dogs and overloaded fronts, too short overall appearance, too light or too heavy in build, steep-set limbs or any other feature which detracts from the reach or endurance of the gait are faults.

Chest: should be deep (45–48 per cent of the height at the shoulder) but not too broad. The brisket is long and well developed.

Ribs: should be well formed and long, neither barrel-shaped nor too flat; correct ribcage allows free movement of the elbows when the dog is trotting. A too round ribcage will interfere and cause the elbows to be turned out. A too flat ribcage will lead to the drawing in of the elbows. The desired long ribbing gives a proportionately (relatively) short loin.

Belly: firm and only slightly drawn up.

Back: the area between the withers and the croup, straight, strongly developed and not too long. The overall length is not derived from a long back, but is achieved by the correct angle of a well-laid shoulder, correct length of croup and hindquarters. The withers must be long, of good height and well defined. They should join the back in a smooth line without disrupting the flowing topline, which should be slightly sloping from the front to the back. Weak, soft and roach backs are undesirable.

Hindquarters

The thighs should be broad and well muscled. The upper thigh bone, viewed from the side, should slope to the slightly longer lower thigh bone. The angulations should correspond approximately with the front angulation without being over-angulated. The hock bone is strong and, together with the stifle bone, should form a firm hock joint.

The hindquarters overall must be strong and well muscled to enable the effortless forward propulsion of the whole body. Any tendency towards over-angulation of the hindquarters reduces firmness and endurance.

Feet

Should be rounded, toes well closed and arched. Pads should be well cushioned and durable. Nails short, strong and dark in colour. Dew-claws are sometimes found on hind legs; these should be removed two or three days after birth.

Gait

The GSD is a trotting dog. His sequence of steps therefore follows a diagonal pattern in that he always moves the foreleg and the opposite hind leg forward at the same time. To achieve this, his limbs must be in such balance to one another so that he can thrust the hind foot well forward to the mid-point of the body and have an equally long reach with the forefoot without any noticeable change in the back line.

The correct proportion of height to corresponding length of limbs will produce a ground-covering stride that travels flat over the ground, giving the impression of effortless movement. With his head thrust forward and a slightly raised tail, a balanced and even trotter displays a flowing line running from the tips of his ears over the neck and back down to the tip of the tail. The gait should be supple, smooth and long-reaching, carrying the body with the minimum of up and down movements, entirely free from stiltiness.

Tail

Bushy haired, should reach at least to the hock joint, the ideal length being to the middle of the hock bones. The end is sometimes turned sideways with a slight hook; this is allowed but not desired. When at rest the tail should hang in a slight curve like a sabre. When moving it is raised and the curve is increased, but ideally it should not be higher than the level of the back. A tail that is too short, rolled or curled, or generally carried badly or which is stumpy from birth, is faulty.

Coat

(a) The normal-coated GSD should carry a thick undercoat and the outer coat should be as dense as possible, made up of straight, hard, close-lying hair. The hair on the head and ears, front of the legs, paws and toes is short. On the neck it is longer and thicker, on some males a slight ruff. The hair grows longer on the back of the legs as far down as the pastern and the stifle, and forms fairly thick trousers on the hindquarters. There is no hard and fast rule for the length of the hair, but short mole-type coats are faulty.

(b) In the long-haired GSD the hairs are longer, not always straight and definitely not lying close and flat to the body. They are distinctly longer inside and behind the ears, and on the back of the forelegs and usually at the loins, and form moderate tufts in the ears and profuse feathering on the back of the legs. The trousers are long and thick. The tail is bushy with light feathering underneath. As this type of coat is not so weatherproof as the normal coat it is undesirable.

(c) In the long open-coated GSD the hair is appreciably longer than in the case of type (b) and tends to form a parting along the back, the texture being somewhat silky. If present at all, undercoat is found only at the loins. Dogs with this type of coat are usually narrow-chested, with narrow, overlong muzzles. As the weather protection of the dog and his working ability are seriously diminished with this type of coat it is undesirable.

Colour

Black or black saddle with tan, or gold to light grey markings. All black, all grey or grey with lighter or brown markings (these are referred to as sables). Small white marks on the chest or very pale colour on inside of legs are permitted but not desirable. The nose in all cases must be black. Light markings on the chest and inside of legs, as well as whitish nails, red-tipped nails or wishy-washy faded colour are defined as lacking in pigmentation. Blues, livers, albinos, whites, (i.e. almost pure white dogs with black noses) and near-whites are to be rejected (Abbreviated KC Standard: 'are highly undesirable').

The undercoat is, except in all-black dogs, usually grey or fawn in colour. The colour of the GSD is not in itself important and has no effect on the character of the dog or on its fitness for work and should be a secondary consideration for that reason. The final colour of a young dog can only be ascertained when the outer coat has developed.

Height

The ideal height (measured to the highest point of the wither) is 57.5cm (23in) for females and 62.5cm (25in) for males. 2.5cm (1in)

51

either above or below the norm is allowed. Any increase in this deviation detracts from the workability and breeding value of the animal.

Faults

Any departure from the foregoing points should be considered a fault and the seriousness with which a fault should be regarded should be in exact proportion to its degree.

Note   Male animals must have two apparently normal testicles fully descended into the scrotum.

Interpreting the Standard

Characteristics and General Appearance

The Breed Standard, from the outset, places great emphasis on temperament and stresses the fact that the GSD must be confident and reliable, with the intelligence and energy to work with enthusiasm. Nervous, vicious or apathetic dogs are untypical of a good Shepherd. Hyperactive or over-excitable dogs are also undesirable, the salient words being 'calm self-assurance'. The GSD never looks shifty, mean or apologetic – the word 'nobility', still retained in the Standard even in these egalitarian times, suggests a dog of dignity and good looks with a certain mental and physical poise. He possesses an innate protective instinct but is so amenable to training and sensible discipline that he makes a dependable member of the human household.

Head

The assessment of some breeds such as the Boxer and Rottweiler places considerable emphasis upon the particular formation of the head. While this is not so with the GSD, there is no doubt that a Shepherd's head and expression are an essential part of his appeal, especially to the layman. Over-large, coarse heads with doleful eyes, loose lips and unfirm ears often accompany a heavy, plodding dog that lacks the firm, athletic constitution envisaged by the Standard. A head that is too small detracts from overall balance and harmony. It should be possible at a glance to distinguish between male and female, but even the latter should display sufficient strength in the muzzle and foreface. Ideally, when the mouth is shut, and provided the lips do not overlap loosely, it should be possible to discern the underjaw when viewing the head from the side.

The 'stop' is the slight declivity between the eyes where the forehead narrows down to join the beginning of the foreface. If, when the head is viewed in profile, the stop is hardly apparent, as in a Rough Collie, it is criticized as 'shallow' and is untypical of a Shepherd, as is the too 'obvious' stop which breaks the gentle line of the profile, resulting in a harshly accentuated forehead above the eyes. Sometimes the forehead itself may be spoiled by obvious furrows, giving a quite untypical taut, worried look to the expression. The lips should be clean-fitting, not hanging loosely, although a male's head may often exhibit an acceptable degree of looseness, provided it is not overdone. Occasionally, the lips are too turned up at the corners of the mouth when the dog is panting and this creates an untypical 'grinning' expression quite foreign to the correct head.

The superb head of Odin von der Tannenmeise, an outstanding German male.

Eyes

The Standard allows a range of eye colours, though the preference is for darker rather than lighter shades. Essentially, the colour should blend with that of the surrounding head colour so that, for example, light eyes do not stand out glaringly against a dark background. Very light eyes, however, are undesirable no matter how lightly coloured the head. They often lack the intelligent, kind expression characteristic of the Shepherd. Round eyes are untypical; the almond shape is accompanied by a slightly slanting set of the eye, though any exaggeration of this will lead to an untypical look. A dark muzzle or 'mask' contributes to a more imposing head, especially with males. A uniform colour throughout the head without markings often lacks interest. Any markings, however, should preferably be well shaded in and not be loudly obvious.

Ears

Over-large ears are unfortunately not uncommon. Often these are rather thin in substance and may flap when the dog is moving. It is quite natural for the Shepherd to pin back his ears when moving at speed, but there should be no suggestion that the ear-tips are flapping loosely. The ears of some dogs are set too widely on the head and cannot lift to, and sustain, a keen, erect position in which the inner line is almost, but not quite, vertical. Sometimes, but less often, the ears are set too closely on the top of the head, or may incline inwards. Sometimes too, the point of the triangular-shaped ear is rounded rather than clearly defined as it should be.

Mouth

The number and disposition of the teeth is called the 'mouth' in canine terminology. This has nothing to do with the tongue, gums or the Shepherd's capacity to express himself! The number of teeth is specified and most judges will penalize missing teeth, with varying degrees of severity depending upon where the gaps are. An absent premolar one may not be regarded as seriously as a missing molar (one of the big crushing teeth at the back of the jaw). Occasionally extra teeth are present, usually a double first premolar. If your dog has a correct mouth otherwise, the presence of a single one of these will not disqualify him from an excellent grading, even under SV judges who are committed by German breed regulations to consistent strictness towards teeth faults. The 'bite' is the term used to describe the way in which the upper incisors (front teeth) meet the lower. The upper teeth should touch the lower ones but slightly overlap them to form the scissor-bite referred to in the Standard. If they meet without overlap, the top resting upon the bottom, then the bite is 'level' and therefore faulty. If the overlap is pronounced, obscuring the lower incisors and forming an obvious gap between the upper and lower teeth, then the dog is overshot, a serious dentition fault. If the under-jaw protrudes slightly so that the lower teeth 'underlap' the upper, the bite is 'undershot', a quite rare fault in the German Shepherd. Sometimes the incisors are irregularly set out of line, resulting in an unacceptable 'wry' mouth. The teeth should be strong, healthy and without obvious fleshy spaces between them. A black blotch on the tongue is occasionally seen and is of no importance whatsoever.

Neck

A high head carriage on an almost perpendicular or 'swan' neck may look showy, but is incorrect. As the German Shepherd's trot acceler-ates, he should naturally lower his head and neck as he reaches over the ground with a long stride. The neck should flow into the back smoothly without a disturbing break in the flowing outline. An over-long, narrow neck is untypical, as is a short, stuffy one. An obvious 'dewlap' (floppy folds of loose skin underneath the neck) detracts from a clean, firm outline. A strong, well-muscled neck is an asset in a working dog and usually indicates good muscularity generally.

Forequarters

It is impossible to eavesdrop on a conversation between exhibitors or breeders of the German Shepherd for long without hearing the term 'angulation'. This concept is introduced in the Standard in the words describing the forehand and is used in discussing other parts of the dog's construction too. The shoulder blade and upper arm are described as meeting or joining at the shoulder joint at an approxi-mate right-angle (90 degrees) and the pasterns at about 23 degrees to the foreleg if you imagine the latter to be the base-line (perpendicu-lar). An angle greater than 23 degrees would result in too much slope of pastern, probably indicative of weakness, whereas an angle less than 23 degrees will result in a steep pastern, as in some terrier

Ch. Gayvilles Nathalie, demonstrating excellent fore hand angulation.

breeds. Sufficient slope or 'spring' of pastern is necessary for the foreleg to absorb any potential concussion as the front foot makes impact with the ground at the end of the stride. Steep pasterns will lead to a jarring effect on the forehand that will affect endurance.

The shoulder blade should be set 'obliquely' or be 'well laid back'. By running your finger down the centre of the blade you will detect a bony central ridge. If you can imagine a chalk line following roughly the course of this ridge, you will be able to assess the approximate angle to a horizontal line drawn through the centre of the dog's body from shoulder joint to its back end. The closer it is to 45 degrees the better, as this will ensure that the blade is of good length. The longer the blade, the broader it is likely to be, giving plenty of room for the attachment and development of the good long muscles necessary for a trotting dog. It is important to remember that the angles quoted are not to be understood as geometrically exact. A set-square and protractor are not a necessary part of a judge's equipment! The figures are there as an approximate guide to the desired relationship of part with part in the dog's anatomy.

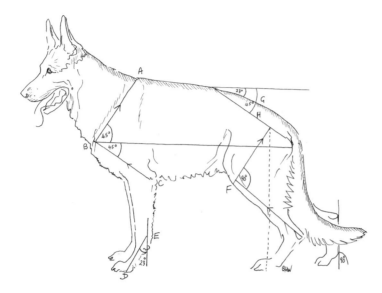

Angulation. The shoulder blade (AB) laid at approximately 45 degrees to the horizontal, meeting the upper arm (BC) at approximately 90 degrees. When the hind foot is positioned below the hip joint, the upper and lower thighs meet at the knee joint (F) at 90 degrees. Visible croup line (G) slopes from the horizontal at about 23 degrees, while the pelvis (H) may slope at up to 45 degrees from the horizontal. The pastern (DE) slopes at 23 degrees from the vertical.

The upper arm should ideally be equal in length to the shoulder blade but short upper arms are regrettably the norm. Limitation in length of the upperarm may affect the scope and fluency of the front stride, particularly if combined with a steep shoulder. It is often difficult to assess the angle of the upper arm. If the dog stands too erect in the neck, he will automatically steepen the upper arm. He must be standing with his forelegs quite perpendicular to the ground so that his feet are well under his withers. If he has a well-developed forechest with an obvious pre-sternum or breast-bone, the eye can be deceived into confusing the resulting outline of the forechest with the actual angle of the upper arm.

The elbows should be well set in to the body and well laid back along the ribcage. Viewed front on, there should be a clean line from the shoulder joint down through the elbow to the pastern and foot, creating the impression of a straight, stable column of support. Thick, bulky muscles over the upper arm, loose elbows, thickening of the bone on the forearm, and turned-out feet and pasterns will all spoil the clean line. The chest should not be too broad, nor too narrow,

Ir. Ch. Willowdale Feigh demonstrating perfect fore and hind angulation.

though immature animals will look decidedly less filled-out in the forechest.

The feet should be rounded and with thick pads, never thin or splayed. The nails should be dark. Pale nails will usually indicate some weakness in pigmentation.

Body and General Proportions

At first view, the German Shepherd should never appear square like the Doberman or Boxer, but neither should one be conscious of a long back and loin. He is slightly longer than he is high, and the Standard is quite specific about the desired proportions. Allowable heights are 22–24in (55–60cm) for bitches and 24–26in (60–65cm) for males, with the ideal being the middle heights of 23in (57.5cm) and 25in (62.5cm) respectively. A dog's correct height is not always easy to ascertain. He must be standing on perfectly level ground and must be neither

58

tautly over-erect nor hunched into his shoulders. His front legs must be absolutely perpendicular so that the measuring line may drop from a point just behind the shoulder blade, through the elbow to the ground. A proper, adjustable measuring-stick is desirable.

The depth of the chest between the elbows should not be greater than the length of leg from elbow to the ground. Sometimes the length of coat furnishing under the chest can deceive the eye into believing the dog is deeper than is actually the case. Immature dogs, too, may look longer in the leg until body development is complete. Early developers are likely to be too deep in body as adults. The ribcage should not be too 'sprung' or concave when viewed from the top, but neither should it be 'slab-sided' or flat. Rounded or 'barrel' ribs usually accompany heavy bodies and broad fronts. The elbows are often pushed out in movement affecting the directness of the front action. While the German Shepherd's body should denote firmness and strength, it must also be flexible and capable of quick unhindered shifts of direction as the dog carries out his herding work. Flat ribs often indicate a general narrowness and lack of substance throughout the dog's build, though maturity may bring with it an improved 'spring' of rib. The brisket should be long and must not

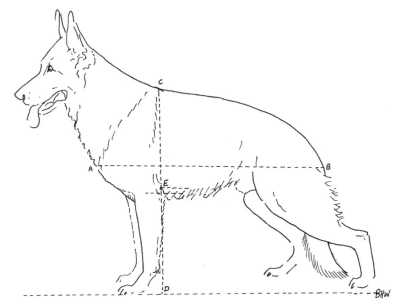

Measuring the German Shepherd Dog: length = AB; height = CD; depth of brisket = CE.

tuck up too early into an exaggerated waist. Short briskets create an undesirable 'pear-shaped' body, particularly if they are too deep as well.

A beautiful body shape is the product of a correct 'topline' as well as 'underline'. Both lines should please the eye through graceful, gentle curves: 'flowing' is the word used by the Standard. A neck that meets the back at a sharp angle; a back that is dipped or roached or a croup that is flat or steep; a rear that is higher than the top of the shoulder; even a hooked or twisted tail, will all spoil the flowing line from ear-tip to tail end. A comparison of the top-winning German Shepherds of today with those of thirty years ago demonstrates clearly the progress made in breeding a more harmonious and pleasing topline. Unfortunately, the German Shepherd Dog has too often been assessed in the show ring in an artificially exaggerated 'show stance' with one hind leg stretched out behind, creating a completely false picture of the topline. This is particularly so in the USA and among some sections of the fancy in Britain. Thankfully the majority of breeders are not fooled by such manipulation and realize that the correct topline of a German Shepherd can only be properly appreciated when he is standing quite naturally.

Overlong, poor topline; poor underline; flat croup. Short, steep upper arm. Excessive hind angulation. Weak pasterns.

To demonstrate the flow of topline it is necessary only to encourage your Shepherd to stand poised and alert, but not too erect in neck, and to place his hind foot just behind him, to show off a *gentle* slope down from the withers through the back, loin and croup. A good natural topline will not alter significantly when the dog is walking.

Whereas in the horse the withers are obvious to the eye as an undulating prominence at the base of the neck where it meets the back, the Shepherd's withers should blend smoothly into the line running from the neck into the back. They are actually formed by the first three dorsal vertebrae of the back. These should ideally be slightly prominent above the top of the shoulder blade when the neck is erect. The withers should flow well back into the back proper and remain the highest point of the back-line in stance and movement. Long, well-placed withers contribute to the topline of graceful curves already discussed.

The back, including the loin, should be strongly developed and must not be narrow when viewed from above. It should be straight but not level or horizontal in stance, showing a slight, unexaggerated slope and joining the croup imperceptibly so that, ideally, it should be impossible to see where the back ends and the croup begins.

Square proportions: steep shoulder and upper arm. Raised back. Short brisket. Tucked-up loin; ugly tail-set; poor hind angulation.

The croup is made up of the pelvis and the muscle and coat covering it. When your dog is in full coat and good muscular condition, the croup-line that your eye follows should slope gently away from the back to complete the flowing overline. The angle of the croup should be assessed when the German Shepherd is on the move. The length of the pelvis is measured from the bony points at the end of the loin to the 'sitting-bones' at each side of the dog's anus. Good length of pelvis offers scope for the development of strong muscles in the hindquarters, while the angle contributes significantly to the mechanics of the Shepherd's gait.

Probably nothing divides the opposing 'factions' in the German Shepherd fancy more than the assessment of topline. One side holds rigidly to the view that a straight back means a level one and any suggestion of a curve is dismissed as a 'roach' back. A roached back occurs only when the back itself is higher than the wither, and is very uncommon in Shepherds. A slight rise in the loin, often an indication of muscular strength in that area, should not be confused with a roached back. The horizontal, level back, wrongly assumed by some to be correct, is more common in dogs that are overlong in the back, particularly if this is accompanied by a tendency to short forelegs and croup. The back is best assessed when the Shepherd is walking purposefully without pulling on the lead, or at a slow trot. The natural outline, without any handler manipulation, will then be apparent. At the extended trot, with his neck lowered, there will inevitably be some loss of static wither height and the back should then be horizontal to the ground, though the loin may well show a slight curve down to the croup as the Shepherd reaches powerfully under his body with well-angulated hindquarters. The best specimens of the breed maintain a 'flowing' outline of gentle graceful curves at all speeds.

The Hindquarters

As these provide the 'motor' for the German Shepherd's movement, they must be strong, stable and well-muscled. The Shepherd has long bones in the upper and lower thigh which produce a distinctive length of stride. When he is standing with his hind foot directly underneath his hip-joint, the angle between the upper and lower thigh at the knee-joint should approximate to the angle at the shoulder-joint. He is then said to possess 'balanced' angulation. The lower thigh should be only slightly longer than the upper. An overlong lower thigh may look impressive if the dog is required to pose in an artificially exaggerated, stretched stance, but it has nothing to do with *correct* angulation and may often lead to weakness in the hindquarters. Powerful muscles are necessary to contract the angle at the knee as the dog moves forward and, more particularly, to enable him to open up the angle and produce the characteristic thrust behind that launches the German Shepherd's body smoothly over the ground. Thin, weak or unsteady hocks will affect the effectiveness and endurance of the gait.

The Gait

Evaluation of movement is probably more important in the German Shepherd than in any other breed, a fact only too obvious at any dog show where the breed has classes. Trotting once or twice around the ring will not satisfy most specialist judges, who feel the need to compare the dogs closely as they move together. The Standard, after all, seeks to describe a dog capable of moving with great economy, covering the ground with no waste of energy or unnecessary muscular effort, possessing both endurance and ease of movement. His length of limbs and angulation will be so beautifully balanced that he will move smoothly and freely with rhythm and poise. There will be little up-and-down movement of the back, which will remain firm and steady at all speeds without rolling or swaying over the pelvis. His feet will remain close to the ground without lifting up his legs in front or kicking up the hocks behind, which simply wastes energy

A free outreaching gait: Chipsi von Bad Boll.

63

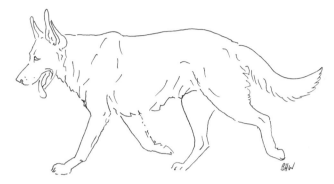

Poorly angulated dog. The short upper arm and steep shoulder with flat wither causes the dog to fall on to the forehand when trotting. Short bones in the hindquarters result in limited length of stride and poor hind thrust.

Over-erect head carriage and steep shoulder, contributing to faulty, high front action. Excessive slope of loin and exaggerated hind angulation result in lack of 'follow-through' at completion of each stride.

and may reduce endurance. There must be no suspicion of jarring or restriction as he moves, nor any sense of a cumbersome heaviness in his general build. At the walk and slow trot his limbs will move towards you and away quite soundly on maintained parallel lines with a minimum of deviation. The hind foot will immediately be placed on the spot vacated by the forefoot. As he increases speed and extends his hind foot well forward under the body, he will place this

Fully extended, reaching gait, with optimum front reach and extension behind; ideal topline in movement.

significantly past the point vacated by the forefoot. This is termed 'over-reaching' by some judges and is regarded as faulty in other breeds. In the Shepherd, however, this is an observed characteristic of what is termed the 'period of suspension', when the dog launches himself forward with such smoothness and momentum that all four feet are off the ground for a split second. 'Over-reaching', however, must never occur when the dog is walking or trotting slowly as this will indicate a lack of balance between fore- and hindquarters. Such a fault in movement is called 'crabbing'. During movement the croup should not be raised higher than the withers, in which case the dog is said to be moving 'overbuilt'. Nor should the dog create the impression that he is carrying most of his weight on the forehand, as if his centre of balance had been pushed forward. This will lead to throwing out of the elbows and a lack of endurance. He will be described as 'falling on the forehand'.

The Tail

The Standard leaves little to be said on this. Short tails are rarely seen nowadays, the tendency being towards overlong ones which often form a pronounced hook at the end, disturbing the flow of the over-line when compared with the gentle curve of the 'sabre' formation.

The 'tail-set' at its root or beginning at the pelvis should not be obvious to the eye but should blend in smoothly with the overline. A slightly pronounced tail-set is, however, a minor blemish and may have little to do with the length or angle of croup, which is of far greater importance anatomically. The tail-tip should be black. Pale colouring indicates weakening of pigmentation.

The Coat and Colour

Again the Standard is very specific. As a working dog, the German Shepherd needs a resilient 'hard' coat rather than a soft one to the touch. The dense undercoat protects him against the weather and even in torrential rain his skin will remain dry. Long coats will attract and hold mud and other accretions and are less serviceable than the correct coat.

The Standard asserts that the colour of the German Shepherd is of secondary importance, and there is an old saying that 'a good horse can't be a bad colour'. Nevertheless, fashions come and go in dogs, as in other things. The prevailing colour in the GSD is that of a black saddle with varying degrees and shades of tan to accompany it, from pale cream to red tan. Blacks, sables and bi-colours are very much in a minority. As a consequence very few German Shepherds of these colours make a show title in the breed ring. The bitch Ch. Sabre Secretainaire, who gained her title in 1951, was the only all-black champion in Britain since the war. Sables vary from a dark iron grey through to a pale silver and various shades of tawny fawn, all with black tips to the adult hair. Of all colours, these are the most reminiscent of the wolf colouring. Black and tan puppies usually get lighter as they get older, whereas sables darken with age. Sometimes puppies born black and tan fade so that, with maturity, their black saddle has receded to a mere flecking across the back. These are sometimes termed 'sable' by the novice. The term 'bi-colour' is also often misused to describe a very dark Shepherd with slight tan markings. A proper 'bi-colour' is always characterized by black markings on the back of the hocks and often on the tops of the toes. He will have slight tan or grey markings on an otherwise all-black appearance. There have been only three bi-colour champions in the last twenty-five years in Britain.

Pale or washed-out colours are undesirable, and strong pigmentation is to be preferred. Though the white German Shepherd attracts an enthusiastic following among the pet-owning public, it is unacceptable in the show ring and, though not debarred from competition, is even less likely to win any prize than is the faulty long-coated Shepherd.

Understanding the Standard

Simply to read the Standard is not enough: you need to understand it. The most effective way to do this is to attend breed shows, sit at the ringside and watch the judging. The judge *should* be judging with the Standard in mind but remember that he or she will be interpreting it with his or her own particular emphasis in mind. Not all judges agree, or the same dogs would win every time! Try to see as many of the best specimens of the breed as you can and pay particular attention to developing an eye for correct movement. Unless you can appreciate the German Shepherd in motion you will make little progress in understanding the Standard.

Seek out the acknowledged experts in the breed, particularly those who watch the judging rather than those spending the day in the bar. Conversation with such enthusiasts can be a most helpful way to increase your grasp of correct construction and type. Avoid the exhibitor who has failed to win and who feels the need to let everyone know how bad the judge is. You are unlikely to get an objective point of view from that quarter.

Type

The idea of 'type' is perhaps the most elusive of concepts to define yet the word is used regularly by breeders, exhibitors and judges. A dog may possess a number of shortcomings such as a light eye, steep upper arm or short croup and yet still be described as 'of good type'. Some judges may reveal quite personal preferences or prejudices and demote a dog in its class for being 'not my type'. Loose talk around the rings will employ expressions like 'old-fashioned type' or 'Germanic type'. Good type is best understood by considering those features that undermine it. Correct general proportions are paramount, so that overlong or short-legged dogs fail in type. Similarly, weak, shelly or soft, flabby constitutions betray weak type. Any obvious exaggeration that strikes the eye is also undesirable. Ultimately, the correct type is that envisaged by the Standard and by the interpretation laid upon it by the country of the breed's origin and development. There ought to be no room for widely disparate views about what constitutes good type.

American Kennel Club Breed Standard
(Reproduced by kind permission of the American Kennel Club.)

General Appearance

The first impression of a good German Shepherd Dog is that of a strong, agile, well muscled animal, alert and full of life. It is well balanced, with harmonious development of the forequarter and hindquarter. The dog is longer than tall, deep-bodied, and presents an outline of smooth curves rather than angles. It looks substantial and not spindly, giving the impression, both at rest and in motion of muscular fitness and nimbleness without any look of clumsiness or soft living. The ideal dog is stamped with a look of quality and nobility – difficult to define, but unmistakable when present. Secondary sex characteristics are strongly marked, and every animal gives a definite impression of masculinity or femininity, according to its sex.

Size, Proportion, Substance

The desired height for males at the top of the highest point of the shoulder blade is 24 to 26 inches; and for bitches, 22 to 24 inches.

The German Shepherd Dog is longer than tall, with the most desirable proportion as 10 to 8½. The length is measured from the point of the prosternum or breastbone to the rear edge of the pelvis, the ischial tuberosity. The desirable long proportion is not derived from a long back, but from overall length with relation to height, which is achieved by length of forequarter and length of withers and hindquarter, viewed from the side.

Head

The head is noble, cleanly chiseled, strong without coarseness, but above all not fine, and in proportion to the body. The head of the male is distinctly masculine, and that of the bitch distinctly feminine. The expression keen, intelligent and composed. Eyes of medium size, almond shaped, set a little obliquely and not protruding. The colour is as dark as possible. Ears are moderately pointed, in proportion to the skull, open toward the front, and carried erect when to attention, the ideal carriage being one in which the centre lines of the ears, viewed from the front, are parallel to each other and perpendicular to the ground. A dog with cropped or hanging ears must be disqualified.

Seen from the front the forehead is only moderately arched, and the skull slopes into the long, wedge-shaped muzzle without abrupt stop. The muzzle is long and strong, and its topline is parallel to the topline of the skull. Nose – black. A dog with a nose that is not predominantly black must be disqualified. The lips are firmly fitted. Jaws are strongly developed. Teeth – 42 in number – 20 upper and 22 lower – are strongly developed and meet in a scissors bite in which part of the inner surface of the upper incisors meet and engage part of the outer surface of the lower incisors. An overshot jaw or a level bite is undesirable. An undershot jaw is a disqualifying fault. Complete dentition is to be preferred. Any missing teeth other than first premolars is a serious fault.

Neck, Topline, Body

The neck is strong and muscular, clean-cut and relatively long, proportionate in size to the head and without loose folds of skin. When the dog is at attention or excited, the head is raised and the neck carried high; otherwise typical carriage of the head is forward rather than up and but little higher than the top of the shoulders, particularly in motion.

Topline : the withers are higher than and sloping into the level back. The back is straight, very strongly developed without sag or roach and relatively short. The whole structure of the body gives an impression of depth and solidity without bulkiness.

Chest : commencing at the prosternum, it is well filled and carried well down between the legs. It is deep and capacious, never shallow, with ample room for lungs and heart, carried well forward, with the prosternum showing ahead of the shoulder in profile.

Ribs: well sprung and long, neither barrel-shaped nor too flat, and carried down to a sternum which reaches to the elbows. Correct ribbing allows the elbows to move back freely when the dog is at a trot. Too round causes interference and throws the elbows out; too flat or short causes pinched elbows. Ribbing is carried well back so that the loin is relatively short.

Abdomen: firmly held and not paunchy. The bottom line is only moderately tucked up in the loin.

Loin: viewed from the top, broad and strong. Undue length between the last rib and the thigh, when viewed from the side, is undesirable.

Croup: long and gradually sloping.

Tail: bushy, with the last vertebra extended at least to the hock joint. It is set smoothly into the croup and low rather than high. At rest, the tail hangs in a slight curve like a saber. A slight hook – sometimes carried to one side – is faulty only to the extent that it mars general appearance. When the dog is excited or in motion, the curve is accentuated and the tail raised, but it should never be curled forward beyond a vertical line. Tails too short, or with clumpiness due to ankylosis are serious faults. A dog with a docked tail must be disqualified.

Forequarters

The shoulder blades are long and obliquely angled, laid on flat and not placed forward. The upper arm joints the shoulder blade at about a right- angle. Both the upper arms and the shoulder blade are well muscled. The forelegs, viewed from all sides, are straight and the bone oval rather than round. The pasterns are strong and springy and angulated at approximately a 25-degree angle from the vertical. Dewclaws on the forelegs may be removed, but are normally left on. The feet are short, compact with toes well arched, pads thick and firm, nails short and dark.

Hindquarters

The whole assembly of the thigh, viewed from the side, is broad, with both upper and lower thigh well muscled, forming as nearly as possible a right- angle. The upper thigh bone parallel to the shoulder blade while the lower thigh bone parallels the upper arm. The metatarsus (the unit between the hock joint and the foot) is short, strong and tightly articulated. The dewclaws, if any, should be removed from the hind legs. Feet as in front.

Coat

The ideal dog has a double coat of medium length. The outer coat should be as dense as possible, hair straight, harsh and lying close to the body. A slightly wavy outer coat, often of wiry texture, is permissible. The head, including the inner ear and foreface, and the legs and paws are covered with short hair, and the neck with longer and thicker hair. The rear of the forelegs and hind legs has somewhat longer hair extending to the pastern and hock, respectively.

Faults in coat include soft, silky, too long outer coat, woolly, curly and open coat.

Color

The German Shepherd Dog varies in color, and most colors are permissible. Strong, rich colours are preferred. Pale, washed-out colors and blues or livers are serious faults. A white dog must be disqualified.

Gait

The German Shepherd is a trotting dog, and its structure has been developed to meet the requirements of its work. General impression – the gait is outreaching, elastic, seemingly without effort, smooth and rhythmic, covering the maximum amount of ground with the minimum number of steps. At a walk it covers a great deal of ground, with long stride of both hind legs and forelegs. At a trot the dog covers still more ground with even longer stride, and moves powerfully but easily, with co-ordination and balance so that the gait appears to be the steady motion of a well-lubricated machine. The feet travel close to the ground on both forward reach and backward push. In order to achieve ideal movement of this kind, there must be good muscular development and ligamentation. The hindquarters deliver, through the back, a powerful forward thrust which slightly lifts the whole animal and drives the body forward. Reaching far under, and passing the imprint left by the front foot, the hind foot takes hold of the ground, then hock, stifle and upper thigh come into play and sweep back, the stroke of the hind leg finishing with the foot still close to the ground in a smooth follow-through. The overreach of the hindquarter usually necessitates one hind foot passing outside and the other hind foot passing inside the track of the forefeet, and such action is not faulty unless the locomotion is crabwise with the dog's body sideways out of the normal straight line.

Transmission: the typical smooth, flowing gait is maintained with great strength and firmness of back. The whole effort of the hindquarter is transmitted to the forequarter through the loin, back and withers. At full trot, the back must remain firm and level without sway, roll, whip or roach. Unlevel topline with withers lower than the hip is a fault. To compensate for the forward motion imparted by the hindquarters, the shoulder should open to its full extent. The forelegs should reach out close to the ground in a long stride in harmony with that of the hindquarters. The dog does not track on widely separated parallel lines, but brings the feet inward toward the middle line of the body when trotting, in order to maintain balance. The feet track closely but do not strike or cross over. Viewed from the front, the front legs function from the shoulder joint to the pad in a straight line. Viewed from the rear, the hind legs function from the hip joint to the pad in a straight line. Faults of gait, whether from front, rear or side, are to be considered very serious faults.

Temperament

The breed has a distinct personality marked by direct and fearless, but not hostile, expression, self-confidence and a certain aloofness that does not lend itself to immediate and indiscriminate friendships. The dogs must be approachable, quietly standing its ground and showing confidence and willingness to meet overtures without itself making them. It is poised, but when the occasion demands, eager and alert, both fit and willing to serve in its capacity as companion, watchdog, blind leader, herding dog or guardian, whichever the circumstances may demand. The dog must not be timid, shrinking behind its master or handler, it should not be nervous, looking about or upward with anxious expression or showing nervous reactions, such as tucking of tail to strange sounds or sights. Lack of confidence under any surroundings is not typical of good character. Any of the above deficiencies in character which indicate shyness must be penalized as very serious faults – and any dog exhibiting pronounced indications of these must be excused from the ring. It must be possible for the judge to observe the teeth and to determine that both testicles are descended. Any dog that attempts to bite the judge must be disqualified. The ideal dog is a working animal with an incorruptible character combined with body and gait suitable for the arduous work that constitutes his primary purpose.

Disqualifications

Cropped or hanging ears, dogs with noses not predominantly black, undershot jaw, docked tail, white dogs, any dog that attempts to bite the judge.

3

Choosing a German Shepherd

The German Shepherd Dog is one of the most popular breeds of pedigree dog. Over 25,000 were registered by the Kennel Club in 1996 alone, and in Germany the SV issued its two-millionth pedigree to a bitch puppy named Zari von Augrund, whelped on 3 September 1997. So if you intend owning a German Shepherd you will find plenty of consumer choice, ranging from puppies bred from a wide range of parentage in a variety of circumstances to, sadly, adults languishing in rescue kennels or dogs' homes.

Older Dogs

This chapter is intended to offer advice to those seeking a puppy to be proud of, but what if you decide to take an older dog into your home? Firstly, it is essential that you are confident in your dealings with an adult dog. Unlike a small puppy, he may have habits which will necessitate a firm, controlling hand. If you have any reservations about your ability to cope, or you lack any previous experience of the breed, you would do better with a puppy so that you can learn about the development of Shepherd character and play your part in shaping it. An older dog may be unused to living in a house, or be inexperienced with children. His reaction to other dogs and animals must be considered.

Getting to know an adult dog will be a journey of exploration lasting several weeks, and you must be prepared to behave sympathetically and firmly. He will bring with him all the formative influences that have made him the dog he is. Most breeders offering you an older dog will be prepared to allow a probationary period for you to assess the dog's suitability, but it is unfair to return a dog on the basis of a mere whim, without putting in any genuine effort of your own. If you really want him, be prepared to commit yourself. But don't be so impressed by a dog's good looks that you overlook failings of character. A shy, nervous adult will only cause you headaches and embarrassment, while an unreliable, aggressive dog could be a danger to your family and acquaintances. Remember that by adulthood the Shepherd's character is rarely capable of much significant modification.

Puppies

If you decide to start with a puppy, the question of which sex to choose will doubtless be uppermost in your mind. Bitches are smaller, will eat less and be satisfied with less exercise than will energetic males. Unlike the latter, they are less likely to assert their dominance and test your authority as they develop. But they will find more subtle ways of getting their own way! Twice yearly seasons require sensible handling but, provided you have a kennel available and can exercise her away from your immediate neighbourhood, there should be few problems. German Shepherd bitches are usually excellent with children and make good house-dogs.

Both sexes need plenty of space but a male, in particular, will soon be frustrated if denied freedom and plenty of exercise. The German Shepherd is essentially an active, working dog and his innate energy and intelligence need to find constructive expression. Before you invest in a puppy, make sure you will have the time available to train him properly and allow him sufficient physical activity in all weathers.

Choosing a Breeder

Impulse-buying of any commodity is hardly likely to prove successful, but particularly where puppies are concerned. Before choosing a puppy, take the opportunity to visit local breeders and find out which bitches are to be bred from in the near future. Visits to local clubs will put you into contact with people who may have a bitch you admire and from whom you would like a puppy. Don't be influenced by the impressiveness of the breeding establishment or the sheer number of dogs kept. A small breeder with one or two bitches and the time and experience to bring to the rearing of a litter is often

Three-week-old puppies bred by Jayne Swan of the Starhope prefix.

as good a bet as the larger commercial concern. It is unwise to book a puppy before the litter is born; no breeder can guarantee what a particular mating may produce and it is essential that you ultimately feel that you have a puppy that suits you, rather than one you feel an obligation to have because of a previous booking. If you do express an interest in a puppy make sure the breeder realizes you are prepared to make only a provisional reservation.

Assuming you want a promising puppy, with the aim of showing and breeding eventually, you should seek out breeders who have proved successful in these activities. Many litters, however, fail to produce a single puppy worth showing, no matter how impressive the breeding, and you will be lucky to find a breeder who, recognizing an outstanding pup, will want to let him go. Nevertheless, breeders often cannot keep all the dogs they would want to and it is possible to turn up trumps. But even if a puppy bitch fails to hit the high spots in the ring, she can prove a useful brood if she is well-bred and of above average quality. A dog puppy is unlikely to achieve a reputation as a stud-dog, however, unless he has gained top honours at shows.

Any breeder worth his salt will expect you to ask to see the dam when you go to inspect the litter. Ideally you will have got to know

75

her before she gave birth and before the demands of motherhood have taken their inevitable toll on her condition. A caring breeder will, however, try to make sure the pups do not pull her down too severely and should have a photograph of her in good condition in case you have not seen her before. Away from her puppies she should be relaxed, good-natured and glad to see you. The dam has a significant influence upon the temperament of her puppies so make sure she is not nervous or shy. Be suspicious of any obvious indications of skin-trouble as this may prove to be hereditary.

Choosing your Puppy

At seven to eight weeks old the puppies will have been fully weaned and, apart from occasional social visits from the dam, will have been independent of her for two or three weeks. They should be solid, chunky babies, well filled out without being flabby, and you should be impressed by their thick knobby legs with plenty of 'knuckle'. Avoid puppies with narrow loins and shallow chests, and look for broad, thick thighs and strong hocks. The ears will probably not be erect at this age but they should be well placed on the top of the head and tip towards you like those of an alert terrier. Large, heavy ears set widely at the base and hanging low may be slow in going up and may even continue to fail to do so without assistance. The expression should be lively and alert with no sign of apprehension or anxiety. At this age puppies should be in love with the world and everyone. Even at this early age you should expect to see a clear difference between a dog pup and his sister. The male will have a bigger, stronger head and more substance generally than the slighter, more graceful female. Little can be predicted about the final size of the adult at this age, but the length of pasterns and hocks are often an indication of how tall the puppy may grow. Strong skeletal substance is reflected in thickness of pasterns and breadth of skull. The tail, too, is a good indication of the potential strength of the mature dog. Look for a thick broad tail at the root, especially in a male.

A promising puppy will have a good, dense undercoat, thick and woolly to the touch. The close-lying top coat with its glossy, straight hairs will not develop until some eight weeks later. The puppy destined to develop the long coat, unacceptable in the show ring, will be obviously more fluffy than his litter-mates at this age. He will have lengthy tufts of hair at the base of his ears and fluffy frills down the

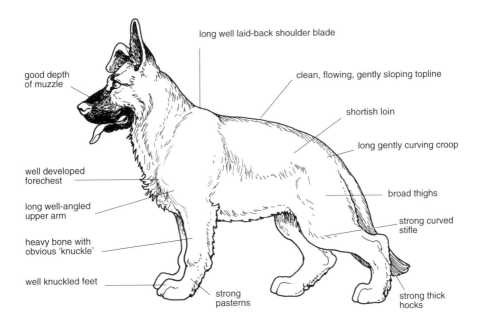

long well laid-back shoulder blade

good depth
of muzzle

clean, flowing, gently sloping topline

shortish loin

long gently curving croop

well developed
forechest

long well-angled
upper arm

broad thighs

strong curved
stifle

heavy bone with
obvious 'knuckle'

well knuckled feet

strong
pasterns

strong thick
hocks

Points to look for when choosing a nine-week old puppy.

back of his front legs. Often the hair is longer on the top of the skull. The final colour of the eyes cannot be determined until maturity, but light eyes are often transmitted from parents to offspring so this is a factor to consider when examining the dam.

Make sure you examine the puppy's milk teeth. These appear during the third week, with the six incisors of the lower jaw followed by those in the upper jaw. The four canines and twelve premolars appear in the fourth week, giving a total of twenty-eight milk teeth. (Adult dogs have forty-two teeth.) The puppy does not have premolar number one, nor any molars. Look carefully also at the bite. Some puppies are very slightly overshot at this age but, provided there is no obvious gap and no suggestion of a receding underjaw, this should rectify itself as the underjaw grows and strengthens and the larger adult teeth break through, from around four months.

If the puppy has been regularly handled he will be delighted to be lifted up and fussed. You should feel an enthusiastic tongue on your face, a soft well-filled belly in your hand and the regular thump of a wagging tail against your lapels. A fresh, clean smell, bright eyes and a healthy skin will provide the clinching signs that this is the pup for you.

Choosing the best-constructed puppy with show potential is very problematic at eight weeks, especially if you are inexperienced in assessing litters. An understanding of the faults and virtues of the sire and dam is important in determining how the puppy may develop. If, for example, the bitch has a poor topline, you can at least look out for the presence of this failing in some of the litter.

To begin with you should arrange to see the puppies in a run or area where they are accustomed to playing around freely. It is essential that they are relaxed and natural, not suddenly transported to a spot where they feel inhibited or uncertain, as this will result in their crouching or sniffing around and you will see little of their natural shape and balance. You cannot choose the best puppy if the litter is leaping all over you or jumping up the run fence. So take a fold-up chair, sit and be patient, and let the puppies forget you and play. Avoid the puppy whose back dips or who looks too long in the middle-piece. Look instead for one with pleasing deportment, carrying himself well as he trots, with an obvious rhythm and good co-ordination. As he moves he should retain a gently rounded outline and create the impression of a one-piece pup. When something attracts his attention, he will stop and offer you a pleasingly balanced picture. He will have good wither height and a long, gently sloping croup. Well-rounded stifles and good length of lower thigh will result in his adopting an attractive, slightly extended stance. As he trots off again you will notice the thrusting, piston-like action of his strong, short hocks.

Now is the time to examine him more closely. You should stand him on a firm table-top and make sure the shoulder blade is well laid back and that the upper arm is of good length, with the elbows well back along the lengthy ribcage. While hind angulation can alter as the

A promising dog puppy at eight weeks.

An attractive long-coat puppy at eight weeks.

pup develops, the forehand remains substantially the same. Your fingers should detect the pin-bones at the beginning of the pelvis along the back and you should look for a good length of croup. The actual angle of the croup will alter with growth, as will the tail-set. Hope to find good strength and width of loin and straight, sound legs.

The forelegs should be straight at this age. Any tendency to turn out the front feet is unlikely to improve later. The feet themselves should be well knuckled and not flat or open. White nails may indicate a lack of pigmentation as will a red (rather than black) tail tip. A young puppy often carries his tail gaily as he plays, but it should not curl over the back or be twisted at the end.

You should check that both testicles are present in the male puppy. These will be very small and sometimes they may not have descended into the scrotum. It is essential that they do so if you wish to show the puppy later with any chance of success, so you should seek an assurance that the breeder will take the puppy back if he fails to become entire. Better still, arrange for the breeder to retain him until both testes have descended.

The colour of your puppy may change as he grows unless he is a jet-black with no markings, or all-white. Whites make attractive pets but are undesirable in the show ring. Occasionally other deviations from acceptable colours also occur in a litter, such as browns, livers and blues. Blues are sometimes confused with grey sables but there is

Good companions.

a clear difference to the practised eye. Apart from the tell-tale, pale smoky-blue body colour, a true blue will usually have tan markings similar to his black and tan litter-mates. In effect he will be a black and tan, whose black colouring has been diluted. Sable puppies vary from silver grey to various shades of fawn. The only body colour they may have at eight weeks is a black stripe on the back or tail. The distinctive wolf-like flecking will only become apparent as the adult coat develops later. Every sable puppy must have at least one sable parent, so be suspicious if two black and tans produce a 'sable'. Puppies with pale fawn markings may go lighter as they grow, as the colour spreads and the black areas recede. Sometimes they can pale off so radically that only a limited broken saddle remains on their body at maturity. Puppies with very pale inside legs and no markings on the head are most likely to be affected in this way. Often a muddy tan at eight weeks can deepen with age into an attractive red. Bi-colours are practically all black with distinctive markings on the back of the hocks and on the top of the toes. These are unlikely to alter later, and will remain very dark. A rule of thumb to remember is that black and tans will lighten in adulthood, while sables will darken.

Having discovered the puppy you want, ask if you can see him on his own away from the litter. If he bounces around you playfully, shows a keen interest in investigating objects you throw for him and trots round proudly with your car-keys in his mouth, you have not only the prospect of a German Shepherd that will attract admirers because of his handsome good looks, but a dog that will have the enthusiasm to learn whatever you have to teach.

4

Caring for Your German Shepherd

Most German Shepherd puppies settle into their new homes with few problems, but you can help ease the transition. Your puppy will appreciate a sleeping box placed in a cool, quiet area of the house where he can rest undisturbed. Remember he may be unused to the centrally heated warmth of a modern home and to the comings and goings of people around him. You and your family will now replace the litter he has left and he will soon overcome his feeling of separation by bonding closely to those who share his daily life, particularly the one who is responsible for feeding him regularly.

Early Days

It is a good idea to place a piece of blanket carrying the scent of his litter-mates in his box on arriving at his new home. A ticking clock can sometimes lull him into sleep during his first night. You should not feel too guilty if, succumbing to his protests at being left alone, you go downstairs to comfort him. Sooner or later, however, he must be prepared to be left on his own without making a fuss. Place his food in a separate room and leave, closing the door behind you. If you can give him a bone to chew on, do so, as this takes his mind off the fact that he has been left. If you do this regularly he will soon accept the fact that you have gone. Never give in to him if he scratches at the door or he will soon learn that he has *you* under his control! A collapsible cage is a useful substitute for a sleeping box. You can move it easily if desired and the puppy can be conveniently shut away if circumstances demand, though you must never keep him enclosed in such a confined space for long.

You will need to spend plenty of time in contact with your puppy for the first few days, especially if he is to live in the house. Training him to be clean is straightforward as long as you are quick and observant. As soon as you spot him sniffing and circling around, you should be ready to carry him outside so that he can empty himself on a spot of your choosing. If he has been kennel-trained to perform on newspaper or sawdust, you can make sure the same materials are available to encourage him. Inevitably, accidents will occur in the house. If they do, ensure that you immediately expunge the spot of any trace of the offending scent, as its persistence will only attract the puppy to empty himself in the same place again. A disapproving 'Aah-aah!' or 'Noo!' as he is about to squat, will elicit an embarrassing self-consciousness on his part and will soon result in his seeking the door. Do not be tempted to hit your puppy or to 'teach him a lesson' by pushing his nose in the mess. Both tactics are unkind and ineffective.

You should have received a diet-sheet from your puppy's breeder. Try your best to follow it and feed at the times suggested. As the puppy grows you can vary his food and establish a routine to suit yours, but make any changes gradually.

Your puppy will have been wormed before leaving his kennel, but you should be prepared to worm again at twelve weeks, and at three-monthly intervals until he is an adult. See the vet for advice on the correct preparations and dosage.

From eight weeks onwards the puppy is ready for vaccinations against distemper (hardpad), leptospirosis, hepatitis and parvovirus, which your vet will administer in two stages with a four-week gap in between. Any natural immunity he will have gained from his dam's milk will be negligible at eight weeks, so he is particularly susceptible to infection. Common sense will keep you from allowing him to sniff around areas frequented by street dogs, but it is quite impracticable to imagine you can quarantine him from all outside contacts until he is twelve weeks old. Such isolation may affect the development of his confidence with people and traffic during an important phase of his growth. He can still be taken out in the car to get used to the noises of urban life. Provide him with a soft leather collar and light lead and let him sit with you in a quiet spot close to a road and watch the traffic pass. Carry him into friends' houses to lap up the fuss strangers will give him. The more you introduce him to pleasant experiences in different situations, the more his confidence will develop.

Most German Shepherd puppies take particular delight in using their teeth, often with painful results for unprotected feet or ankles.

Once they have grown out of the toe-chasing phase, they may turn to 'mouthing' your hands and wrists. This is perfectly natural and has nothing to do with any intention to devour you! Male pups, in particular, seem to take a roguish pleasure in seeing how far they can close their teeth on your flesh before you protest. They actually need to learn the limits you will tolerate, just as they must when playing roughly with their own kind. You should offer a disapproving sound to discourage a pup's hard use of his teeth and substitute a plaything for your hand. But make sure your utterances are calm and low. If you react in an angry or heated way, you may simply stimulate the pup to an over-excited reaction. He must, of course, never be allowed to take liberties with children in play.

Sensible discipline begins early. Your puppy should develop sensitivity to your tone of voice as you communicate disapproval and praise for the way he behaves. You should never have to hit a puppy: your voice should be the most effective instrument of control and encouragement. It is essential that both you and other members of the family can remove food, bones and playthings from him at any time. He must never be allowed to resent your attempt to do so, nor to succeed in intimidating you by growling. Teach him the word 'Give' and offer him a tit-bit in exchange for the object you have taken and he will soon gladly relinquish his possessions. Avoid confrontation, but if it does occur he must be left in no doubt that you will have your way. During the normal course of a day many opportunities arise which allow you to gradually convince the pup that you are his 'pack' leader. Before grabbing a tit-bit he can be taught to wait for the words 'Take it'. He can be encouraged to sit at the door until you allow him to go through. If he wants to jump up to lick your face, you can step back and restrain him, allowing him to do so only when you choose. In these and other ways you will be unobtrusively asserting your dominance over him. Harsh treatment will only confuse and subdue him. Your aim should be a happy, confident yet amenable puppy.

He should be accustomed to being physically examined at an early age so that you do not have problems later if he has to be taken to the vet. A very dominant puppy will often resist any attempts at making him lie on his back, but you should insist on his doing so while he is a baby and easy to control. Anticipate a frantic wriggling, but quietly yet firmly hold him in a supine position until he submits. Praise him for lying still and then release him. If you repeat this regularly he will get used to 'playing dead'. As you groom him gently, make sure he will allow you to brush his tail and inspect his teeth.

The Growing Pup

By four or five months of age your puppy will have grown a glossy new coat to cover his woolly undercoat, his ears will probably be erect and, although he should still have plenty of bone and knuckle in the forelegs, he will begin to look like a chunky miniature adult. At this age you will often get a glimpse of the dog he is to develop into. He will probably be ungainly and loose as he moves, especially if he is very well angulated. Because his skeleton is still developing and his bones are still soft, you should not allow him to grow fat and heavy. Excess weight will spoil his backline and contribute to weak pasterns and loose elbows. His body should be well covered with a healthy, loose-fitting coat but he should be slim and flexible at this age without being thin, taut-stomached or ribby.

Exercise should be confined to freedom to romp around in play without tiring over-exertion. Lead-walking should be restricted to brief pleasurable forays into the wider world for socialization. Long walks on the lead while he is soft and uncoordinated can often do more harm than good to his growing joints and ligaments. You should wait until he has finished growing before introducing a fitness programme aimed at optimum physical condition.

Teething

He will begin to lose his milk teeth at about four months of age and by six months he should have a fine pristine set of forty-two adult teeth in place. The teething process can be helped by giving him plenty of hard marrow bones to chew on. Occasionally the emerging, large canine teeth protrude behind the remaining puppy canines, pushing the latter awkwardly awry. Normally the puppy teeth will soon be displaced but should they continue to cause a problem, your vet may need to attend to them. Not uncommonly during this period, a Shepherd puppy's ears will assume a wide variety of comic positions and may even alarm you by dropping completely down. Usually, if they have once been convincingly erect for a period, they will resume the correct position once the teething process has been completed.

Ch. Mortoff Marcus at five months. *Ch. Marcus at maturity.*

Ears

It is often difficult to predict precisely when a puppy's ears will become erect, but most will have the desired ear carriage by five months of age. If you have doubts about your puppy you should first consult the breeder. He will tell you if the puppy needs help with his ears. Some lines are slow in developing erect ears and may simply need time. On the other hand, you may come to the conclusion that the ears should be carefully taped to encourage the correct carriage. Since you can do more harm than good by a botched attempt to interfere with this sensitive part of a dog's head, it is always better to seek help and advice from someone who has had experience of artificially strengthening a dog's ears. The inside of the ear must be carefully shaved, dried and left for a few hours before the process begins. A piece of chiropodist's felt is then cut to the size and shape of the ear and tapered at the bottom so that it will fit well down into the ear between the 'knobs' at its base. The plaster should be comfortably warm and tacky as you press the felt well down into the ear, smoothing it from the base upwards until it is firmly and neatly fixed. The felt should remain in place for several weeks. If there are any indications that it is becoming loose so that the shape of the ear is affected, it must be renewed as soon as possible.

Remember that no matter how effective this operation may prove, if your puppy is subsequently used for breeding he will pass on to his offspring a tendency for soft ears. Alert, erect ears are an essential part of the German Shepherd's distinctive head and expression, and you should therefore think seriously about whether your dog should be bred from at all.

Eight-week dog puppy – ears yet to move.

At twelve weeks: 'Who says I can't put them up?'.

The Kennel

If your puppy is to be a kennel dog you must provide at least the following: a dry, draught-free sleeping area protected from the weather, a floor area of at least 8ft × 5ft (2.5m × 1.5m), adequate light and ventilation, and access to an outside run. The sleeping box should be raised from the ground and allow the dog freedom to curl up or stretch out. The run need not, as its name might suggest, be an area where you expect your dog to exercise himself. Unless he has constant distractions to keep him on the move, he will simply amble around, and will still look forward to his daily free exercise away from the kennel. Your run should provide enough room for him to play, sunbathe, observe the world and empty himself. Thick, heavy-duty weld-mesh should be used in constructing the run. Anything lighter will buckle as the dog jumps up it. The mesh can be fastened to wooden or angle-section steel supports. The whole frame should be firmly carried on the run base, which is best formed of concrete or coarse slabs. It is surprising how slippery some surfaces can become. Ash or earth floors may be difficult to keep clean of excrement, with the consequent risk of recurring worm infestation. A sloping roof with suitable guttering is an asset, as it will protect the run from rain and snow. You should provide a raised bench in the run on which the dog can lie protected from any damp. You will need to ensure that the access door the dog uses to enter the run is different from the main kennel door. This will be important when you wish to confine him in the run, while you carry out necessary tasks in the kennel itself. Make sure, too, that the doors open inwards and that you can open them easily with a minimum of fuss.

German Shepherds are a hardy breed and do not need expensive bedding materials. Blankets and rugs need constant washing and changing if they are not to prove unhygienic and many dogs delight in pulling them around. A thick layer of newspapers will suffice in his sleeping box. These can be easily and quickly replaced, and prove absorbent if he returns damp to his kennel. The kennel floor itself can be spread with newspapers and sprinkled with a fresh layer of clean-smelling sawdust. Any accidents while he is shut up can then be easily removed.

Dogs very rapidly adapt themselves to routine. You should feed at regular times and try to give your dog the opportunity to empty himself some five or six hours after a meal. If you stick to your routine, you will minimize the chances of the dog's fouling his kennel.

Feeding

Never feed your German Shepherd after strenuous exercise, and always allow him the opportunity to rest after his meals. Some dogs are alarmingly greedy and will wolf down their food almost before the dish has settled in front of them. Obsessively competitive eaters are best fed alone and should not be given bones to swallow posses-sively as another dog approaches. A healthy dog should need no

This lovely four-month bitch puppy grew up to become Romainville
Esta, the bitch CC winner at Crufts, 1998.

coaxing to eat. If he becomes too fastidious about his food, remove the dish after a few minutes and let him go hungry until the next meal. Never leave uneaten food with him.

As your Shepherd grows he will need plenty of the right food. From four to nine months he will need three meals a day, with two daily feeds thereafter until he reaches maturity. With such a great number of prepared foods specially designed for dogs of differing stages of development from puppyhood to old age, there can be no excuse for feeding your Shepherd incorrectly. It is simply a matter of choosing a food that suits your dog and then following the manufacturer's instructions. Dry foods are best fed after being soaked in warm water for about twenty minutes. This not only releases the flavour but discourages the dog from drinking excessive amounts of water. Unless there is a particular health problem, such foods need no further vitamin or mineral supplementation. To do so will upset the balance achieved by the makers. Nevertheless, additional fresh protein can be added now and again by offering red meat, tripe, fish or chicken with the complete food. Lightly cooked vegetables can also be chopped in. A sliver of raw lamb's liver twice a week is excellent, while some dogs relish grated carrot or apple.

Your dog's stools will indicate whether his food agrees with him. They should be well formed without being hard. Overfeeding, particularly of some processed foods, may lead to looseness. Often the colour of the motions will reflect the colour of the food he gets. His digestive system was originally designed to cope with foods that required much chewing and tearing, and so he is capable of coping with bony bits, fur and flesh. If you do decide to feed him chiefly on processed foods, remember to give him the occasional bone or hard biscuit to exercise his teeth and jaws. Shepherds are perfectly capable of digesting a whole rabbit, fur and all, without leaving a trace, and raw chicken portions are crunched and devoured with avidity. Never, however, feed cooked bones as these can splinter and cause internal problems.

Exercise and Play

Most Shepherds can be maintained in good condition with half an hour's exercise twice a day, though much depends on the nature of the activity and the constitution of the dog. A slow amble on the lead will be of little benefit. He must have the freedom to trot and gallop, developing his muscles and expanding his lungs. Watching two dogs at play, running, lunging and rolling, panting till they drop, suggests how vigorously we must participate in the dog's exercise if he has no canine companion. We can throw a piece of hose-pipe or rubber ring for him to chase and retrieve and indulge in a tug-of-war encouraging him to pull and twist about. Balls can unfortunately be easily swallowed unless they are large enough to make such alarming incidents impossible.

Sticks are dubious playthings also. They can splinter or, more dangerously, catch awkwardly on something as the dog runs, suddenly jarring or piercing his mouth. Galloping exercise must be avoided on hard surfaces or after a stiffening frost as the dog can easily sprain his muscles. Running up slopes will strengthen his hindquarters and back, though he should be discouraged from galloping down an incline as this can loosen his elbows and pasterns. Swimming is excellent and the Shepherd's thick undercoat will protect him from skin-chill. You should combine his free exercise with a regular amount of controlled lead work on a hard surface. This will keep his feet and pasterns in good trim and strengthen his hocks. On three days of the week he should be given at least an hour's brisk walking. If you cannot walk fast enough for him to sustain a slow trot and you wish to condition him for the show ring, a bicycle may help, but only if you have access to cycling tracks away from the dangers of traffic. Specially made spring-like attachments are commercially available which fix on to the cycle. The dog is then fastened to this, allowing you both hands free to control the handlebars. Some owners invest in an electrically powered trotting machine with a rotating belt that can be set at a speed suitable to the dog. These are undoubtedly an asset if weather conditions or personal circumstances make normal exercise impossible. They can never, however, satisfy the dog's need for mental as well as physical stimulation. The most productive exercise is that in which the dog is enthusiastically involved. Remember, too, that a dog may sometimes be off-colour and disinclined to vigorous exercise. You must be sensitive to his moods and, if he is lethargic, you should not compel him to work but allow him to rest. Bitches, in particular, can sometimes be subject to hormonal changes that affect their enthusiasm for physical activity.

Grooming

As a natural breed, thankfully free from the cosmetic 'improvements' of some show dogs, the German Shepherd's coat needs little special attention to keep it in good order. A good brushing with a stiff brush twice a week will suffice. The twice-yearly moult will require rather more regular attention from you, however, The moult usually begins with a loss of bloom on the top coat and a loosening of the undercoat, particularly on the hindquarters. After brushing you should massage the coat to loosen the dead hair, then thin it out using a large plastic comb. If you neglect to do this daily, the dead coat will accumulate and you will be faced with an apparently inexhaustible supply of dead hair to strip out, much of which may be tough and resistant, especially in dogs carrying a thick undercoat. Recourse to a metal stripping comb may then be necessary, but you should take care in its use. Bladed combs are particularly risky and must not be used near the sensitive parts of a dog's body. You can expect the change of coat to take ten or twelve weeks from the onset of the moult to the completion of the new coat. Bitches often lose their coats before they are due in season.

Ears need no more than a cursory check and you should not clean out the naturally protective wax that forms inside. Dirt or dust can be easily removed by the light application of a damp cloth.

During grooming you should check for any signs of impending skin trouble. Examine the armpits and inside thighs, and use your fingers to detect any growths or cysts that may be developing on the neck or body. Regular, methodical attention will help to prevent the development of problems which, if neglected, can lead to costly treatment later.

Early Training

As a youngster your German Shepherd should be regularly exposed to the experience of modern traffic. The more often you can take him into town conditions, the better. He needs to gain confidence in coping with staircases and different floor surfaces. Buses with pneumatic brakes, lorries that backfire, cars moving just inches away from him: all provide an assault on his finely tuned senses that he must gradually manage to accept. In such conditions you must make sure he cannot slip out of his collar or chain if suddenly alarmed, so ensure it is not too loose. Let him take his time, distract him with a tit-bit and talk quietly and soothingly to him. Forcing him roughly and impatiently to confront whatever alarms him will simply reinforce his fears. Teaching to sit on command is a useful aid in situations where he is likely to flap, for he will be drawing upon a degree of self-control in responding to your command.

Inevitably in our car-oriented society, your dog will be expected to travel in your vehicle without causing problems. If he is prone to carsickness you should not feed him for several hours before travelling. Your vet can prescribe tablets to help, and a trailing chain suspended from the back bumper can reduce the effect of static electricity.

A travelling cage tailored to fit your vehicle is essential if you intend journeying to doggy events. On hot days the tailgate can be opened to allow necessary ventilation during those unavoidable periods when he will have to stay in the car. You should firmly discourage any tendency to bark or whine while he is in the vehicle, and he should not feel free to react aggressively to other dogs passing. Once you allow your dog to get away with such behaviour while

91

you are driving, he will conclude that you are quite impotent to stop him. A noisy, distracting canine passenger is not conducive to happy motoring!

Most German Shepherds have an innate guarding instinct and need no special training to express this. They are 'one-family' rather than 'one-man' dogs and will closely bond with members of the human pack and be naturally protective of its territory. A certain suspicion of outsiders is common to many of the breed but this must never be confused with nervousness. If a young puppy barks anxiously at visitors with his hackles raised, you should not shut him out of the way. This will simply increase his concern. Instead, calmly control him on a lead and encourage the stranger to stroke him gently while you offer a tit-bit. You should take every opportunity to introduce him to strangers while he is young so that he finds their company pleasurable. He will soon learn to accept them as long as you are present, and such friendly relations will not affect the later development of a natural guarding tendency. Your dog must be completely reliable at home and accept whomever you wish to enter. If you keep him in a kennel where his opportunities for social contact with visitors are limited, you must make even greater efforts to take people to meet him. Many first-time owners of the breed may still harbour a residual feeling of distrust towards it and this anxiety transmits itself to the dog. Because he is a German Shepherd Dog, he is not destined to become an aggressive biter. He is simply an intelligent, discriminating animal who deserves a sensible owner that will have faith in him and treat him normally.

When you are out and about with your dog, remember that the breed still appears intimidating to some people. Do not allow him to behave in such a way that they are alarmed by his approach. This is particularly true if young children are involved. A playful, bounding German Shepherd with the most innocent of intentions can, unfortunately, cause panic in those suspicious of the breed. Never allow him to hurtle towards other small dogs unless you are certain they will not turn tail and run away, otherwise your dog will develop a chasing tendency which can be difficult to check.

The Adolescent Dog

Adolescence can be a difficult time for your Shepherd as he changes from a submissive puppy to an adult. The hormonal changes inherent in sexual maturing can affect his reactions to you, to other dogs and to the environment generally. At this time hitherto unnoticed quirks of behaviour can become magnified. Some dogs become wilful and disobedient, apparently forgetting all they have been taught. Others can display signs of insecurity, as if they are discovering their environment all over again for the first time. A previously happy, equable puppy may develop uncertainty in his response to strangers. In some cases he may attempt to challenge your authority as 'pack-leader'. This phase can last from about ten to fourteen months of age. Provided you handle him consistently, firmly but kindly, he will come through it positively.

The Older Dog

Longevity in German Shepherds depends as much upon family background as upon feeding and keeping. Some lines mature late and live longer. With ordinary luck your Shepherd should not show signs of slowing down until his ninth or tenth year provided you keep up his regular exercise and make sure he does not get fat. He needs no special food, though later he may prefer a number of smaller meals rather than one large one, and in old age he will require less protein in his diet. Old dogs, in particular, need to be protected from lying on damp surfaces which may exacerbate any predisposition to arthritis. And when he is no longer capable of a life with dignity and free from discomfort, you must be prepared to take the difficult decision ultimately faced by all dog-owners. Euthanasia is a quick and humane end, and though your sense of loss will be acute you will find some comfort in knowing that you prevented further suffering. And however great the pain of parting you will be able to look back on years of unquestioning loyalty from your German Shepherd.

> We have not to gain his confidence or his friendship: he is born our friend: while his eyes are still closed, already he believes in us: even before his birth he has given himself to man.

5

Training

The German Shepherd Dog is the world's most versatile working dog. To be allowed the opportunity to use his innate talents is his birthright. If you have purchased a well-bred puppy, the chances are that many of his immediate ancestors carry working qualifications, especially if they are German imports. They will have demonstrated their abilities in obedience, tracking and protection work. As your puppy develops into adulthood you can find much pleasure and satisfaction in giving him, too, the chance to work. Obviously, only a minority of dogs will fulfil an actual working role such as that carried out by police dogs, guide dogs, and drug-detection dogs, but even your family pet can be encouraged to use his physical and mental abilities in a satisfying way. The happy dog is one that is allowed expression of his instinctive canine drives in a directed and socially acceptable way. The frustrated dog is denied such opportunities. Training should be just as much about 'educating' a happy and reliable Shepherd as it is about discipline and control.

Laying the Foundations

All dog-training is based upon the relationship between a dog and his owner. Too often this is seen as a one-way process: the owner imposing his will upon the dog. But all good trainers realize that a two-way process is always involved. The dog's reactions will affect the trainer's attitude and subsequent behaviour. No two dogs are alike and training methods will invariably be adapted with that truth in mind if they are to succeed. It is essential, therefore, that you know your dog. It is very difficult to generalize about typical German Shepherd Dog character. Some are sensitive and submissive, others bold and wilful. As your puppy grows you should have formed a sound understanding of his nature so that you may employ the right training techniques for *him*. Of course, you will probably learn by

94

trial and error whether you are being too harsh or too soft with your dog, but much frustration for dog and handler can be avoided with a little forethought. If you decide to attend a dog-training club, don't necessarily follow the advice of a trainer who treats every dog in the same way. Attend to the trainer who has attempted to assess your dog's particular needs, and don't be offended if he makes some constructive observations about the way *you* should respond.

For formal training, many people replace their dog's leather collar with a check-chain. Chains are very effective, but it is essential that they are the right size, correctly fitted and used properly. Incorrect use of a check-chain can be dangerous.

This check-chain is correctly fitted. You can see that if the handler yields the lead, the chain will loosen. The handler should exert pressure only when necessary, and then only momentarily.

This check-chain is incorrectly fitted. If the handler yields the lead, the chain will not loosen; in fact, as the weight of the lead pulls downwards, it will force the ring towards the dog's neck, tightening the chain.

The Recall

The basics of training should begin in puppyhood. An instant recall to you is essential, and is the foundation of all later progress. Decide which word you intend to use to call your puppy to you and don't let anyone else use it at the beginning. Since most of the family may be using the dog's name casually during the day – to attract his attention, to reprove him, to make a fuss of him – it is better to use a word that you want the puppy to understand solely as an invitation to rush to you as quickly as possible, as if his life depended upon it! In the first weeks of puppy training you must arrange things so that as soon as he hears the magic word he runs to you. Never give him the chance to be deflected or to lose interest. Exploit his natural greediness as a puppy; let him know you have a tit-bit he wants, and then get someone to hold him while you walk away. He should be wriggling with excitement to get free. Give your word at the precise moment he is released and let him have his reward as soon as he reaches you. After you have repeated this several times and you are sure he will rush to you, let someone hold him in a different room and then call him out of sight. Now you will see whether he is responding to the word and not simply to your presence with the food. Once he has learned to rush from another room to you, you can increase the time-lag before you call, or call him into the house from the bottom of the garden and so on. Later, away from the house, you can practise in the park, amongst distractions, but with the dog on a long line so that he is never given the chance to fail to return. A good recall is the basis of good control, both for the family pet and for the dog destined to compete in obedience or working trials.

The Retrieve

The competitive aspect of dog-training can offer a leisure activity with much to offer. If you intend to be involved in competition, the other basic ability to develop in your pup is a willingness to retrieve. Most young puppies will run after a moving object and you should capitalize upon this. Make a firm but not too hard toy that the puppy can be encouraged to pick up and carry. If it can roll a little after you have thrown it, it will hold the pup's attention and stimulate what dog psychologists call the 'prey drive'. Vary the object, and praise the pup for every attempt to pick it up. Do *not* call the puppy back to you unless you are certain he will come (remember a recall word ignored is a recall word weakened). *Never* pursue the puppy while he is carrying the toy. This will simply increase his tendency to possess it for himself and run off, the very opposite of what you will ultimately be aiming at: a willing retrieve back to you. Carry out the above in a confined space and wait until the puppy comes back to you, then praise him for every movement in your direction. Introduce the word 'Fetch' to coincide with the *exact moment* that the pup picks up his toy, not as a command or order but simply as a sound that he will

Stuart Nye's Schutzhund bitch, Dora, demonstrates the retrieve over the bush jump.

associate with the activity of picking something up. Your eventual aim will be to get him to pick up a variety of stationary toys when you tell him to 'Fetch'. Once you are sure he will do that in the house, you can practise on the lead outside. Simply drop a toy and tell him to 'Fetch', with enormous praise as he picks it up. Then let him parade around proudly carrying it, but still on the lead so that he cannot avoid your control. Remember 'Fetch' does not mean 'bring back' at this stage. Be more than happy if your pup is keen to pick up whatever you indicate to him in a number of different places and situations. If he begins to lose interest in toys, then make sure they move, by kicking or throwing them for him or encouraging him to play tug-of-war with them. It is worth spending a great deal of time on this aspect before even considering the bring-back.

In parallel with this activity you should have kept up your recall work. Now is the time to marry the two. As the pup picks up on the word 'Fetch', give the recall word and be ready with the tit-bit as soon as the pup comes to you. Do this with the puppy very close to you so that he hardly has to move to come to you. This will minimize the chance of his dropping the toy. Quickly take the toy and give him the reward. Always do this on the lead, and remember that your aim will be to associate the word 'Fetch' with pick up, coming in and instant reward. The smaller the time-lag between these three elements the better. Avoid any lengthening of the distance between you and the toy, until you have thoroughly conditioned the pup to expect

Tom Nye and Paco demonstrating a perfect present in the retrieve exercise.

a reward as soon as he picks up and comes in. Gradually lengthen the distance and soon the word 'Fetch' alone should suffice to encourage the pup to pick up and return without the need for the recall word. Although you have increased the distance, never allow the pup to take his time in returning. Use the lead to get him back, and move backwards yourself to ensure he returns quickly. He must never be nagged for dropping the toy at your feet (it was your fault for not taking it in time, anyway!). Remember he must experience only pleasure at coming up to you at all times. If he has unpleasant experiences on coming in, he will be hesitant and never perform the retrieve you should be aiming at.

The next step is to teach him to hold the toy as he is walking on the lead and then to keep hold of it as you stand still. Most dogs will drop it as soon as you stop, so try to make sure this does not happen. If it does, simply give the word 'Fetch', walk on further and slow your pace right down, taking the toy just before he stops. *Don't* praise him as you take it: reserve the praise for his holding it.

Finally you must teach him to 'Hold it' as he is in a sitting position. (It is useful if you have taught the Sit–Stay exercise – *see* The Down Stay, page 100 – before this point so that the pup knows he must not move.) Gently put the article in his mouth with the inducement 'Fetch', and stroke him quietly with words of encouragement as he grasps it for a few seconds. Never take it as he spits it out; try to be one step ahead and take it before he can do that. He must learn that he is not free to let it go when *he* wishes. If he does release it when you don't want him to, make a strongly disapproving noise, place it quickly in his mouth and immediately change your manner into soothing encouragement. Gradually increase the time you expect him to hold it and when you are sure he will not drop it you can move away from him as he sits proudly holding his toy. Don't kill his interest in it; throw it for him to play-retrieve periodically.

You have now taught a quick recall, pick up and return and your young dog will sit on command while holding the article. He is ready to be told to stay at your side, while you throw the article in front of you. He should go out on the word 'Fetch' and return ready to sit in front of you. You now have the basics of a good retrieve. Remember to practise on the lead to avoid any loss of control. When you are confident he will always come back to you off the lead, you can reward him by immediately throwing the article for a play-retrieve with the minimum of formal control as he presents it to you. He will soon learn that coming back to you means a game will follow. Once he is keen to retrieve you can throw articles into long grass and encourage him to use his nose to find them. Then drop them as you walk, without his realizing you have done so, and encourage him to go back to find. This is not only a great game in his eyes but it forms the basics of the scenting work you may wish to develop further, should you take up the sport of working trials with your Shepherd.

Teaching the Immediate Down

Your Shepherd should be taught to lie down immediately on command and stay down until released. Do not try to force your dog to 'Down' while he is standing. Wait until he is sitting, but do not 'Down' him immediately after a command to sit, or you will confuse him. As he sits, you will find it easy to pull his offside foreleg under him towards yourself, so that he trips over on to his side in a down position. The aim is to get his brisket on to the ground as quickly as possible with the command you use. There should be an element of shock in this command; it needs to be a sharp, incisive word. The German word *Platz* is a particularly effective sound when contrasted with the longer, more muted consonants of the English 'Down'. You must insist he hits the deck as soon as he hears the command, so there can be no room for coaxing, cajoling or awkwardly manipulating him down. The more forceful and decisive you can be in physically compelling him down, the better. After he has learned the

99

response, continually reinforce it while he is running free. When he is not looking at you, throw your bunched-up lead at him as you command him sharply 'Down'. This element of surprise will ensure he does not become blasé about the order.

The Down Stay

Teaching your dog to stay should present few difficulties provided you do not rush things. Do not be tempted to leave your dog until he will stay in the sit or down position by your side without moving. You will find it better in the early stages of training to keep exercises where you require the dog to be active, such as heel work and recall, quite separate from 'Stay' training. Find a separate time and place if you can. After a while you should be able to signal to your dog by your own behaviour just when he is expected to be ready for action and when he is required to compose himself and wait. For 'Stay' work you need to be calm and unhurried in your approach and avoid behaviour that would unsettle or excite the dog. Do not casually leave your dog in a 'Stay' position and then release him to search for objects or he will soon be breaking his stays out of excited anticipation. And avoid doing recall work at the same time as you practise stays. Similarly, do a 'Sit, Stay' and a 'Down, Stay' at different times to avoid confusion in the dog's mind.

Once your dog is in the required position, tell him to stay using your hand before his head to reinforce the command, and step away from him while holding the lead. Sometimes the presence of the hanging lead will induce the dog to come forward to you, particularly if you have been using the lead to call the dog to you. If that is happening then drop the lead so that you can put your foot on it if necessary. Be content with a few feet of distance at first and, when returning, make sure your dog does not move until you signal to him that the exercise has finished, by either a word or a particular body movement. Never let him move on any other action of yours. Indeed, before you start to move more than a few paces from him, make absolutely certain he has learned the routine of remaining still and never moving until you give him the signal. If he moves, give a sharp repetition of the command to stay with a forceful 'No'. Try to be one step ahead of him and at the slightest suspicion of movement intervene immediately. You must never take your eyes off him but do not stare him in the eye. This may unsettle him and make him want to show submissive behaviour by crawling towards you. Never lose your temper or berate him too harshly or again he will recognize your dominance as pack leader by crawling to you. Simply put him back on the exact spot, talk to him quietly to settle him down and then repeat the exercise. The more contrast you can get into your voice in this work the better: soothing for the correct position, harshly unwelcoming for any attempt to move to you. The dog must recognize the difference in your tone, so indulge in a little dramatic exaggeration.

After a while you can increase the distance and, when you are certain he is reliable, begin to go out of sight. Go behind a tree or fence where you can still see him though he is not aware of it. Again, be ready with instant intervention if he shows the slightest inclination to move or tense himself up. Sometimes he will want a sharp word to remind him, at other times he may just need the reassurance of your voice to assure him that you are still in contact. Do not have to return too far during the early stages, because as you come back into view he will naturally be keyed up to see you again and may be tempted to get up. So the sooner you can get back to him and execute a correct finish to the exercise, the better.

Heel Work

Walking to heel means different things to different people. To the pet-owner it simply describes the behaviour of a dog walking calmly under control at its owner's side without persistent pulling. The obedience enthusiast must aim at a highly disciplined, formal heel-work in which every movement of the dog is closely scrutinized for deviations from the ideal routine. A slightly wide about-turn, or a crooked or non-aligned sit, could mean the loss of valuable marks in competition. Should you wish to aim at such precision, books specially written by obedience experts will help, as will attendance at a training club that specializes in training for competition.

Most problems with pulling for the pet-owner are caused in the earliest days of a puppy's experience of the lead. Often the lead is too short or is held too tightly so that, right from the beginning, the pup associates the lead with pulling and forms the habit of leaning into it. The simple rule is: never let him pull! If he does, let the lead suddenly loose and he will fall on his nose: an unpleasant experience he will not want to repeat. Or, just as suddenly, turn right round and walk in the opposite direction but do not pull him round with you. Let the lead loose and call him to follow, having a toy or tit-bit ready when he catches up with you. Unless you are teaching formal heel-work you will be content with a dog walking slightly ahead of you at a comfortable pace.

Competitive heel-work demands a great deal of sustained concentration from the dog, as those who have watched the obedience championships at Crufts each year will have observed. You can lay the foundations for future success by systematically developing your dog's attentiveness to you. Sit him close to your left side and attract his attention with his toy in your right hand. Tell him to 'Watch' and, after he has gazed fixedly for a few seconds, throw his toy or play tug-of-war. Gradually extend the time he must spend attending before he wins his reward. Repeat this later when there are distractions about. Only when you are sure you can hold his attention when you need to, should you begin formal heel-work. Then walk forward four or five paces, to see if his watchfulness is maintained as you walk, and give him his toy. Be very satisfied if, after several days' practice, you can walk in a straight line for thirty paces or so without losing his attention. Only then should you think about teaching him to keep close as you turn left, right and about, and to sit straight and close as you halt. Don't harass your dog by pulling and shoving him into position when you stop. The less physical contact with him the better. Assuming he sits quickly on command and you have his attention at heel, try walking along a pavement with the dog at the very edge of the kerb. When you halt, he will sit very close to your left leg in order to avoid toppling off the kerb-edge. And you will not have to put a finger on him! Practise this regularly and sitting close will become a habit.

Tracking

If you have encouraged your dog to be fanatically keen on his toy, you should find no difficulty in teaching him to track. Tracking is not only an absorbing activity which will take you and your Shepherd out in all weathers, but it is an essential part of training if you wish to progress in working trials competition.

The simple idea is that your dog will follow the track of scent left by the footsteps of the track-layer with the main purpose of finding articles he or she has laid on the track. The dog must learn that only by keeping his nose close to the line of scent can he find his toy. He must realize that he cannot succeed by using his eyes or by lifting his nose and scenting the article on the wind currents around him.

Competitor and judge following a German Shepherd in the tracking tests at the Dutch Schutzhund National Trial, 1996.

He will know all about using his eyes and wind-scenting while searching for a toy you may have thrown for him during play. Tracking is a different game. Begin by fastening your dog to a fence, making sure he knows you have his toy. Excite him with it so that he is mad keen to get it from you. Say or do nothing to restrain his enthusiasm. Now walk in a straight line away from him for about twenty-five paces; let him see you hide the toy in the grass, then carefully retrace your exact line back to the starting point. You have 'double-laid' a short track in doing this. The dog should have one thought only in mind: to find what you have placed in the grass. Untie him and, holding his lead, take him to the start of your track. He may put his nose down straightaway. Alternatively, he may want to drag you to the spot he is convinced holds the toy. As long as he is going directly along the line, don't interfere with him. He will have to use his nose to find the article, so steady him slightly so that he does not miss it. Make it easy by using a large toy, but make sure he cannot see it in the grass. As soon as he finds it make a great fuss and enjoy a game with the toy.

Once you are sure he will follow your short track, you can begin developing the set of associations that will always accompany tracking in the dog's mind and prepare the mind-set necessary for him to attempt a track anywhere and in any conditions. Purchase or make a set of tracking poles. These are simply easily transportable spiked sticks about 2.5ft (75cm) long. Stick one in the ground at the spot where your track begins and get into the habit of marking a scent pad at its base before you lay your track. Simply scuff your feet to make a triangular shape with the apex of the triangle pointing in the direction of your track. Encourage your dog to investigate this intensified pad of scent before he begins to track. Buy a leather or nylon tracking harness and tracking line and put on the harness *immediately* before he starts to work. He will soon learn to associate the pole, the harness and the line with the business of tracking. If you have laid the foundations correctly and made haste slowly, your Shepherd should show obvious signs of excited anticipation as soon as he hears you rattle his harness.

Try to avoid the temptation to lay long or ambitious tracks until you have built up this keen enthusiasm in your dog. The right attitude is a priceless asset and well worth the time spent developing it. In competition he may well be required to track in difficult weather conditions or over demanding terrain. Only a committed attitude will see him through. If you and your dog have enjoyed elementary tracking it would be a pity not to develop it further. Indeed, you will probably be keen to discover how your dog will react if he has not seen you lay the track, or if it has been laid some time before he is asked to work it. But be patient! Get the basics right first. Many a dog has been spoiled by a handler pushing him too ambitiously, so that the dog becomes confused, loses the track and fails. It is essential that the dog always succeeds and finds his reward. If he is in difficulty at any point on the track, you must know *exactly* where it is so that you can help him back on to it and conclude positively. Both you and your dog will learn from experience in tracking. You will begin to

Kate Coleridge's Santrovaso Ivy C.D.Ex., U.D. concentrates on her tracking work.

'read' your dog on the track and detect those signs he gives you that he is following the scent. Handling the tracking line will improve with practice and you will begin to take notice of the impact of wind direction and natural obstacles.

There are certainly few experiences in working a dog that can equal the sense of achievement in successfully completing a track, the course of which is unknown to you, and which may be up to three hours old. And if your dog finds the articles on the track, your cup will be overflowing! There are several excellent specialist books on tracking and if you are attracted by this rewarding aspect of training, do invest in them. In addition, the help of an experienced triallist, well versed in tracking, will be invaluable. Although you should lay your own tracks during most of your training, it is important that you also have occasional experience of working an unknown track, laid by someone else. You will then be forced to trust your dog, and to read the signs indicating he is tracking properly. Your track-layer can follow close behind and make sure you do not lose the track and confuse your dog.

Agility

Agility is not only a compulsory part of working trials but is now a well-established sport in its own right, enjoying growing popularity throughout the world. In trials the requirements are straightforward. The dog must jump, on command and under control, a 3ft (90cm) hurdle, a 9ft (2.7m) long jump and a 6ft (1.8m) scale. As in all other aspects of training, the right attitude on the dog's part is paramount. He must enjoy jumping and you can do much to foster a positive approach well before you begin the formal training needed for competition. Although you should not expect your dog to do any physically demanding jumps until he has finished his growth and skeletal development, at around sixteen months of age, you can encourage him to jump over low objects on your walks and teach him appropriate words such 'Up' or 'Over' as he does so. Combine this with much praise or a reward, and he will soon enjoy the game. It is useful to take him to the same obstacles every day so that he will develop a keen sense of anticipation as you approach them. Restrain him from jumping for a few seconds and give the word 'Ready'. You will want to arouse his sense of anticipation whenever he hears the word. He will then realize he is expected to jump whatever obstacle you indicate. You will have laid an excellent foundation for further agility training if you can see him eye up a log or a low fence with poised excitement as soon as you say 'Ready'. Encourage him to clamber up on to wooden boxes or low walls so that he grows up with no inhibitions about jumping on to whatever you wish. As long as he experiences nothing unpleasant, he will grow to trust you and jump with confidence.

Eventually he will have to learn literally to clear the hurdle. Any slight touching of the top will dislodge the top bar and he will have failed. Gradually increase the height and always jump the dog on the lead. You should go past the jump as he does so. You must then progress to the situation where he will stay at your side, either sitting or standing, until you send him over while you remain on your side of the jump. You must gauge the correct distance to position your dog in front of the jump. If you or a friend can observe him jumping from the side it will be clear whether he is contacting the top bar because he is too close or far away or simply because he is not jumping high enough to clear the full height. If the latter is the case, encourage him to clear a solid obstacle a little over 3ft (90cm) high. If you detect that he is becoming lazy or careless about clearing it, you may tie some fisherman's twine across the jump about 3in (75cm) above the maximum height. The unexpected contact with his toes will galvanize him into trying harder next time. Remember that, like most dogs, the Shepherd is a very observant creature and, particularly when he is poised to jump, the slightest body movement on your part can send him into action. So make sure you do nothing inadvertently to release him to jump until he is properly positioned and ready. Control and timing are essential for success. Remember, too, that any hesitation, anxiety or nerves on your part may be communicated to the dog and affect his jump.

Long-jump equipment is easy to make and transport, giving you the opportunity to practise in different situations. Your dog will be required to jump over the boards spaced out to cover a length of 9ft (2.7m). He must stay in a position of your choice as soon as he has cleared the jump and *you* will not be allowed to pass behind the first board during the exercise, until you are told to join your dog. If you have encouraged your dog to jump very obvious obstacles, he may find skipping over a couple of low boards, just inches from the ground, rather uneventful. Begin with a low hurdle about 18in (45cm) high and place one of your boards just in front of it. These will give him an obvious target to jump. Run with him on the lead and give him his toy as soon as he lands. Then throw his toy over the

Kate Coleridge's Santrovaso Flora C.D.Ex. makes easy work of the 9ft (2.7m) long jump.

hurdle, making sure it lands in the correct position to encourage him to jump straight. Never let him jump at an angle or you will be building problems for later progress. When he is keen to get over you can gradually place three or four boards together in front of your hurdle so that he is having to stretch out a little to clear it. The boards should be very close and create the illusion that he is jumping an almost solid box-top. You can then place other boards behind the hurdle so that the dog has to describe an arc in the air as he leaps, as well as stretching to cover the length. Very gradually and over several days, widen the distance between the boards and increase your run up to the jump. Always run past the jump with your dog on the lead to keep up momentum and to make sure he does not run out and avoid the jump. He must learn that *only* by jumping can he get at the toy you have positioned on the other side. On no account must he be allowed to 'paddle' through the boards. At the slightest sign of this you must immediately revert to positioning the boards together so that such behaviour is impossible. By the time he is jumping 5–6ft (1.5–1.8m) without the hurdle and with enthusiasm on a centre line through the boards, you will find it difficult to run fast enough to keep up with him and you may find that keeping him on the lead will result in your distracting or hindering him. Now is the time to teach him to wait at the appropriate distance from the jump. Give him the word 'Ready' that you have used before, to arouse his sense of anticipation, and then walk a few paces from him before suddenly bursting into a run towards the jump, encouraging him with the word 'Over'. If your earlier work on the lead has been thorough, he should now run keenly to the jump and clear it. Throw his toy at him as soon as he has landed and let him enjoy it. Do not extend your jump beyond 5–6ft (1.5–1.8m) until you are confident he will stay, poised to move, and then run towards the jump enthusiastically (off the lead). It is then simply a matter of gradually increasing the length to the 9ft (2.7m) necessary and commanding him to stay at the other side. Do not overemphasize the control to begin with. It is better for your dog always to expect fun after jumping rather than a repressive command.

Scaling a vertical height of 6ft (1.8m) on command and under control is the third necessary element in working trials agility. Your dog has to learn how to spring up, reach for the top of the jump, pull himself over and scramble down the other side without leaping off the top. You should have laid the foundations by encouraging him to jump on to boxes, ledges or table-tops (not in the dining-room!) to find his toy there, so that he has learned how to spring up and to make contact with the obstacle. Make sure you begin your scaling work proper on a strong, stable jump. Avoid narrow jumps with angle-iron supports and anything that might seem insubstantial to your dog. He must feel comfortable and secure in his training. With the boards at a height of approximately 3ft (90cm), and with the dog on the lead, encourage him to jump over and back. When he is keen to do this, gradually raise the height and bring the dog close to the jump so that he cannot clear it but must hook his forelegs over the top and fold his hindquarters underneath him. Once you are certain that he is contacting the jump comfortably and with confidence and is turning to come back over, you can gradually increase the height. At each increase you will be positioning him a little further from the jump so that, at the maximum height of 6ft (1.8m), you will expect him to jump from a spot some 6–9ft (2–2.5m) away.

A common problem encountered on the return jump is that caused by the dog coming in too close to the base of the scale, making it difficult for him to gain the height necessary. Plan to avoid this by moving with the dog as he goes over on his initial jump and positioning him at an appropriate distance from the scale with the order to 'Wait'. Then return to the front of the scale and call him over to you. With repetition of this, he will eventually learn to move away from the scale on his own. You can help him, too, by placing a piece of carpet on the spot you wish him to aim for on landing. As with all jumping exercises, pleasure and confidence in the activity must be fostered at all stages. Try to minimize unpleasant experiences and your Shepherd will enjoy demonstrating his physical prowess in agility. He cannot be expected to take pleasure in jumping if you push him beyond the limits of his previous experience so that he fails, or if you forget that he needs to be in the right physical condition for the task. Always limber him up before jumping and never expect him to perform 'cold'.

Before your dog's jumping ability is tested at a trial do make sure he has gained experience of jumping different types of equipment in differing situations where distractions may have to be overcome. Unfortunately, the Kennel Club does not specify the type of scale-jump used in trials competitions. Some have slats to enable the dog to gain some purchase as he goes over. Others are simply sheer. Though the height is specified, the width is not, and you may also find that, having trained on a naturally coloured scale, your dog is confronted with one recently painted a dazzling white. The same applies to the long jump and hurdle, which may differ in appearance. The element of unpredictability is what makes trials an interesting test for dog and handler, but it also means you have to train your Shepherd to cope confidently with the unexpected.

If you feel that the demands of formal obedience tests and the rigours of working trials will ask too much of your German Shepherd, you may find the increasingly popular sport of timed agility competitions an enjoyable outlet for your dog's physical and mental exuberance. The sport had its origins in Britain, where it mirrored competitive horse-jumping in its early days, with a variety of 'show-jumping' obstacles to be negotiated against the clock. But soon it spread to the Continent and beyond. Specialist books have been written on the sport and formal rules and regulations established by the Kennel Club and the FCI (Fédédération Cynologique Internationale – the organization governing canine affairs in a number of countries, the most notable exceptions being Britain and the USA). These regulations mean that a high degree of training and control is necessary for success. Your Shepherd will need to be quick, athletic and responsive in order to compete with other breeds noted for their speed, like Border Collies. He must clear hurdles, negotiate weaving-poles and tunnels, climb angled ramps and traverse the see-saw, all in the order you point out to him. And you must be reasonably athletic yourself! Agility appears to be a sure-fire winner with the dogs, whose enthusiasm for the activity is only too apparent. But remember you will need to develop a special relationship

109

with your Shepherd so that he feels free to jump with speed and confidence, yet is always aware of and responsive to your guiding control, especially when he is required to lie down on one of the elements for a specified time and when following the course stipulated by the judge. Whereas you can train for obedience competition and trials without special equipment, apart from the jumps we have discussed earlier, if you want to take up agility you will need to find a club in your neighbourhood with the necessary obstacles.

Competitive Work for the Shepherd

Obedience

Obedience shows run under the jurisdiction of the Kennel Club are held on almost every weekend of the calendar somewhere in the UK, such is the popularity of the sport. If you wish to add to the numbers of the addicted, you will be warmly welcomed at one of your local training clubs, most of which are run by those already hooked. They will be keen to help you achieve the high standard necessary for success and leave you under no delusions about the persistence and commitment you will need. You can make excellent progress provided you follow the dictum 'a little and often'. Two twenty-minute sessions a day, broken up with play, will suffice. Trying to compensate for a lack of training over four or five days by imposing a hour's unremitting work upon your dog will get you nowhere fast. You need to be a repetitive perfectionist without becoming a harassing nag! And the best thing about obedience training is that you need no special equipment or facilities (apart from a wooden dumb-bell) and you can train in the park, the living room or the garden, at your place of work, or anywhere where you can keep your dog's attention and have ten minutes to spare. Remember if you are teaching something *new* to your dog, avoid doing so with distractions around. Train with distractions only when you are sure he knows what is required of him. And whatever you are teaching him, always make sure you end the session positively. If he has failed in one area, conclude your lesson with something you know he can do well and then praise him enthusiastically. Never end with your dog dispirited and confused.

Obedience shows are usually advertised in the specialist magazines devoted to the sport. Your local training club may also publicize forthcoming events in your area and have entry forms for

Guide dog, Muffin, at eleven years of age, still working with owner, Cliff Vawda, in a Lichfield park.

you to fill in. Most shows are open to all breeds of dog but occasionally breed clubs organize limited shows at which entries are confined to German Shepherds only. You may find such an event is a good one to start you on the competitive trail: you will be relieved, also, of the rivalry of the ubiquitous Border Collie who will dominate most obedience shows you will subsequently attend.

The classes to work your way through to the top are Pre-beginners, Beginners, Novice and Classes 'A', 'B' and 'C'. The winner of the most difficult class 'C' at a championship obedience show, provided he or she has gained sufficient overall marks, is awarded the Challenge Certificate (CC), three of which, won under three different judges, will confer the title Obedience Champion. All certificate winners in the year preceding the annual Crufts Show are invited to that event to compete in the prestigious KC Obedience Championship and the winner is awarded the title of Champion if not already in possession of it. Shepherds are very much in a minority at this event, dominated as it is by the Border Collie, but a good German Shepherd is capable of taking on the best of any breed. Unfortunately some obedience judges expect a Shepherd to work like a Border Collie and forget that all breeds have their own distinctive ways of moving and reacting.

The Beginners and Novice classes will require your dog to heel on and off the lead, recall to handler and stay on command for no more than two minutes with you in sight. In Novice your dog will also have to retrieve a dumb-bell. Because the exercises are pretty elementary and limited you may think these classes will be a doddle for you and your Shepherd. Not a bit of it – many a good dog has found it difficult to win a Novice class, because the work must be done with great precision. Entries are often huge, with several dogs at the top losing just fractions of a mark for very minor imprecisions. Classes A, B, and C require even greater exactitude because you will not be allowed to give any extra commands, either by voice, body or gesture. Stays will require you to go out of sight for up to ten minutes and your dog's scenting skills will be tested in tests of increasing difficulty through the classes. Heelwork will become more complicated and involve different speeds and your dog will have to be taught the sendaway exercise. The detailed requirements of each class, together with the marks allocated, will be found in the schedules for shows which are distributed with entry forms.

Working Trials

There is no doubt that trials work is for the 'outdoor' German Shepherd enthusiast, who has access to jumping equipment and land for tracking and long sendaway training. You must be prepared to train in all weathers for, unlike in Obedience, your dog will have to perform no matter what the conditions. At the great annual Christmas Trial at Scarborough, for example, dogs have had to stay down with snow falling while their shivering handlers went out of sight, then track over frozen hillsides. But if you like being out in beautiful rural areas of the country and enjoy watching dogs work against a backcloth of the changing seasons, trials may be for you. Most German Shepherds will thrive on trials work, for it allows expression of their natural capabilities in agility and nose-work but places less emphasis on formalized perfection of execution. A dog may be his natural exuberant self, enjoying the task, and not be penalized for it!

Although prizes are awarded for the winners in each class or stake, most competitors regard these as a bonus, the main objective being to gain a Working Trials qualification with your dog. To do this you need to receive 70 per cent of the total allocated marks in each of the specified areas such as agility, obedience (control) and nose-work. A mark of 80 per cent or higher overall will gain the qualification 'Excellent'. The C.D. (Companion Dog) stake is the lowest step on the ladder, but still requires a substantial amount of training in preparation. Your Shepherd must have learned the 3ft hurdle, the 6ft scale and the 9ft long jump (*see* page 106). He must be proficient in heelwork at normal, fast and slow pace and at retrieving a dumb-bell. 'Stay' exercises require him to sit for two minutes and lie down for ten minutes while you go out of sight. The judge will expect your dog to perform a sendaway of about 50 yards (45m) in a direction indicated to you. Finally the judge will arrange for small articles to be hidden in a 25-square-yard (20sq. m) area, to test your dog's ability to find them using his nose and retrieve them to hand within the time allocated. You may enter the C.D. stake at a championship trial without any previous qualification, but to enter the higher stakes you must have gained a certificate of merit (awarded for an overall qualifying mark) at an open trial. Only after qualifying at a championship trial are you allowed to place the qualification after your dog's name.

All subsequent stakes involve tracking work of increasing difficulty. The U.D. (Utility Dog) stake will include a track which is half an hour old with two articles left on it carrying the track-layer's scent. Your dog must find at least one article to qualify on the track. The W.D. (Working Dog) stake expects the dog to work a longer track which is one-and-a-half hours old and which contains more 'legs' (straight sections) and angled turns. Most triallists will aim to qualify through the stakes to enable them to enter the T.D. (Tracking Dog) stake at championship level. Here the track is three hours old and can often be incredibly complicated. Twenty legs of differing length and unpredictable turns in disorientating directions are not uncommon. The sendaway will cover distances of up to 250 yards (225m) and include redirections on command. To gain the award T.D.Ex. (Tracking Dog Excellent) is the dream of most triallists but the really committed will aim at winning the Challenge Certificate for the best qualifying performance in the stake overall.

To gain the title of Working Trials Champion you must win two certificates under two different judges in the T.D. or P.D. (Patrol Dog) stake. The latter is the only stake involving 'criminal' or 'man-work'. Your German Shepherd will be expected to range over an area to find a hidden 'criminal' and bark (but not bite) on discovering him. He must pursue a fleeing man and stop him from escaping by holding him fast by the arm. His courage will be tested in a number of unpredictable ways and, most difficult of all, he must be recalled to you, on an indication by the judge, while he is in full pursuit of the 'felon'. At all times he must be under strict control. The tracking in this stake is not as demanding as that in T.D. but all other aspects require a high standard of preparation.

Compared with obedience competitions, there are fewer trials organized especially in the high summer months when tracking land may not be so easily available. If you enter a tracking stake you will be required to indicate your preferred day for tracking and include a stamped addressed envelope so that the organizers can inform you of the day and time you are expected to attend for your track. Championship trials usually involve your attending for two days, one devoted to completing your tracking and search work and the other to control and agility. At open trials you will usually complete all your work on the same day. Your dog must be at least eighteen months old to be eligible for working trials competition.

Schutzhund Trials

Schutzhund literally means 'protection dog' and is the term used on the Continent to denote the working tests in operation there. You may have noticed that your German Shepherd's imported ancestors often have the abbreviations Sch.H. I, II or III after their names to indicate they have passed such a test at a particular level. In Schutzhund trials in Europe, dogs belonging to the 'guarding' breeds such as Dobermanns, Boxers and Rottweilers, as well as German Shepherds, are expected to demonstrate their ability to protect their owners as well as proficiency in tracking, agility and nose-work. The British Schutzhund Association has been in existence for over a decade and has a number of member clubs in different parts of the country. Although it is not officially recognized by the Kennel Club, it actively seeks to demonstrate the excellence and reliability of dogs trained by its members by holding its own Schutzhund trials. Several British dogs have qualified Sch.H. III under Continental judges.

The British working trials system involves 'protection' work only in the Patrol Dog (P.D.) stake. To enter that your dog will have to qualify up the ladder through the preceding stakes. A relatively small number of trainers decide to aim at P.D., the majority setting their sights on the T.D. qualification. Schutzhund tests, however, will

*Steve Dunn's Vidbar Jago
retrieves the dumb-bell over
the 'A' frame at a
Schutzhund test.*

include protection work from the outset. You will not be allowed to enter Sch.H. I until your dog has passed an elementary B.H. (Companion Dog) test which simply assesses whether your dog is under basic control and is safe with people and other dogs. Simple recall and heelwork are the requirements. Your dog does not even have to be taught the retrieve, the main point of the test being to see if your Shepherd is stable and sociable. Aggressive, unreliable and nervous dogs are excluded from Schutzhund training in this way. Owners who want to encourage their dogs to be aggressive are given short shrift by Schutzhund enthusiasts!

Working trials tests run by the Kennel Club allow considerable freedom for the judge to devise the exercises. In T.D., for example, one of the tasks requires the dog to bark on command and cease when required to do so at the judge's discretion. The judge decides precisely how the test will be carried out. Sometimes the dog must 'speak' as he is heeling, or when the handler is out of sight or at a distance at the end of the sendaway exercise. It is this element of the unpredictable that tests both dog and handler and makes trials so interesting. Schutzhund tests, on the other hand, make every effort to minimize the element of unpredictability. The exercises are rigidly circumscribed and formalized so that dog, handler and judge know exactly what is expected of them. Certainly no Schutzhund judge can set a test that might be regarded as unfair or confusing to the dog, an accusation sometimes levelled at the working trials judges. Because the Schutzhund exercises are so clearly defined, the judge will mark with corresponding exactitude.

The difference in approach may be clearly seen by contrasting aspects of a P.D. stake with those of a Sch.H. III test. At a recent KC championship event, spectators looked out over a wide expanse of grazing land flanked by hedgerows on one side and thick woodland on the other. An 'abandoned' vehicle stood in the middle of the field. The judge instructed the handler to go with his dog to search the car and informed him that a suspected 'criminal' had left the vehicle and made off towards the hedge. As the handler approached the vehicle, the 'criminal' was to fire a gun from his hiding place. Both dog and handler were required to crouch behind the car, while the man, unseen by dog and handler, would leave the hedge, race across the field and find refuge in the woods. The dog was then sent to find the man while his handler remained out of sight, unable to give him any help by voice or signal. The dog had to use his initiative and bark on apprehending the man without biting.

The corresponding exercise in a Schutzhund III test is quite different. Six artificial 'hides' are positioned formally in the working ring or stadium, three on each side. As the handler proceeds down a centre line between the hides, the dog is directed to investigate each hide

Hindering the criminal's escape – a Schutzhund dog shows his courage.

*Stuart and Pauline Nye's Ary von Haus Ming C.D. Ex., U.D.Ex.,
W.D.Ex. in combative action.*

in turn until reaching the sixth, when he will discover the 'criminal' and detain him by forceful barking. This format is followed in all tests with little variation. No attempt is made to simulate a 'real-life scenario' as in P.D., and neither dog nor handler will be required to display initiative or adaptability during the test, unless things go wrong!

In Schutzhund work – the essence of protection dog training – the animal's courage and resilience, together with the handler's complete control, has been distilled, formalized and perfected. In tracking, too, the handler will know the prescribed pattern so that less emphasis is placed upon the partnership of dog and handler in following a completely unknown track as in working trials. What matters is the formal execution of the task and, rather like obedience, marks are lost for the slightest deviations.

Any training involving 'man-work' must be done with expert guidance. Unless you seriously intend to aim at P.D. or Schutzhund trials you would be advised to concentrate on other areas of Shepherd training.

6

Showing

A rose-grower gazing in rapt attentiveness at a flower's colour, petal formation and leaf texture; a pony breeder absorbed in watching a magnificent Welsh stallion arrogantly whinnying into the wind at the end of his show-line; a song-bird fancier drawn to the cage of the champion exhibit to admire perfection of shape, plumage colour and poise: all share with the dog-show enthusiast the same appreciation of beauty in flower, fur and feather. All are fascinated by the challenge of shaping the raw material nature offers into the impossible dream of perfect form.

But people become involved in showing dogs for many reasons. For some, the appetite for success increases through that on which it feeds: they cannot amass enough prizes to sustain a swelling pride in their animal's wins. The sheer number of prizes matters more than the quality of those awards. They forget that a prize is only as good as the judge who awards it and the strength of competition in which it was achieved. Others will be commercially motivated, seeking to increase the value of their stock as potential merchandise or breeding material. Some enjoy shows as social occasions, offering regular opportunities to meet friends whom they would not otherwise see. But the interplay of such varying motives should not blind us to the main point of dog shows. They exist to improve the quality of a breed by providing a competitive context in which the products of breeding may be assessed. In addition, they provide an area for aesthetic pleasure, for all who find great satisfaction simply in looking at a beautiful representative of its breed

Showing German Shepherds is an absorbing, time-consuming hobby and can be enormously rewarding. Imagine the satisfaction of planning a mating, rearing the resulting litter, choosing a puppy to retain, developing it physically and mentally, bringing it through months of careful preparation to peak show condition and finally beating the best to achieve the title of Champion. Such an outcome remains in the imagination for most exhibitors, however, since merely a handful of all dogs shown will ever reach such an elevated height. Yet hope springs eternal in most dog breeders' breasts, and each litter offers new dreams!

If you have purchased a puppy with the intention of showing him, you will have to wait patiently until he has finished his growth before you can decide whether he is worth showing. By seven or eight months you should see whether he has developed faults which would put paid to a show career. Ears should be properly erect by this age, though in very rare cases they may hang until nine or ten months of age. In any event, you cannot show your pup with any hope of success until his ears are correctly carried. Similarly his adult dentition should be complete at this age. Occasionally a small first premolar may be delayed in breaking through the gum but it will probably remain underdeveloped even after appearing. Sometimes a pup may be very slightly overshot at this stage and the correct scissor bite may form later. But an overshot mouth at eight months is unlikely to improve. His coat must be correct and obviously a male must be entire, possessing two descended testicles. He must not be nervous or aggressive, and he must allow a stranger to examine him. If he has been bred by an experienced exhibitor, you should seek that person's opinion of his show quality. He should also be able to tell you whether any puppy faults are likely to disappear as the pup grows.

Lasso von Neuen Berg, Sieger 1977.

Your pup should be comfortable travelling. Any dog that suffers from persistent travel-sickness will not enjoy the experience of showing. It is unacceptable to impose unnecessary physical and mental stress upon any dog in the pursuit of show success.

Training for the Ring

Long before you reach your first show ring, you need to make careful preparations. First, your dog must be used to responding to you when other dogs are around. Joining a local training club will help. To begin with, simply give him the chance to feel at ease and make sure he is not unnecessarily harassed by any canine 'yobs' present. Classes held outside are better than those in confined halls, where the congested conditions often make dogs tense or inhibited. The more restrained he feels, the less relaxed he will feel. Take his favourite toy or tit-bit with you and simply concentrate on gaining his attention during the session. Be content to begin with if he is happy and relaxed, watching the proceedings with interest.

It is best to begin show-ring training proper at a German Shepherd Club, for there are aspects of showing a Shepherd which are different from the presentation of other breeds. This applies particularly to movement. Whereas most breeds are required to trot by the side of their handlers once or twice around a ring, Shepherds are assessed at three speeds: the walk, the slow trot and the extended trot. Specialist judges will expect your dog, in company with the rest of the class, to sustain good movement for several circuits of a roomy ring. He must be schooled to move out purposefully in front of you, maintaining good front reach and hindthrust, especially at a fast pace. If he hangs back or clings to your side he is unlikely to be demonstrating his full abilities on the move. He must be used to gaiting around the ring perimeter and negotiating corners without losing co-ordination and concentration. The presence of other dogs running behind him must not distract him.

If you have been training your dog to do heelwork, you will have encouraged him to stay close to your side and pay you complete attention. Now you require him to do just the opposite! To help him avoid confusion the following should be kept in mind. Your dog will be very conscious of your body language and the way you use your hands. Be consistent when training for heelwork and he will read the signal and anticipate what is expected of him. Use a relatively small-link chain for heelwork, with one ring loose so that he can respond to the rasping noise as you tighten and relax it. Put on a larger-link chain for other informal occasions, with both rings fastened to the clip so that he will feel free to pull into his chain. When you are out for a walk and you sense he is keen to pull out in front of you, give him the command 'Gait' and let him go ahead. Control him to a steady rhythm and don't let him lunge or scrabble. There are usually stretches on your walk, perhaps nearing home, where you know he would go on ahead without you if he could. Utilize these areas. Let him stand in front of you, looking in the direction he wants to go. Don't let him move forward until he hears the word 'Gait'. Allow him four or five strides only and then abruptly stop, still letting him face the direction he wants to go. Your aim will be to condition him to pull forward on command. Repetition in places where there is an incentive for him to go ahead of you will soon lead to success. Remember, he must not move a limb until commanded. Later you can apply gentle persuasion to drive the message home. If he starts to lag or relax the lead, deftly contact his hocks with your toe. This will compel him to move smartly forwards. But never hurt him or he will be anxious of your presence behind him and you will not achieve your aim. If you have kept your hands close to your body during heelwork training, make sure your dog senses them in a different position, holding the lead at a different angle, as he gaits.

At this stage you have simply taught a different physical response to the words 'Heel' and 'Gait'. Your dog still has to cope with the ring. Stake out a square or rectangular 'ring' with sides of around 30–40 yards (25–35m) in length. Enlist the co-operation of someone whom the dog knows and likes. This assistant must stand at one corner with the dog's toy. From a stationary position, give the word 'Gait' and let the dog run in a straight line on a taut lead from one corner to your assistant, who then lets him play with the toy. Then the attractor moves to another corner so that the dog has to negotiate a turn before reaching him. Soon your dog will be gaiting around the ring in front of you, eagerly anticipating a reward at one of the corners. You will not be allowed to attract him at a show, but if you adopt these measures every time you train him, he will quickly master the routine. Good handlers know how to move in harmony with their dogs, and you should set the best pace to suit your Shepherd. If you move too fast for him, he will lose his trotting rhythm and break into a gallop. Teach him to move in a controlled way towards and away from the judge and in a straight line. If he pulls at an angle it

A top German male, Olk von Bergmannshof, demonstrates a superb gait before a packed stadium at the Sieger Show, 1996.

will be impossible for the judge to assess the relative soundness of his action.

Your dog should be used to having his teeth examined. The judge may wish to do this himself or he may ask you to do it, so prepare your dog for either eventuality. Some dogs simply object to being held steady by the muzzle and regard the whole business as an indignity. Often this can be traced back to insensitive handling, especially during puppyhood, or to a handler's incompetence. No dog will enjoy having clumsy fingers obstruct his nostrils or obscure his vision. You should begin gently in puppyhood. While stroking your pup informally simply place your fingers unobtrusively around his muzzle, while soothingly tickling his chest with your free hand. Don't impose yourself upon him, and be content with a few seconds' compliance on his part. When you feel that he is relaxed enough about this, you can gently lift his lips slightly. As he gets nearer to showing-age, accustom him to the routine you will adopt in the ring. Remember you will need both hands free to show his bite and the rest of his teeth including the big molars. During the examination your dog must be under control, either standing still or sitting with his back against your legs so that he cannot pull backwards away from the judge. The judge will also need to see his teeth with the mouth closed so that he can examine the bite.

You will notice from visits to shows and from photographs in breed books that the German Shepherd is usually shown in a distinctive 'show pose', with the rear leg (nearest the judge) extended behind him as if he had stopped mid-stride. Dogs are moved in an anti-clockwise direction around the ring with you on your dog's right side, so that when you stop to stand by your dog, it will be his left rear leg that is slightly behind him.

Teaching your dog to adopt a pleasing show stance is easy if you begin early and proceed unobtrusively. Wait until his attention is fixed on something in the distance, so that he is taking little notice of you. Ease him forward slowly in the direction he is facing. With your hand on his chest, try to stop him half-way through his hind stride and hold him still, saying nothing to distract his attention from the distant object. He should now be posed with one hind foot extended behind him. Don't bother at this stage about which leg it is. Just condition him to adopting the stance when you stop him. Continue to restrain him with your hand on his breast-bone, until he is prepared

Handler allowing his dog to stand 'east-west' in front. Note the flat, open feet.

Even the tail cannot hide the cow-hocks!

to sustain the stance with just the tautness of the lead to hold him in position. Eventually, practise the procedure with nothing to attract him. You can stand in front of him with a toy or tit-bit, but only if he has been taught to stay on the spot. If you find that he puts his ears back if you use a command, it is better to stand at the side of him and allow him to take note of what is going on around him.

Eventually you must learn how to pose him to his best advantage so that his best points are emphasized and the weakest disguised. Expert advice at a training club is useful because a good handler must understand his dog's anatomy and movement very intimately. Each dog requires slightly different treatment. An overlong dog with a slightly soft back will need to be presented in a way that these faults are minimized. A shorter, only moderately angulated dog may be spoiled if compelled to adopt a pose in which he appears uncomfortable. A dog with short forelegs may need to be encouraged to lift his neck and head high to lessen the impression of a low forehand. Go to as many shows as you can and watch the best handlers at

124

work. If you are able to watch yourself handling on video, nothing is more revealing! You will be able to see just how easy it is to hinder the dog from presenting himself well by unnecessarily fiddling with his legs or leaning obstructively over him. The aim should be to create the illusion that the dog is showing himself off with the minimum of interference from you. The judge's attention should be drawn to the dog, not to his handler.

Avoid the temptation to present your German Shepherd in an unnatural, exaggerated manner. You will still see occasional demonstrations of this form of handling, which are an insult to such a noble breed. The handler will employ a fine slip-chain tightly noosed under the ears and against the throat. He will grasp the poor, submissive creature tightly by the muzzle and by squeezing will compel the dog to crouch in an attempt to create the illusion of 'angulation' and to disguise a faulty topline. Such manipulation robs the Shepherd of his dignity, apart from making it quite impossible for the judge to assess his actual shape. Regrettably, some judges are still impressed by such exaggerated presentation. Finally, don't assume that your dog must stand in dulled immobility all the while – most enlightened judges

The author handling Mr and Mrs Hood's Majestic Black Beau into a natural stance at the Two-day Show (Weston Hall in the background).

A bitch shown in an unnatural, overstretched stance with exaggerated slope of backline.

will not mind if he shifts his position, as long as you can present him in a natural, controlled way to enable his construction and soundness to be properly assessed.

Show Condition

As a working dog, the German Shepherd should be presented in firm, athletic condition. Young animals can be excused some degree of looseness in elbows, hocks and pasterns but by fourteen or fifteen months they should be relatively firm all through. Weaknesses in the back so that it dips or rolls will be penalized heavily by most judges. He should not be showed in thin condition, so that his ribs, spinal vertebrae and pelvis bones are obvious to the eye. Neither should he be soft and flabby. The large 'rearing' muscles at the back of his hindquarters should be strong and well developed.

Although most judges will consider your dog's construction more important than a temporary loss of coat, you will be well advised to show him only when he is in excellent condition. In the ring, your dog is on 'show' and you should make sure he is clean and looking his best. He needs no special grooming apart from the regular attention you give him. If his legs, furnishing and underparts have become rather grubby, then these can be bathed the day before the show, while a damp towel, impregnated with a spray-type cleansing agent, will be sufficient to rub through the rest of his body. If you have to bath him completely, do so a couple of days before the show

126

as his coat will lose some of its natural lustre after bathing and will appear soft and stand-offish.

If you have given him sufficient walking on a hard surface his nails should certainly not be long. If you need to trim them, the chances are he will not be in show condition.

You want to feel proud of your dog in the ring, so make sure his condition does you credit and reflects the commitment and care you have put into preparing him for competition.

Choosing your Show

Shows differ greatly in size, status, the quality of the dogs and the competence of the judges. There will undoubtedly be canine societies in your area recognized by the Kennel Club and licensed to hold shows for all breeds. Sometimes separate classes may be scheduled for German Shepherds but often you may have to enter your dog in classes for Any Variety, open to all breeds. Yours may be the only German Shepherd in the class! Occasionally at such shows a judge with specialist knowledge of the breed is invited to judge the German Shepherd classes, but it is more common for someone judging several breeds to be given the task. Such a non-specialist may be less concerned with detailed aspects of construction and gait and more with general attractiveness, head and expression and soundness. If your dog has an excellent temperament, and is sociable with members of other breeds, he can do much good in all-breeds shows as a representative of the breed before the general public. Some exhibitors are perfectly satisfied to limit their aspirations to wins at such shows. Most committed enthusiasts, however, will seek to win under knowledgeable specialists at shows specially for German Shepherds.

Classes at shows are based on one of two criteria: the age of the dog or the number of prizes he has been awarded at previous shows. Age classes are Minor Puppy (six to nine months) Puppy (six to twelve months), Junior (six to eighteen months) and Special Yearling (six months to two years). You will notice that it is possible to enter, say, an eight-month-old puppy in all four classes, but the difference in development and maturity between the pup and a Junior or Yearling would make it highly unlikely that the youngster could hold his own. In many cases a minor puppy finds it difficult to compete with puppies of eleven or twelve months old, especially in males.

127

Other classes employ a number of qualifications for entry which become progressively more exclusive, so that the greater the number of top prizes your dog has won, the fewer classes he will be allowed to enter. Age classes are restricted to dogs of a certain age, irrespective of their previous wins. A champion may therefore enter a Special Yearling class provided he is under two years old. A Maiden class, in contrast, is limited to dogs that have not yet won a first prize (puppy wins excluded). Novice classes admit only those dogs who have not won three first prizes, and so on through Undergraduate, Graduate and Post-Graduate Limit to the Open class. The last, as the name implies, is open to any dog exhibited, regardless of age or previous wins. In practice, however, it is the class for exhibits who have won awards that exclude them from earlier classes. All champions ineligible for an age class must enter the Open class.

Limited shows are restricted to members of a particular canine society and must be held in its own locality. Class regulations exclude dogs that have won at a high level. Entries are usually small and in fact there are hardly any such events run by German Shepherd Dog Clubs.

You will probably find at least one KC-recognized breed club in your area which will normally hold two Open shows annually,

Ch. Markoy Eiko at Jemness, Best of Breed at Crufts, 1998.

judged by breed specialists. There are forty-three German Shepherd Dog clubs represented on the KC Breed Council, with a mere four or five operating independently.

A number of clubs are granted championship show status by the KC depending upon their age, experience or geographical situation. This allows them to hold shows, usually every other year, at which Challenge Certificates are awarded to the best animal of its sex in the show. Since winning three of these CCs under three different judges qualifies a dog for the coveted title of Champion, such shows attract good entries of the best Shepherds in the country. Exhibitors chasing a title may well travel many hundreds of miles to championship shows up and down the country at considerable expense. Runners-up to the best dog and bitch are awarded the Reserve Challenge Certificate. Regrettably, such an award does not contribute to a Champion title, no matter how many you win. The officiating judge may award the Challenge and Reserve Certificates only if he is of the opinion that the winners deserve the title of Champion. If for some reason the CC-winner is disqualified, the reserve dog is granted the major award. Crufts Show, run by the Kennel Club itself, is the only championship show in the year requiring a qualification to enter. Your dog will need to have won one of a number of specified prizes in certain classes at a championship show in the twelve months prior to the Crufts event. In spite of this, and prestige apart, a Crufts win is of no greater value than any other championship show award. A number of large all-breed societies also possess championship status and Challenge Certificates are on offer at their events, as are Crufts-qualifying wins.

In addition to the title of Champion, the KC also offers an award known as the Junior Warrant to young animals up to eighteen months old which have won consistently from six months of age. Since the GSD is a later-maturing breed and it is not advisable to overshow youngsters, few sensible owners deliberately aim at a Warrant. To win one you must gain a total of twenty-five points. A minimum of twelve points must be won at open shows, where you are awarded one point for a class win. Winners of a Junior Warrant are awarded a Stud Book number, which qualifies them for Crufts for life.

The Stud Book contains details of all the major winners at championship shows and, apart from qualifying by gaining a Junior Warrant, your dog may also gain inclusion by winning First, Second or Third in Limit or Open classes at a championship event.

The Kennel Club has extended to the German Shepherd fancy the privilege of holding an annual two-day Championship show, which has established itself as the premier show in the calendar. Hosted in turn by the national clubs in Scotland, Wales, and Northern Ireland, and by the GSD League of Great Britain, it attracts a large entry of dogs for international judges to evaluate.

There is only one feature of dog-showing that you can be sure of: you will be out of pocket! The practice of paying prize-money has long been discontinued. The only people who profit financially from shows are the professional handlers, who will charge for presenting your dog to the judge. Curiously, the larger the event, the less you will take home with you if you win. Topping a class at Crufts will gain you a modest piece of cardboard indicating your win. Do the same at one of your local breed shows and you may well arrive home replete with a prize-card, a splendid rosette, a trophy or commemorative plaque, and perhaps a bag of dog food thrown in for good measure!

Your First Show

Assuming you have come to the conclusion you would like to show your German Shepherd, you will need to find an event in your area. Weekly magazines like *Dog World* or *Our Dogs* usually include advertisements for forthcoming shows, giving date, venue and judges. You will need to contact the club secretary to request a show schedule which sets out the 'classification' or classes on offer, and includes an entry form. You will need to think well ahead. Entries usually have to be received by the secretary by a closing date which may be anything from a fortnight to six weeks before the event. Entries arriving late are normally returned. Make sure you get a proof of posting from the post office. It is not unknown for an exhibitor to arrive at a show expecting his or her dog to be entered, only to find the entry has been lost in the post. If you can demonstrate your entry was dispatched properly, most clubs will make allowances.

It is sensible, at the beginning of your dog's show career, to enter him in an age class or in one of the lower classes like Maiden or Novice. If he is a promising youngster he should soon win his way out of these. Any wins he may have achieved at earlier shows which affect his eligibility for a particular class are taken into account only up to the closing date for entries. Any wins after that time but before the show will not affect his eligibility.

The schedule will indicate the time the show opens officially, though there is nothing to stop you arriving earlier if you wish. Judging will normally begin some time later. The time of the first class will be stipulated. Succeeding classes must be judged in the order in which they occur in the schedule. Be careful at all-breed shows: where there are several judges, and a number of rings, different breeds may be judged at the same time and it is not so easy to predict when your class will be called. In any event, arrive in good time to settle your dog down after his journey and give him the chance to get used to the venue.

The first thing to do on arriving is to attend to your dog. Ask where the exercising area is, and do not allow your dog to relieve himself anywhere else on the show-ground. If he does so, you will be expected to clean up after him. Accidents happen even with the most considerate animal, but provided you do not display a careless indifference towards your dog's fouling, it will be accepted with good humour.

You will need to purchase a show catalogue, which will include your dog's name, parentage and the class in which he is entered together with your own name and address. Check to make sure he is entered in the class you indicated on your entry form. Your dog will be allocated a number in the catalogue and this is his 'ring number', which you or his handler must display in the ring. Sometimes your ring number will be given to you at the secretary's table. Alternatively, the ring steward will offer it as you enter the ring for your class. Ask what the procedure is when you buy your catalogue. Some shows are 'benched'; this will be indicated on the schedule when you make your entry. The bench consists of a wood and metal partitioned space allocated to each dog. Your bench will display your ring number. Your dog must be fastened on the bench during the course of the show and is allowed to leave it only for grooming, appearance in the ring and exercising. It is your responsibility to ensure your dog behaves himself on the bench. You will need an extra lead and leather collar to attach him to his place, making sure the lead is not long enough for him to jump off, and not short enough to distress him. Loose chains around the neck are dangerous; it is easy for a dog to entangle a foreleg and panic.

At an 'unbenched' event you may allow your dog as much time around the ring as you wish, but never allow him to interfere with other exhibits. If you decide to leave him in your vehicle until his class, make sure he has time to limber up and prepare himself for the ring. Common sense will lead you to consider ventilation and shade for your vehicle on hot, sunny days.

So the judge is ready; there are already a number of dogs in the ring and the ring steward is calling for all dogs in your class to enter.

In the Ring

Your class will be announced by the ring steward probably while the winning dogs from the previous class are just leaving. Wait until the ring is emptied before entering. Make sure your ring number is clearly visible and firmly attached. Some of the larger German Shepherd shows use special ring vests which you pull over clothing and which indicate your ring number very clearly. The vests do not fit comfortably over a jacket! The ring steward will take your number and inform you of the judge's wishes. You may be required to walk around the ring in numerical order. Keep plenty of space between your dog and the one in front. If your ring-training has been consistent, your dog should know he must *not* walk to heel but pull out purposefully in front in a controlled manner. After an assessment of the dogs on the walk, the judge will then look at each dog individually. He will ask your number and the dog's age, before examining his teeth. No judge should ask about your dog's name, breeding, previous wins or ownership and you should never provide any information of such a nature. Attempting to influence the judge is regarded as a heinous offence.

After examining your dog in stance and taking any notes he needs, the judge will usually ask you to trot or walk your dog in a straight line away from him and back. In a very large ring the judge will usually call to you to indicate when he wants you to turn around and come towards him. If you turn back too early, the judge may suspect that you are trying to hide some weakness in the dog's hind action. Similar suspicion may be aroused about his front action if you fail to return in a straight line directly back to the judge. Next you will be required to move your dog around the ring to demonstrate his side-gait. Before you move into a trot, let him collect himself on the walk and when he is properly co-ordinated gradually increase his speed. You should not stop until the judge or steward indicates. When your turn is over you must wait in the position assigned to you by the steward. Never stand in the way of other dogs who need the perimeter of the ring to perform individually after you. After the individual examinations are completed, the steward may call for any dogs present who have been judged in a previous class and who are also entered in yours, to join the competition. You will all then be placed in order by the steward, either numerically or according to some provisional order of merit determined by the judge. Normally you will then be required, as a class or in smaller groups, to move together around the ring, while the judge compares the movement and outline of the dogs. Keep your dog smoothly co-ordinated and rhythmical, avoiding sudden jerking and interruption in his flowing gait. If you feel the dog in front is lagging behind and there is a danger your dog will interfere unless he is held back, simply allow your dog to continue moving past on the right-hand side of the other dog. Never overtake a dog on its left, as you will be obscuring him from the

A perfectly balanced natural stance without exaggeration or handler manipulations: Lasso von Kämpchen, V32 Sieger Show, 1997, and highest-scoring breed winner at the Sieger Working Championships in the same year.

133

Ch. Peterwell Wasp.

judge (and be pretty unpopular with his handler). If you are lucky enough to be leading the class, make sure you maintain the speed asked of you by the judge. It is not your privilege to dictate the pace at which the dogs should be moving. Be attentive to the judge and to your dog at the same time if you can.

At the end of the class the judge will line up the winners in the middle of the ring from left to right and the prizes will be distributed. Do not leave the ring until the judging has been completed. If you have won a class and are subsequently unbeaten by another exhibit in any later class, you will be called into the ring at the end of the class judging to compete for the Best of Sex award. The Best of Sex winners then compete for Best of Breed.

Remember that, in the end, judging depends upon the personal opinion of the judge. You are sure to attend shows where you disagree with the judge's decisions. The more blind you are to your dog's failings, the less prepared you will be to accept his defeat. If you are unable to be objective about your dog, or to see the virtues of other exhibits, then showing is not for you. Most judges will be ready to give you an opinion of your dog, even if you did not win. But wait until the classes have finished, before you ask, so that you do not hinder the judge in his work.

7

Judging

The development of any breed is significantly shaped by the influence of the people who judge it in the show ring. The dogs they select for top awards are likely to be used for breeding, and breeders aiming at success in the ring must breed animals that will appeal to contemporary judges. If the latter consistently elevate dogs with fashionable exaggerations or faulty character then there is a real possibility that the breed may be subsequently afflicted by such shortcomings. The more uniform in type that top winners are, whether in the right or wrong direction, the more clear it is that the majority of judges share a common understanding of the requirements of the Breed Standards. An obvious lack of uniformity betrays a corresponding lack of agreement amongst judges. For better or for worse, your understanding of what makes a good German Shepherd Dog will be strongly influenced by prevailing attitudes and fashions, especially when you begin your judging career, and your actions will either contribute to or detract from the positive development of the breed.

Judging, therefore, should not be undertaken lightly. You may feel flattered to be invited to judge and relish the apparent power and importance it promises but egotism and self-display should play no part in your acceptance. Only if you feel you are knowledgeable enough, and capable of handling the task, should you consider occupying the centre of the ring.

The Demands of Judging

The job may look deceptively easy from the outside, but the spectator is free from the pressures operating upon the judge. Discussing casually with a friend or two around the ring how you would place the exhibits may convince you that you could do the job equally well, if not better. But inside the ring there are many factors operating that

136

make the business far more demanding. To begin with, you have an audience who will carefully scrutinize your every move, often not too sympathetically! The awareness that the spectators are inevitably discussing your performance throughout each class is something to which you must be completely indifferent. You may be only too conscious of the fact that the audience may want you to select a particular animal, and that you would gain immediate approval and popularity if you did so, but you must please only yourself. Some otherwise knowledgeable people will never make good judges because they are unable to resist these intangible but significant pressures. They lack the independence of mind to be confident in their own decisions.

In the ring, too, the judge sees far more (or should do!) than the spectators can. He will be aware of details like eye colour, mouth faults, poor feet and less obvious failings in movement, all of which may be difficult for the ring-side critic to notice. He must take all these points into consideration and, most importantly, come to a decision quickly and confidently. Judging is all about making up your mind and if you cannot do this in reasonable time, you will never make an acceptable judge.

Int. Ch. Gayvilles Nilo, top-winning male.

You must be the kind of person who is unswayed by sentiment, whether it presents itself in the form of concern for an exhibitor who you know has been through a rough patch domestically and for whom a win would be a real tonic, or consideration for a person whose dog only needs one more CC to make him a popular champion and who has missed the award so many times he is inclined to give in. The more you are personally involved with people who show under you, the more you will have to stiffen yourself against sentiment. And you are bound to displease some of those who do not win.

Finally, judging will be demanding in other ways. You will need to sustain your concentration, particularly if you have a large entry. The very last dog you assess on the day will have to be judged as carefully as the one you first looked at. You may find yourself judging outside in all weathers, for German Shepherd exhibitors are a hardy lot, usually preferring outdoor rings with room to move their dogs properly. Travelling distances to show venues may mean leaving home at some unearthly hour in the morning, and you will be expected to write a report on the winning dogs after the event. You may have to miss a day's work, or pay for someone to look after your own dogs in your absence, and you will not be reimbursed for all your efforts. It is not regarded as good form to demand a judging fee for your services, though you should receive travelling expenses from any self-respecting club that invites you.

If all these considerations have not dissuaded you from wanting to judge, you may wonder how to begin.

Becoming a Judge

Traditionally, a judging appointment is regarded as a privilege bestowed upon an enthusiast because of experience and success in exhibiting and breeding. To judge at Limited or Open shows you need to be invited by the committee of the club concerned, who will have decided that you are capable of judging and are respected enough amongst the showing fraternity to draw a decent entry. To do anything which smacks of actively seeking appointments or canvassing is seen as highly irregular, a form of self-advancement to be deplored. There are judging cliques in the show world who have influence upon various committees and who are not averse to advancing their own interests, but you should avoid such circles.

Accept an invitation only if you feel it has been honestly and openly proffered with no strings attached or favours expected.

Breed clubs are required by the Kennel Club to keep lists of approved judges, which are reviewed and updated annually. These lists can be used by other societies seeking judges for their own shows. You do not have to be a member of the club to be included on its list.

Judges with substantial experience in officiating at Open shows may be offered the opportunity to judge at championship level. Even though they will be included on a club list of judges considered capable of operating at that level, they must still obtain the Kennel Club's official approval before they can do so. A championship show judge is entrusted with the responsibility of awarding the most coveted prize in the show ring: the Challenge Certificate, which is given to the best of sex, provided the judge is clearly of the opinion that the dog deserves the title of Champion. In the past, each judge invited to officiate at the level for the first time had to complete a questionnaire, giving full details of all previous shows judged and the number of exhibits, together with information about his or her own breeding and exhibiting successes. Completion of a first judging assignment in no way guarantees automatic appointment to

Ch. Sagenhaft Tamara.

a second. Each subsequent invitation has to be passed by the Kennel Club, which reserves the right to withhold permission.

From January 1999 aspirants towards championship judging status will have to meet much more stringent requirements. For the first time, the Kennel Club has laid down a set of objective criteria with the intention of improving the quality of championship show judges. A minimum of seven years' previous judging at Open level is necessary, together with stewarding experience. Furthermore, judges will have to attend educational seminars and be formally examined by a panel of breed experts to assess their knowledge of the German Shepherd Dog. It is probable, then, that all future championship show judges will have served at least twelve years' apprenticeship in breeding, exhibiting and judging before being allowed to award the highest honours.

Ring procedure, judging methods, etiquette and report-writing are essentially the same no matter what type of show you judge at. And the application of your interpretation of the Standard to a class of generally poor dogs at a Limited event may be just as taxing as sorting out a class of very good ones. How then should you approach your first judging assignment?

You should first make sure that you receive a formal contractual invitation from the club secretary, writing on behalf of the committee, which you should return promptly. Never accept word-of-mouth or telephone invitations. Once you have accepted, you are contractually committed and are not expected to renege on your commitment. Invitations are offered usually well in advance of the event so make sure you check your diary! Sometimes the club will lay down particular conditions for acceptance, such as your agreement not to judge other events within a prescribed radius and time-period. Details about travelling expenses or accommodation should also be agreed at this stage. Don't be tempted to win favour and future appointments by declining expenses, even if you can afford to do so. You have a responsibility towards other judges who may not be as favourably situated as yourself.

Your First Show

After the closing date for entries has expired and the secretary knows the total number of dogs to be judged, you should receive a breakdown of the numbers entered in each class. An experienced judge may be able to assess each individual in two minutes or so; you may require a little longer. Unless you have a particularly large entry, you should be able to complete your judging well within the time allocated.

If the show is to be held out of doors, make sure you take wet-weather clothing. You are hardly likely to make a good job of judging if you are wet, cold and miserable. Decide how you will handle the necessary note-taking. If you use a clip-board and notepaper, you will need plastic covering to protect it from the rain. Some judges employ a portable tape-recorder, which has several advantages. You can keep your eyes on the dogs all the while they are presented to you. The frustrations of wet or flapping papers are avoided, and the recorder can be easily be placed in a pocket when you need both hands free to examine a dog's teeth. But beware of the pitfalls! An exhausted battery or a button inadvertently mispressed can result in blank tape when you get home. Finding a particular report to give to an owner who approaches you during the show for your opinion can be difficult, necessitating an irksome rewinding and search procedure. Since dogs are not always presented to the judge in the order in which they occur in the show catalogue, you should keep a note in a small pocket book of the sequence of numbers. This will help you find a report quickly on the tape when you later come to preparing a written report for the canine press.

You should arrive at the show about half an hour before judging is scheduled to start. This will give you ample time to acquaint yourself with your ring steward, deal with any particular queries the secretary may have, and relax after your journey. Sometimes clubs will invite you to bring along your own steward, especially if the show concerned is scheduling several breeds and there is a shortage of willing personnel. It is better, however, to request the club to provide its own, unless you can take an experienced person along. A capable and efficient steward can make your job easier. But no matter how effective your steward is, you are in ultimate control of what happens in the ring. You cannot shuffle off responsibility on to a steward who is there simply to carry out your instructions. Most shows proceed smoothly, but occasional difficulties can arise, so avail yourself of the *Guides for Judges and Stewards*, published by the Kennel Club, which will clarify any procedural problems.

Your steward will accompany you to your ring and will take responsibility for checking prize-cards, rosettes or other prizes on offer so that they are ready for you to present to the winners at the

Ch. Starhopes Kassie.

end of each class. He will set the ball rolling by calling for all the dogs in the first class to enter the ring, but before he does so, make sure he knows the procedure you intend to adopt. It is usual for the dogs to follow each other in numerical order at a steady walk around the ring. The steward can then check all the numbers and make a note of absentees.

The initial walk around can give you the opportunity to assess the general quality of the class. You should be actively searching for what appear at first glance to be the best four or five exhibits. Keep a mental note of these dogs clear in your mind so that you can recollect them later when they present for individual examination. If you are fortunate enough to have all the exhibits present and are not waiting for handlers to arrive from another ring with other dogs, you can, at this stage, put the dogs in provisional order of merit as they walk or trot slowly around the ring. This order can then be modified if necessary after you have seen each dog individually, examined teeth, assessed movement coming and going and other details. Unfortunately the prevalence of professional handlers at many shows may mean that dogs will enter a class in haphazard fashion since a handler may often have a dog to handle in a ring for the opposite sex and in a class which is being judged concurrently with yours. You may be asked to wait a few minutes until he is free to handle a dog under you. As the judge, you are certainly free to decline such a request especially if judging is being unacceptably prolonged. But since handlers are often booked well in advance of a show and some exhibitors are dependent upon them, your refusal to co-operate may cause problems. Nevertheless, the situation is unsatisfactory as the job of both judge and steward is complicated by such arrangements. Also, dogs waiting in the ring for the late arrival of a handler-presented animal may become bored with the proceedings, while the latecomer enters fresh and on his toes.

To keep a clear head when judging, divide a page of your notebook into three columns headed 'A, B, C' or 'excellent, very good, good'. Keeping in mind that the four or five dogs you initially selected will be in your first column, you should then begin judging each individual. After you have finished examining each dog, assign him a place in the appropriate column. Write his number towards the top of a column if he seems to you to deserve such a ranking. You must then decide where the other dogs should be provisionally placed in your lists, as you begin mentally comparing them with each other. When you have completed your assessments of the individual dogs, you can instruct your steward to place them in a provisional order according to your list. Having 'rough-hewn' the class in this way you can begin the final stages of your judging.

Most shows will probably offer five or six prize-cards in each class: First, Second and Third; Reserve for the fourth with Highly Commended and Commended for the fifth and sixth dogs respectively. Continental shows, on the other hand, award Grading Certificates to every exhibit so that no one goes home empty-handed. Though grading is sometimes adopted at British shows, it is practised unofficially and has no Kennel Club status or sanction. Grading is a controversial issue, requiring as it does a convincing consensus between judges as to what constitutes an Excellent, Very Good or Good dog. Since there are no guidelines available to you, nor a background of established practice, you are probably best advised to leave grading to more experienced judges. Nevertheless, the exhibitors at specialist breed shows will expect you to place every dog in the class right down to the last one. You should not simply concentrate on the six possible card-winners and discard the rest. Each exhibitor has spent time and money in preparing his dog for the show. He deserves a full and conscientious examination and, even though he may not win, his owner expects you to offer your honest assessment of his dog.

As your final placings may, in part, be influenced by the comparative gaiting ability of each dog, you may find it useful to run-off four or five dogs together. This will avoid the hectic cavalry-charge of all the dogs running around together, exciting each other and confusing you. Make sure the rest of the class stands clear so that your gaiting group is not obstructed as it moves around the ring. Begin with the four or five dogs you have placed at the end of your provisional running order and then work up through the class to the top group. You can alter any of your positions at this point, demoting or elevating individuals as you think fit. Your provisional order is just that – provisional.

The German Shepherd at his best is a calm, self-possessed, confident dog and, as a judge, you should ensure that your ring provides the right context and atmosphere for him to display those aspects of his character. Over-enthusiastic ring-siders, alarmed and confused

Quena vom Haus Sommerlade, Siegerin 1996.

144

dogs, ambitious handlers abrasively jockeying for position: these are the features of a bad show in which the judge lacks the ability to control his ring. Ring control is essential and you must quietly but firmly insist that the dogs are presented to you in the way *you* wish. You, not the handlers, must dictate the speed at which the dogs move around the ring. Make sure the handler in front does not set a pace that suits his dog but handicaps those immediately behind him. Watch out, too, for the handler who stops without your permission when his or her dog loses interest. You should warn handlers who persistently allow their dogs to interfere with or overrun other exhibits that they are likely to lose their place. Professional handlers worth their fee will obviously do their best to present dogs to the best possible advantage, minimizing their failings and highlighting their virtues. But good handlers will also take into account the way in which a particular judge wants the dogs presented. If you make it clear from the outset that you are not impressed by an artificially exaggerated dog strung up on a tight chain, a sensible handler will avoid such a practice.

Because so much importance is placed upon an enthusiastic, sustained gaiting performance in judging German Shepherds, the practice of owners or family acquaintances calling the dogs from outside the ring has grown in recent years, even though it infringes KC regulations. You should not be over-zealous in this matter, feeling you must be on the look-out for every movement or sound outside your ring that may attract a dog's attention. Excited shouting and running along the perimeter are, however, unacceptable. Your steward should be instructed to inform you of unsporting behaviour and, in extreme cases, you are entitled to stop judging until the offending activity ceases.

It is a good idea to view the dogs from different positions in the ring so that you combine your close-up assessment with an appreciation of their outline and proportions at a distance. Movement coming to and going from you can be re-assessed if necessary from an appropriate vantage point at the corner of your ring. If the majority of the spectators are gathered at one particular side of the ring, arrange for your final line-up to be presented along the opposite side. This will give the audience the opportunity to view your top placings in stance.

KC rules require you to bring the prizewinners into the centre of the ring, where they should be placed in order before receiving their awards. Your steward will enter the results in the official judge's

Shanto's Xano, a superb V.A. male bred in Holland.

book, which contains three detachable columns for each class you judge. You must sign each column, which will record your placings and an indication of absentees. One column is usually displayed on a board for public consultation, one is retained by the secretary for administrative purposes and you have ownership of the book containing the third column.

When the judging of your classes has been completed, all unbeaten dogs are mustered to compete for Best of Sex. Traditionally, the exhibitors anticipate that you will compare all the dogs together as if they were competing in another class. You are not obliged to do this, however. If you are of the firm opinion that a particular animal is the best you have judged on the day, you can dispense with any comparison and simply announce the number of the best animal. This is rarely done, however, and most shows conclude with a 'challenge' for the top award. If an award for Best Puppy is on offer, you must remember that it can be won by any puppy, even if he has not been entered in the puppy classes, provided he has not been beaten by another youngster under twelve months of age.

Appropriate ring etiquette on your behalf can help make the show pleasurable for both you and the exhibitors. While it is regarded as bad form to engage in sustained conversation with a handler, a friendly word or two as you take down details of the exhibit's number and age will help create a more relaxed atmosphere. Smoking and alcohol in the ring are strictly taboo, and you must never be seen in possession of, or referring to, the show catalogue. It may be a charade you have to play, but you are expected to judge the dogs as if you have no idea of their identity, ownership or previous show achievements. Any handler who attempts to influence you by providing such information can be disciplined by the Kennel Club. A handshake for all competitors, winners and losers alike, always creates a good impression. Finally, don't forget to thank the steward and show secretary for all the work they have done too.

After the Show

Your duties as judge will not have finished with the conclusion of the show. You will be expected to write a report on the winning dogs for the canine press. Weekly magazines such as *Dog World* and *Our Dogs* will usually have provided the club, or you directly, with envelopes in which to submit your report. Breed magazines, too, may invite you to contribute.

Before judging your show, you should have read plenty of breed reports and already formed a good idea of what is expected. You will probably also have distinguished those reports that are valuable and informative from those that are mere verbiage. Good, well-considered reports make an important contribution to breed development since they record the main virtues and failings of a dog. Such information can prove of considerable value to future breeders, especially to those who do not have the chance to see the dog for themselves. A combination of photographs and judicious show reports can often help us visualize an animal no longer with us in the flesh but still an active influence in pedigrees. So when you put pen to paper, remember you may be writing for posterity!

A good report should be succinct, clear and well-organized. It should offer a brief 'thumb-nail' sketch of a dog with some indication of why you placed him where you did. You should not indulge in subjective effusions such as, 'This dog appealed to me as soon as he entered the ring. He is certainly a dog I would like to take home with me'. Try to make *objective* comments on his size, proportions and construction, together with appropriate references to gait and temperament. Your report should follow a logical sequence. Begin with an indication of size and weight, assess the head, expression, wither, back and croup. Then move to an appraisal of the forehand, middle-piece and hindquarters. A description of the gait, both coming and going, and in profile, should complete your description. In addition, briefly indicate what the deciding factors were in your placing of the dog.

A conventional, if sometimes imprecise terminology exists for report-writing so avoid departing from it too radically. You may realize that the word 'hock' is loosely used, but if you employ the more anatomically correct 'metatarsus' or the Continental 'hind-pastern' you will simply confuse readers. But do not slip into the habit of using vague terms which, though current, are quite useless in any description. A 'good front' is of little value in conveying information about a dog's forehand construction. 'Moves well' is a similarly vapid term to describe the gaiting performance of a German Shepherd. Sometimes judges unwittingly appear to contradict themselves. It is not uncommon to come across the comment 'good forehand' combined with 'upper arm steep' or 'well-proportioned but front legs could be longer'. Be on your guard against such carelessness, for by your reports shall ye be judged!

Assessing the German Shepherd

Many of us are capable of being moved by a fine piece of music without understanding anything of the techniques of composition. Beauties of rhythm, textures and form are sensed intuitively. Perhaps this is so of all art. Certainly it is true of our response to a show dog. Some people are blessed with an innate ability to detect quality and balance in a dog, even if it belongs to a breed of which they have little or no personal experience. But any judge who declares, 'I like the first dog better than the second because he appeals to me more strongly', or 'the winner was more my type' is likely to receive short shrift from the German Shepherd fraternity, which expects its judges to base their decisions on more objective criteria. Before you judge, therefore, you must have given intelligent thought to the Breed Standard and its interpretation, and grasped the underlying principles that inform it.

Regularly abroad and increasingly in Britain, judges are invited to give oral critiques to the spectators, assessing each dog and justifying his position in a class. Such public accountability requires a confident grasp of the criteria that affect your judging decisions. The days of a judge operating in enigmatic silence before an often bemused audience appear to be numbered.

A breed show used to be referred to as a 'beauty' show. Although old-fashioned, this expression reflects the simple point that we expect winning show dogs to be good-looking, attractive and possessed of that indefinable aura of quality and good breeding. We assume a show dog will be in good, healthy condition, his coat clean and well groomed. But features we might describe as 'showy good looks' can easily deteriorate into the merely cosmetic so that undue emphasis is placed upon a striking colour, glamorous coat and exaggerated pose.

The judge of German Shepherds, however, will want to hold firm to the concept of the dog as a herding dog. Even though the dog seldom fulfils such a role in today's society, the Standard is the blueprint for an animal capable of such a task. As a judge, therefore, you must develop a basic understanding of canine anatomy and be able to see how the requirements of the Standard are to be understood in the light of the Shepherd's traditional role. His size, weight and construction enable him to move in an economical and enduring way. Anything about him that results in wasted effort and unnecessary muscular stress, with a subsequent loss of endurance, must be negatively noted in your assessment. You must study as many dogs as you can while they are moving and develop a quick eye for such deleterious features.

But does the importance of movement mean that judging the German Shepherd in stance is superfluous? Some judges have expressed the opinion that it is in movement that a dog's true shape and anatomical functioning can be assessed. Handlers, too, can manipulate a dog into a false shape when it is standing. Examination in stance, however, is essential for a careful assessment of construction and general proportions, provided that the dog is presented naturally. A stable, sound and balanced stance is just as important from a working point of view as movement. Uneven distribution of weight, unsound limbs and lack of balance may lead to a dog tiring easily as he stands because he will be compelled to use unnecessary muscular effort to compensate for his deficiencies. The stance, therefore, should not be seen simply as a cosmetic opportunity for the handler to present an attractive 'picture' but as a demonstration of

Nadja am Seeteich, an outstanding V.A. bitch at the 1997 Sieger Show.

the dog's overall harmony and balance. It will also enable you to assess details such as eye shape and colour, ear carriage and head formation, feet and pasterns, coat condition and physical constitution. Most importantly, it will give you the chance to develop a feel for the dog's presence and character as you note his expression and response to you.

Nevertheless, it is the dogs moving around the ring that will first occupy your attention. Give them time to settle before you start to form any opinion. Once they have stopped pulling or straining into the lead you can begin to see the genuine dog at the walk. At this pace much is revealed to the attentive eye. Height to length proportions become apparent in that obviously overlong dogs stand out, as do those with briskets too deep for their legs. The topline can be seen for what it genuinely is. Some dogs can raise their back slightly at the walk or show some steepness of croup but you should wait to see what happens in these areas at a faster speed before penalizing. A short-coupled dog pulling on his lead may present a different picture when gaiting later in a more relaxed fashion.

At the walk, you would expect to see the presentation of a firm, well-knit dog with no looseness or rolling, particularly over the pelvis. He will walk smoothly and fluently, the roomy hind stride being matched by an equally free and spacious front stride. His wither will be long and well maintained, and there should be no trace of his rear being higher than his wither. Any restrictions in length and angle of upper arm or shoulder blade will be apparent also at this speed, resulting in a lack of fluency or reach in front. Not all good walking dogs subsequently prove effective at the trot and, conversely, some who show limitations on the walk improve when asked to accelerate. You cannot, therefore, place your dogs simply on the basis of how well they walk.

As each dog is brought to you for individual examination, insist that he approaches you on a long, slack lead. He must not be held tightly or under order to stand. Now is the time for you to assess his temperament. Dogs attracted from outside the ring or intent on spotting their owners may be quite unaware of your presence. This fixation on someone else may disguise weaknesses in character which would surface if the dog were required to acknowledge your proximity and respond to a friendly overture on your part. Any German Shepherd of sound character should be prepared to contact you with an investigatory sniff, allowing you to stroke him without signs of anxiety or panic. If you feel that he is so mesmerized by outside attractions that you cannot make natural contact, you should break the spell that transfixes him. A slight noise you contrive to make may attract his notice. Nervousness is a serious fault in the German Shepherd, so do your best to assess temperament, problematic though the task is in the show ring.

Young, inexperienced or poorly trained dogs can sometimes be upset by a tussle to show the teeth. You may find it better to defer this until after the dog has settled down and been examined in stance. Missing teeth, undershot or overshot mouths are clearly to be penalized. Depending on the strength of competition, you may decide to forgive a missing first premolar. Sometimes these are late appearing in youngsters. The presence of one or more extra premolars is often undetected by some judges, but is also undesirable.

As the handler stands his dog, don't be too insistent that his charge is standing on the same spot and looking in exactly the same direction as the others in the line-up. Be prepared, within reason, to alter your position and allow each dog to adopt an alert calm position in a natural manner.

151

You have very little time in which to assess each dog in stance, so make the most of it. The less you take your eye off the dog the better, so avoid writing copious notes. Little is more discouraging for a handler than to present his dog at his best, only to discover that the judge is absorbed in writing a mini-essay. If you can develop your own personal form of canine hieroglyphics (such as VGUA = very good upper arm), this will allow you to give maximum attention to the dog.

Insist that the dog moves away from and towards you in a controlled manner so that you can assess soundness, and be on the look-out for any tactics adopted by the handler to limit your chances of detecting any failings in movement coming and going. At the walk, the Shepherd should ideally move on direct parallel lines so that when you view him from the front, the forelegs show no tendency to deviate inwards or outwards, practically obscuring the hind legs that follow on the same line. The elbows should neither protrude nor be 'pinned-in', restricting freedom of stride. From behind, the hocks should be strong and stable, moving practically underneath the hip-joint, neither turned out in 'bow-hocked' fashion nor 'cow-hocked', where the points of the hock incline inwards towards each other.

As the dog accelerates into a faster trot, his limbs will incline inwards towards an imagined line underneath the centre of his body, so that his front feet will seem to be converging on the line as he completes his front stride. Similarly the hind feet will fall on a point centrally placed well under the body at the completion of each hind stride. This tendency to 'single-track' is not be confused with 'crossing over', which is a fault, restricting the directness and freedom of leg action. The feet should be neither turned in nor turned outwards as they contact the ground.

Your eye must focus on several important features as the dog gaits round the ring. The general impression must be that of a dog moving smoothly and rhythmically, with roomy, co-ordinated strides. The natural clean lines you should have appreciated in stance should be retained as he moves, and there should be no appreciable alteration to the shape of his topline, though he may lower his wither slightly the more his head is lowered at an extended, fast pace. He must never, however, move overbuilt (with croup higher than withers), nor give you the impression that he is falling on the forehand. Dogs lacking long, correctly angled bones in shoulder and upper arm may lack the ability to extend in the forehand. The power generated by the thrusting hindquarters cannot be utilized in front, so the dog loses

A top bitch at the Sieger Show demonstrates her outstanding gait.

balance. You should make sure the dog has *natural*, rather than artificially simulated, hind thrust. He must show you that he is capable of flexing at the knee-joint, contacting the ground firmly with his hind foot on strong hocks, and then smoothly but strongly thrusting backwards with his hind limb. At the completion of the stride, the metatarsus or hind-pastern should be well extended so that, viewed from behind, the dog would be showing you 'a clean pair of pads'. You cannot assess hind thrust unless the dog is moving on a loose-lead. Pulling may deceive you into attributing to him action which he does not actually possess. Remember that hind thrust is significant *only* if it is effectively transmitted through a firm back to the fore-hand. It has absolutely nothing to do with powerfully pulling against the lead. The German Shepherd is a trotting dog, not a weight-mover, and he must be moving freely and unhindered to demonstrate correct transmission.

The German Shepherd's gait is often described as 'a flying trot' since, for a split second at a fast pace, the propulsion from behind will launch the dog's body powerfully over the ground and his well-angled forehand will reach out with corresponding freedom, creating the momentary impression that he is in suspension, with all four feet off the ground. Perfect anatomical balance is necessary for this to occur. In addition, as he accelerates, he will place his hind foot well under his body and beyond the point at which the front foot has left the ground. This 'over-reaching' is a natural feature of a well-angulated, long-striding Shepherd. It should never occur at a walk or very slow trot, however, nor should the body direction incline to the left or right when viewed from behind, as this indicates a 'crabbing' action.

While the dog is moving you should also note any weaknesses in pasterns, ear carriage and tail carriage. Short, steep pasterns can lead to taut, jarring front action while soft, weak ones lack strength to support the dog in his work over rough, irregular terrain. While he may pin his ears back as he moves, they should not flap loosely. A naturally alert dog should use them as he moves. You may gain useful insights into a dog's temperament from the behaviour of his ears.

The correct, sabre formation of the tail, which should smoothly and unobtrusively blend in with the rest of the croup-line, completes the graceful outline. Some tails protrude at the root, or twist and bend at the end. Make sure the tail does not flap lifelessly around the hocks or, at the other extreme, advertise itself proudly by curving upwards above a line drawn horizontally through the back.

Apart from giving preference to good pigmentation and penalizing washed-out, anaemic-looking dogs, you should not allow colour to affect your placings. You may not like sables or all-blacks, but if their construction and movement are the best in your ring, personal preferences must not deny them their just deserts. Be sure that you do not confuse colour with pigmentation. Some dogs with very light fawn markings may have dark eyes, toenails, tail-tips and solid saddles, whereas a foxy red dog, certainly darker in general appearance, may prove on closer examination to have light eyes, pale toenails and a red tail-tip, all indications of weakening pigmentation.

Finally, avoid the temptation to fault-judge. Always try to assess the dog as a whole, appreciating overall balance, movement and quality. Every dog has faults and you should penalize them according to their degree of severity. That means taking into account how far they would affect the dog's ability to perform his original herding task and how far they affect type and general appearance. A soft-eared, long-coated dog may be excellently constructed and have a superb working gait but, by virtue of these faults, he is untypical. You must always, therefore, balance the need for a sound working animal with the expectations that your winning dogs will be typical, handsome and attractive representatives of the German Shepherd breed. Attempting to do just that is what makes judging such a challenging and fascinating activity.

8

Breeding

Breeding German Shepherds is a demanding and costly activity and should never be undertaken lightly. Your bitch will not suffer in any way if she is never mated; and your nerves and bank balance may find themselves in a much more stable state if she remains a maiden! But if you do wish to breed from her, you should consider seriously whether you can do the job properly, if only out of concern for your bitch's welfare.

The demands upon your time will be considerable: you must be prepared to be in constant touch with a nursing bitch and her litter for at least eight weeks. Both dam and puppies will require careful feeding at regular intervals throughout the day. The demands of hygiene and general cleanliness have to be considered. You need plenty of spare cash to cover feeding costs, advertising and registration fees, together with any veterinary attention that may be necessary. Remember you are dealing with living creatures whom you will have brought into the world. Apart from the demands upon your time and money, the most sobering consideration to keep in mind is the problem of finding the right homes for your puppies. Nothing is more disheartening in dog-breeding than the experience of rearing beautiful pups with lavish care from excellent parents, only to find that they end up in unsuitable homes or are discarded as unwanted. Unfortunately the rescue kennels are full of such sad, rejected dogs – once hopeful, happy puppies wanting nothing more from life than to give themselves completely to a committed and caring owner. You must consider your neighbours, too. A growing litter of puppies will inevitably generate a certain amount of noise, though sensible management should reduce it to a minimum. Sufficient space should be available to keep any puppies that may remain unsold, as they will grow and eat at an amazing rate.

If all these considerations do not dissuade you from going ahead, then you must decide your objectives in breeding. As a German Shepherd enthusiast, you will want to breed dogs that are a credit to

155

the breed, sound in mind and body, and with good qualities to transmit to future generations if they themselves are bred from. In this way you will be making your own contribution to the development of the breed.

The Brood-bitch

Your bitch must be well bred, without serious faults and, most importantly, must be mentally and physically sound. Never breed from a bitch with a poor temperament. If she is shy or aggressive she can easily transmit such failings to her puppies. Simply ask the question: would my bitch make a good, reliable family pet? If the answer is no, then think twice about breeding from her. The great majority of puppies are destined to be pets and it is in the family home, not in the show ring, that the reputation of the breed is put to the test. Even if you wish to breed a potential show winner, always keep this underlying consideration in mind.

Give your bitch a chance to mature before breeding from her. The third season should be the earliest time for mating and, ideally, she should produce her first litter before she is five years old. The Kennel

Int. Ch. Chanask Edison.

156

Club will not normally register puppies from litters produced by bitches over eight years unless special permission is granted. Your bitch should have enjoyed a healthy life and be in good condition generally. Try to find out as much as you can about her immediate ancestors and, if possible, her litter-mates. She will carry the genetic factors for both good and bad qualities in her family. Consult with her breeder, who should be able to help you to research her background and suggest possible partners for her.

Hip-joints

Your cannot tell merely by looking whether your bitch has good hip-joints so, once she is twelve months old, ask your vet to X-ray her and send off the resulting slides to the KC/BVA scrutineers panel for 'scoring'. Experts will assess the formation of the hip and award a number to each hip depending upon any developmental abnormalities. Faultless hips would be awarded a score of 0–0. The current average total for German Shepherds is around eighteen. If your bitch scores appreciably higher, you must make a very low score a priority in any stud-dog she is mated to. Never mate a high-scoring male to a high-scoring bitch. Ideally, you should find out the scores, if any, of her immediate family. A bitch with a score of twenty but from a family with a low average may very well be a better breeding prospect than a low-scoring bitch from high-scoring ancestors and siblings.

The Breed Survey

If you wish to demonstrate that you have chosen your brood-bitch with care, you can have her assessed at a breed survey, where she will be awarded a certificate to prove she is a good breeding prospect. Surveys are held throughout the country under the auspices of the Breed Council. They are non-competitive events in which individual German Shepherds are carefully assessed and their breeding suitability recorded. The surveyor will measure the dog's height, length and chest and note all the details of appearance and construction on a prescribed survey form, one copy of which is retained by the Council for publication in its annual Handbook, another copy being retained by the breeder. In addition the dog's character is tested and described. Surveyed animals are granted Class I or Class II status, depending upon their quality and how well they meet basic standards for size, temperament, teeth and hips. Your bitch must have a hip-score of twenty-five or less and must not deviate from standard size by more than 1in (2cm) if she is to be awarded Class I. Missing teeth will also affect her classification. Males must have been tested for haemophilia and have a hip-score of no more than twenty. Most conscientious breeders will seek to breed from surveyed bitches. Show wins are unfortunately no indication of breeding value as far as hips, size and temperament are concerned, since temperament can only be superficially assessed at a show, size is often ignored, and it is possible for a dog to win the title of Champion even with a high hip-score. Your local breed club will inform you of any surveys to be held in your area.

The Basics of Heredity

Genetics is the study of inherited characteristics and of how parents pass their features on to their offspring. Each animal is made up of minute cells each of which has a nucleus containing tiny thread-like chromosomes. The chromosomes carry the genes, a set of chemical instructions from both parents that determine what physical and mental features will be reproduced in the offspring.

The number of chromosomes varies from species to species, but the dog has seventy-eight, in common with the wolf. At the moment of conception the male sperm cell, carrying thirty-nine chromosomes, unites with the female egg cell, which also contributes thirty-nine to make up the total. Since both sire and dam contribute exactly the same number of chromosomes to their offspring, each plays an equal role in the genetic make-up of the puppy. The chromosomes are arranged in identically shaped pairs, resembling threads of beads, with the chromosome acting as the thread which holds thousands of genes in strung-out formation. Each gene affects an aspect of the dog's appearance and function, so the genes provide the link between parents and offspring. When genes are situated in the same place on a particular chromosome, they will affect a particular characteristic in the animal. The genes function in pairs, one member of each pair being contributed from the sire and one from the dam. What chromosomes actually make up each cell is determined by chance, and the resulting combination of genes that make up the living animal is quite fortuitous. That is why it is so common to see brothers or sisters so totally unlike each other in appearance. Unfortunately, like does not beget like, for if it did we would simply have to mate two champions together to produce a third. So is the breeder entirely at the mercy of nature and its unpredictable genetic combinations, or can he have an influence on the outcome of the proceedings?

Phenotype and Genotype

In a manner of speaking, any dog is really two creatures: the actual individual, with all its observable features, and the hypothetical 'dog' composed of its genetic make-up. The former is termed the phenotype, the latter the genotype. Any given dog carries the genes for all the qualities we actually see in the animal before us, unless they are the product of environmental influences. For example, a dog may be cow-hocked because he has inherited the genes for such a condition. On the other hand, environment, in the form of faulty rearing, may have caused the problem. Only what is genetically determined can be transmitted to the next generation, of course. Some breeders become so concerned with the pedigree of their dog as a clue to its breeding worth, that they forget the features of the actual dog. The dog may, for example, have light eyes but his pedigree suggests that his predecessors had mostly dark eyes, so the breeder may assume he will breed on for dark eyes. His genotype, they imagine, must be better than his phenotype in this respect. But that is simply an inspired hunch based on the knowledge of the dogs on the pedigree. They cannot know what genes the dog carries in his genotype until they breed from him. But they do know for certain that he carries the gene for light eyes. Of course, some dogs do consistently produce better than themselves, but we should not become so obsessed with a pedigree and its hypothetical significance that we ignore the dog in front of us. Aspiring breeders should, as a rule, attempt to breed from the best specimens they can afford to work with. You can begin with a mediocre animal of good breeding, but you will have a harder task in succeeding.

Dominant, Recessive and Polygenic Factors

The difference between phenotype and genotype arises because there are two different kinds of genes: dominant and recessive. In a pair of differing genes, one gene may be dominant over the other, giving the visible attribute of the dog. This is termed the dominant gene and the suppressed one is called recessive. For example, in German

Shepherds there exist two basic coat types: the normal, relatively short coat and the long coat. The gene for normal coats is said to be dominant over that for long coats. Consequently, if a dog carries the gene for a normal coat, he will be normally coated himself. But he may have inherited from one of his parents a gene for a long coat, which has been masked by the dominant gene. If that is the case, his phenotype and genotype differ. He cannot be relied upon to produce only puppies with normal coats, in other words to reproduce himself in this respect.

Unfortunately many of the desirable characteristics of the Shepherd are not transmitted by a single gene, but by a varied number of gene pairs. They are said to be polygenic. Think of the innumerable gene combinations required to determine the shape, for example, of the pelvis, the precise form of the hip socket, the muscle mass over it and so on, and it can be seen how complex the matter is. Though the basic rules of dominant and recessive behaviour may still apply, the possible combinations of genes is enormous, making it difficult to predict the outcome of a mating with any certainty. But the challenge of breeding is to narrow the uncertainty factor and try to realize in the living animal the phenotype we envisage.

Assessing Breeding Partners

Some dogs are often described as 'dominant' for a particular characteristic like a well-angled forehand. The term is used loosely, not in the precise genetic sense we have been considering, but simply to mean that the dog regularly appears to produce good front in his puppies even when mated to partners mediocre in this feature. Obviously, the more dominant the breeding animal is, in this sense, the more predictable the results of breeding. But how do we know if a dog or bitch is likely to possess this valuable dominance? Ultimately only by studying very many of the animal's offspring, but young dogs with few progeny to help us have to be used, and we have to attempt an intelligent assessment of a dog's potential for breeding. This is where a thorough knowledge of your dog's ancestors is of the utmost importance. A pedigree as long as your arm is of little use unless you can discover the dog behind the name. Not only must we be able to make an objective appraisal of the faults and virtues of the dog by assessing him against the requirements of the Breed Standard, but we should also try to discover the extent to which he has inherited these qualities from his ancestors. That is why a pedigree is important.

Unfortunately, the traditional pedigree, recording simply the names of the dog's forebears, is of limited use unless the breeder has seen the dogs concerned or at least a picture of them. The Continental system of the breed survey is of enormous value in this respect, for the results are recorded in a book for breeders to use when they come to plan a mating. In addition, a brief description of each animal in the first two generations is also included on the pedigree. A few hours spent on research in the survey books can provide the breeder with information about the size, weight, anatomical faults and virtues, hip status and character of his dog's ancestors. Without such help the breeder's task is more difficult, but not impossible if he takes the trouble to enquire from the knowledgeable fanciers. For, remember, he must attempt to discover the breeding potential of his dog: what qualities, both good and bad, he is likely to transmit. This is not possible without a sound knowledge of the dog's ancestors.

So what would we look for in a promising breeding animal? We will consider the bitch, if only because most breeders obviously begin with her and face the task of finding a suitable male to mate her to.

Int. Ch. Rosehurst Chris, top winner and important sire.

*The outstanding V.A. bitch Jade von Blue Rose, a daughter of a
Sieger mated to a Siegerin.*

The first question to be answered is: is she of good breed type? Type
is notoriously difficult to define but 'good type' suggests an animal of
good general proportion without exaggeration anywhere, and of correct constitution for her breed, neither soft and flabby nor shelly and
weedy in skeleton. She must be of sound temperament, for she will
influence her offspring in this respect even more than the sire
through the nature of her response to the puppies as she rears them.
Ideally, she should be free, as far as possible, from any faults but that
is not essential for there is no guarantee that she will transmit her
excellence. That will depend upon her genotype and the extent to
which she carries pairs of matched genes (is 'homozygous') for her
virtues. She may have faults, then, but some faults are easier to overcome in breeding than others. With luck, her failings will be the
easier ones to correct. For instance, colour paling is very easy to
improve upon in one generation, whereas steep fronts may take
much longer. Mental and physical softness, too, are often consistently
passed on.

So if the bitch is of a good basic type and a sound mover, the next
thing to determine is whether she is typical of her breeding. This will
depend upon whether her ancestors are of a uniform type or whether
they are significantly different from each other in construction and

general appearance. Remember, however, that type is not synonymous with colour. The more alike her immediate ancestors are to her and to each other, the more likely it is that she will transmit that common type to her offspring. The phenotype of her ancestors will therefore be an important guide to use, but her genotype and that of her parentage will also, in all probability, be affected by the prevailing traits present in the family. So the more we can discover about her brothers and sisters and the other litter-mates of her parents and grandparents the better. Again, the Continental breeder has the advantage of the breed book to help him. He can find out, for instance, whether the sire of his bitch shared his excellent forehand with the other litter-mates or whether he was the only one in his litter to excel in that area. If the latter is the case then he is likely to be less dominant for that feature in breeding and his daughter may have to be bred to a sire from a line known to produce a consistently high number of good fronts. So family research is as important as investigating the individual animal on the pedigree.

The breeder must then decide whether he wishes to stabilize type or whether he is aiming at the improvement of particular features in the resulting litter. If the bitch comes from a very mixed background and seems to owe nothing to her parentage, clearly she will be an unpredictable breeding prospect and it may be sensible to choose a sire known to be dominant for producing a good and consistent type irrespective of any minor faults of construction that may affect the offspring's success in the show ring. Too many breeders, however, are impatient and want to produce the 'star' in the next litter they breed. Such impatience rarely leads to success. Having chosen such a sire, the breeder should retain the best bitch puppy that mirrors the desired type. But sooner or later he will need to improve his Shepherds in one feature or another if he wishes to produce the elusive animal that fulfils the Standard. How should he attempt this?

The Practical Application of Line-breeding

Let us assume that the bitch fails in length and angle of upper arm. First we need to find out where such a deficiency came from. She should not be mated to a sire that carries the same line, particularly if he too fails in the upper arm. Then, examining the bitch's pedigree, we would find an ancestor of above-average quality that has consistently produced excellent fronts in his offspring. It will probably be a male, since he will have thrown more puppies than a bitch, making it easier to assess his dominance for the feature. If the bitch happens to be a granddaughter of the dog chosen, then we look for a sire, preferably of complementary type, who is a great-grandson of the same dog. But, and this is the crucial point, he must excel in the feature you are seeking and, just as importantly, so must his father and grandfather back to the dog common to both pedigrees. In other words, we choose a sire whose line of descent from the dog bred back to is strongly stamped by the presence of the feature you wish to obtain and which you calculate was consistently thrown by that dog. Such a breeding plan is called line-breeding back to a common ancestor. Its aim is to intensify the genetic influence of that ancestor on the litter. It would be pointless to line-breed to the dog just because he has a good front. The animals through whom his influence is transmitted must also carry that feature if we wish to increase the probability of the puppies inheriting it. Novice breeders often forget this and behave as though matching animals with a common outstanding ancestor were a magic formula for success. Far from it. That ancestor may also carry the genes for undesirable features. If the dogs in the generations intervening between him and your stud-dog reflect these in their phenotype, then you are increasing the chance of your litter being similarly blemished.

A brief explanation of how line-breeding attempts to maximize the genetic influence of a particular ancestor may be useful at this point. A dog receives fifty per cent of his genes from each of his parents and twenty-five per cent from each of his four grandparents and so on, in diminishing proportion through the pedigree. If we mate a dog with sire X to a bitch with the same sire X then the resultant offspring have one grandsire rather than two. He will then, theoretically, contribute twice twenty-five, i.e. fifty per cent of the puppies' genes. In other words he will be as significant as the sire or dam. But the matter is complicated by the fact that we cannot assume that the sire and dam have inherited the genes for the good qualities we seek unless they both show them in their phenotype. Furthermore, if we pair together two animals that have a common grandsire, rather than sire, we cannot assume that that common ancestor will contribute twice twelve-and-a-half per cent, i.e. twenty-five per cent, of the genes in the puppy, because we cannot be certain that the sire has transmitted exactly half of his sire's genes. He may be capable of transmitting very little of his father's influence. Here again we realize the importance of the phenotype when we line-breed. But by intelligent line-breeding we can improve our breeding significantly, for we are increasing the chances of fashioning homozygous gene combinations in animals that will then 'breed true' for a particular feature or type.

Line-breeding, however, not only increases the likelihood of good qualities being transmitted, but may also result in the combination of undesirable recessive genes, thus bringing unwanted characteristics to light. The resulting animals may then become dominant for faults rather than virtues. If a brood-bitch is herself line-bred we shall want to make sure she does not show evidence of the failings transmitted by the common ancestor on the pedigree, as these may be difficult to breed out in her offspring. Close line-breeding, that is to a common ancestor in the second generation, such as half-brother to half-sister, may throw up such recessive faults particularly quickly and, in fact, this practice has been disallowed in Germany for a number of years. Certainly it should not be attempted unless the ancestors of the paired animals are of outstanding merit and their families free of major recessive faults, particularly those affecting health and constitution. In any case, the breeder would have to be prepared to cull pretty drastically and make sure that none of the afflicted offspring were used for breeding.

Of course, line-breeding will only bring out what is present in the gene plasm of the dogs bred to one another. If the breeding pair do not carry the genes for, say, good shoulders, then no amount of line-breeding will result in their offspring possessing such a virtue.

Inbreeding is the term used to describe the practice of mating together very closely related animals. It is thus a more concentrated form of line-breeding. Father is mated to daughter, mother to son and

Ch. Lindanvale Rena.

so on. Such very close breeding was practised by those who fashioned the German Shepherd in the early years from a widely varying number of sheep dogs in Germany. By so doing they were able to establish a Shepherd that would breed to type with some consistency. The risk of undesirable recessives surfacing is even greater with inbreeding than with line-breeding, so most breeders prefer to avoid it.

Broadening the Breeding Base

Outcrossing, as it is called, is the practice of mating unrelated animals together. In actual fact, most German Shepherds share some common ancestry within recent generations, though any animals appearing more than once in the sixth generation or earlier seem to be insignificant as far as genetic influence is concerned. An outcross can be used to introduce some feature that the breeder finds difficult to obtain in line-bred animals. He may find, for example, that line-breeding over a number of generations has fixed a tendency to poor feet in his dogs. He will, therefore, need to find a new line that excels in that department, while at the same time proving compatible for type. This last consideration is important, for outcrossing can upset the type established by line-breeding, making the outcome of mating unpredictable. Certainly the products of outcrossing may be more heterozygous (i.e. may have more pairs of differing genes) for specific features than their line-bred counterparts. From the point of view of the breed as a whole, intelligent outcrossing is highly desirable, because there is always a danger that breeders will limit their choice of breeding animals to a restricted number of popular studs or lines that appear to be successful. Particularly in those countries where there is no limit to the number of bitches a stud-dog may serve, the breed may rapidly become saturated with that dog's genes, for good and bad. It can never be desirable to narrow the gene pool available to breeders through an overconcentration upon one or two dogs. In time any inherent weaknesses in such a limited gene pool are bound to surface. So the breeder need to be objective and open-minded in the choice of breeding partners. The person who will choose a stud-dog just because it was born in Germany is as benighted as the one who would shun the dog for the same reason. If such prejudices affect their breeding programmes, both are likely to deny themselves the use of many dogs with something to offer their particular bitches.

The Mating

You should have kept a record of your bitch's seasons, indicating the dates and duration, together with any notes that might be useful to you in predicting the nature of her seasons. Most bitches experience their first season at about ten months of age and then at approximate intervals of six months. Some bitches have three seasons a year, which, though a nuisance, is not detrimental to their well-being. More regular occurrences, however, should be regarded as abnormal and veterinary attention sought.

Obviously the bitch's season will determine precisely when the puppies will be born, although you will be faced with the decision of breeding her in the winter or in summer. Fresh air and sunshine are as important as the right food for growing animals, so that puppies born in late winter or early spring clearly have the advantage over puppies whose growing months occur during the short cold days of winter. Remember, too, that if the sale of your litter coincides with the height of the holiday season or with Christmas, you may face difficulties.

Having chosen the stud-dog you should contact his owner and ask if he will be available for a mating during the time you anticipate your bitch being in season. Stud-dog owners always reserve the right

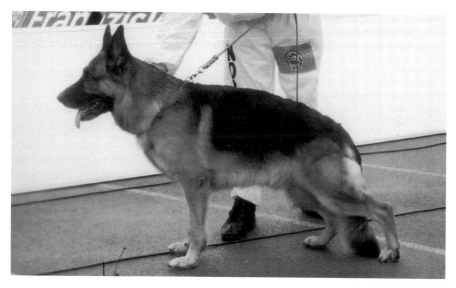

Jeck von Noricum, Sieger 1995 and top sire.

to refuse a mating for what would, in their view, be justifiable reasons; you cannot automatically demand a mating. Usually, if a mating is arranged, the owner will ask you to inform him on the first day your bitch comes into season. This will allow him ten or more days in which to fit her into the dog's breeding schedule. It is most important that you co-operate in early notification, particularly if the dog you choose is a popular stud. Other bitches may be in season at the same time and the dog's owner is often faced with the problem of trying to avoid unnecessary clashes. Normally most bitches can be mated during a period of three or four days at the peak of their season and still conceive. In the event of two bitches needing the dog on the same day, the owner may give priority to the one booked in first. Some owners may be prepared to let a dog mate twice during one day, but they should always let the owner of the second bitch know that the dog has already performed. Usually, healthy studs are quite capable of two successful matings provided the bitch is at the optimum time for conception.

Oestrus or Heat

It is often difficult to notice the first signs of a bitch's season but it is important not to miss them. The period begins with the pro-oestrus, usually lasting about nine days, followed by the oestrus, during which the bitch will be ready for mating with a reasonable chance of conception. The oestrous period varies considerably from four days to nine or more, and you must decide the best time for mating during this time.

If you use newspaper for your bitch's bedding, you should be able to detect the first spots of reddish discharge which you can regard as the beginning of the pro-oestrus. Often the discharge is very slight and you may have to use a clean tissue against the vulva to confirm your suspicions. Some bitches bleed more copiously than others during this period but most should show a gradual swelling of the vulva. If you allow an interested male to run with your bitch she may well flirt with him playfully but be unprepared to allow him to mount and attempt a mating. By the eleventh day or so she should show signs of willingness to stand for the dog. Instead of skipping tantalizingly away she will edge her rear-end towards him, swing her tail to one side and hold it stiffly out, while arching her back and standing on tip-toes behind, as the dog mounts. The vulva will have swollen and be fleshier to the touch, while the discharge becomes pinkish or straw-coloured. Some bitches, however, may show a strong colour throughout the season. This state of readiness varies in its duration, some bitches being prepared to mate as early as the tenth day while others are willing even up to the eighteenth day or beyond. Most bitches, however, are ready around the twelfth or thirteenth day from the beginning of the pro-oestrus. To be doubly sure, ask your vet to take a blood sample at the ninth or tenth day of the season to suggest the best day for mating.

Visiting the Stud-dog

Bitch owners who arrive at unpredictable times are the curse of a stud-dog owner's life, so make sure you settle on a mutually convenient time and try to stick to the arrangement. If you have to travel a long distance, make sure your bitch has the chance to relieve herself before reaching your destination.

Stud-dogs differ in their response to bitches. Some are considerate and careful, others forcefully insistent. The dog's owner will know how best to arrange the initial contact between dog and bitch and much will depend on your bitch's reactions. Allowing time for free play or 'courtship' is a good idea in theory, but if the bitch plays hard to get and the dog is continually frustrated in his attempts, little is gained from such freedom. Usually dog and bitch will be given the chance to investigate each other in a confined space which allows owners to keep in close contact but prevents the dog from unnecessary chasing or harassing of the female. A muzzle should be used on bitches that are obviously aggressive and likely to attack the dog.

After preliminary licking of the bitch's genitals, an experienced dog will soon mount and position himself correctly for an attempted penetration. You should stand in front of the bitch, holding her head firmly but considerately so that she cannot turn around and twist away from the dog, especially at the moment of actual contact. Don't be alarmed if she protests loudly at this stage. The stud-dog's owner will usually kneel at your bitch's rear, gently supporting her under the stomach to avoid any tendency for her to lower herself and make the dog's entry impossible. Her tail, too, can be moved to one side. The dog begins by thrusting very rapidly during the first phase of mating, followed by longer thrusts in the concluding moments, when his hind feet will be seen to tread the ground as he effects the deepest penetration. He will emit varying amounts of clear fluid during the initial stages of ejaculation but these contain few, if any, actual sperm. As he reaches full penetration the penis begins to swell rapidly and at its base a bulbous swelling of the bulbous glandis, grasped by the vaginal muscles, makes it difficult for the dog to withdraw. During this phase, in which dog and bitch are 'tied', or locked together, the dog ejaculates sperm-rich semen.

Once the dog has stopped thrusting he will rest for a moment or two on the bitch's back and he should be quietly held there for a while. He will soon indicate some restlessness in this position. Help him to place his front feet on the ground, and gently move one of his rear legs over the bitch's pelvis so that both animals stand tail to tail. Usually they will need holding together like this until it is clear that the dog cannot slip out and break the tie. When it is time for them to separate, both will begin to show signs of pulling apart.

The 'tied' phase may last for about twenty minutes, but can be over much more quickly. Occasionally it is uncomfortably protracted but there is nothing you can, or should, do about it. Never attempt to separate the couple; simply settle down with something to kneel on and let nature take its course. Interference may injure the mating pair.

After the mating is over, the dog will want to lick himself clean and your bitch should be quietly returned to your vehicle and be allowed to lie still for a while before you begin your return journey. The stud-dog's owner should now provide you with the KC's green litter registration form which should be properly dated and signed. You should also receive a copy of the stud-dog's pedigree.

Stud fees vary depending upon the quality of the stud-dog and his previous record as a producer. An import will often command a higher fee than a home-bred dog, but don't be blinded by pedigree or country of origin. A stud-dog is only as good as his progeny. Naturally, some excellent dogs are denied the opportunity of mating the best bitches and may not have had the chance to prove their ability to produce. Some successful breeders have trusted their intuition and taken a gamble in using an 'unknown' stud, but you should not be expected to pay a top stud fee if you decide to do the same. And don't be swayed in your choice by glamorous photographs and advertising hype. Some unscrupulous owners have been known to falsify photographs to improve the outline of a dog offered at stud. Always see the dog for yourself before your visit with your bitch and make sure he meets your requirements for type and character. Try to assess his temperament away from his immediate kennel surroundings and certainly well away from any bitch in season. Be suspicious if the owner makes excuses for denying you such a sensible appraisal. Normally a stud fee is paid at the time of mating. Most breeders charge a single fee but some require a limited fee for the mating itself and then further amounts depending upon the number of puppies produced. Stud fees are not refunded if your bitch fails to conceive, although most stud-dog owners will offer a free mating at her next season.

Problems with Mating

Apart from the obvious problem of determining the right day or days during which the bitch is at the height of her ovulation and most receptive to the dog, there are other difficulties that may hinder either copulation or conception.

If a mating is affected by discrepancies in size between dog and bitch, the latter should be encouraged to stand on an elevated, non-slip surface to allow the dog access. If the stud-dog ejaculates prematurely before penetration he should be carefully removed to a separate place to allow his penis to retract. After a rest of at least an hour, he may be allowed a second attempt.

Sometimes the bitch's vagina is too narrow. If she is a maiden the hymen (the small ring of skin not far inside) may hinder the dog's intromission. Experienced stud-dog owners will know how to deal with such minor obstructions. Any signs, however, of a polyp-like object pushing through the vulva is often a sign of a swollen vaginal wall and veterinary treatment should be sought.

A successful 'tie' after the dog has penetrated is not essential for conception to take place. It is considered to however, to increase the chances and, unless the dog is known to succeed without one, a mating without a 'tie' should be regarded as dubious. Some dogs tie for a brief period only, however.

It is surprising how many otherwise normal, healthy bitches, even maidens, are hosts to bacteria which may affect fertility. Beta haemolytic streptococcus (BHS) and other infective agents have been found in the vagina and in still-born puppies. A vaginal swab carried out by your vet just before the onset of your bitch's season or during the first days of the pro-oestrus will determine the nature and level of infection and a suitable course of antibiotics prescribed.

After mating, your bitch must be kept well away from other males for about twelve days or until her season is finished. If she is accidentally mated by another dog she may produce puppies by both fathers.

9

Pregnancy and Whelping

The Pregnant Bitch

Pregnancy normally lasts sixty-three days on average. The first few weeks will probably provide you with few signs, if any, of an impending litter. Initially, the fertilized ova move freely around in the uterus until, some eighteen days or so after fertilization, they attach themselves to the uterine wall. Although significant developments occur within each one, rearranging the cells to form the precursors of bodily organs, the embryos do not grow appreciably in size until about the thirty-fifth day. Your bitch will not need any extra food during the first five or six weeks of pregnancy. The emphasis at this time should be on quality rather than quantity, and she should be kept fit and active. There is no need to add extra vitamins and minerals to her food provided she is receiving a well-balanced diet. If she was not wormed before mating, she can be given worming medication during the first three weeks of her pregnancy to ensure she gains the maximum benefit from her food. During the final days of pregnancy special worming treatment is available from your vet which can be safely administered in controlled daily doses to ensure puppies are not afflicted with worm infestation at birth. Roundworms in puppies can not only weaken them seriously but, in extreme cases, can lead to choking and death.

You may not see any obvious changes in the bitch before the fifth week of pregnancy, especially if she is carrying a small litter. Average litter size in German Shepherds is six or seven, though litters of twelve or thirteen are not uncommon. Around the thirtieth day she will begin to thicken somewhat across the loin and slowly increase in weight until the last two weeks, when she will enlarge dramatically. Some breeders swear that they can detect pregnancy by observing slight differences of behaviour in the bitch: increased appetite, morning sickness, unusually dependent and affectionate clinging, or even physical signs such as a fringing of the hair-line at the loin or swelling of the teats. Such reading of the signs is best left to those blessed with a sixth sense. Objectively, only ultrasound scanning at about four weeks can reveal the presence of puppies. There are experts skilled in scanning who offer their services to dog-breeders for a reasonable fee. Seeing the diminutive pulsing blurs of the developing foetuses on the screen can put your mind at rest and give you a good indication of the size of the expected litter.

As your bitch reaches the last two or three weeks of her pregnancy, she will let you know how much exercise she wants. Bitches differ in this respect. Lively ladies may still want to rush around, while others will be content to amble sedately at their own pace. Respond to her wishes but encourage her to keep reasonably active until the last week or so of her pregnancy.

During the final three weeks your bitch will have to provide not only for her own nutritional needs but also for those of her unborn puppies. She will eat at least twice the amount of her normal diet and you should ensure that her food is well balanced and rich in protein. A proprietary complete meal supplemented by the addition of extra meat, chicken or fish should suffice. Her liquid intake will increase, so ensure that fresh water and thinned milk are available. New-born puppies can each weigh an average of around 17oz (500g). Carrying a litter of eight or more can impose quite a burden on your bitch during the final days. With live ballast of 9lb (4kg) or more, plus the volume of foetal fluid, a bitch heavily in whelp will prefer several small meals, spaced throughout the day, to one or two large amounts which will distend her uncomfortably. Make sure she has somewhere comfortable to sleep. Her usual basket or box may now be too small to allow her to stretch out fully on her side or lie on her back with her legs in the air, a posture beloved by some expectant bitches.

Usually German Shepherd bitches experience few problems during pregnancy. Sometimes a slight discharge may persist well after the end of her season and even occasionally throughout her term but, provided it is not dark-coloured or offensive, it is rarely a cause for concern. Resorption of the embryos in the early phase of pregnancy occurs in some bitches. The cause is unknown but the embryos die and fluid is reabsorbed into the bitch's circulation. The bitch will later expel the remains of the embryo and membranes, usually eating them. Actual abortion is very rare in bitches.

After every season, whether a bitch has been mated or not, she will continue to produce the female hormone progesterone. Progesterone production lasts throughout the pregnancy if the bitch has conceived,

Feb	Dec	Jan	Nov	Dec	Oct	Nov	Sep	Oct	Aug	Sep	Jul	Aug	Jun	Jul	May	Jun	Apr	May	Mar	Apr	Feb	Mar	Jan
2	1	3	1	3	1	3	1	3	1	2	1	3	1	3	1	3	1	3	1	5	1	5	1
3	2	4	2	4	2	4	2	4	2	3	2	4	2	4	2	4	2	4	2	6	2	6	2
4	3	5	3	5	3	5	3	5	3	4	3	5	3	5	3	5	3	5	3	7	3	7	3
5	4	6	4	6	4	6	4	6	4	5	4	6	4	6	4	6	4	6	4	8	4	8	4
6	5	7	5	7	5	7	5	7	5	6	5	7	5	7	5	7	5	7	5	9	5	9	5
7	6	8	6	8	6	8	6	8	6	7	6	8	6	8	6	8	6	8	6	10	6	10	6
8	7	9	7	9	7	9	7	9	7	8	7	9	7	9	7	9	7	9	7	11	7	11	7
9	8	10	8	10	8	10	8	10	8	9	8	10	8	10	8	10	8	10	8	12	8	12	8
10	9	11	9	11	9	11	9	11	9	10	9	11	9	11	9	11	9	11	9	13	9	13	9
11	10	12	10	12	10	12	10	12	10	11	10	12	10	12	10	12	10	12	10	14	10	14	10
12	11	13	11	13	11	13	11	13	11	12	11	13	11	13	11	13	11	13	11	15	11	15	11
13	12	14	12	14	12	14	12	14	12	13	12	14	12	14	12	14	12	14	12	16	12	16	12
14	13	15	13	15	13	15	13	15	13	14	13	15	13	15	13	15	13	15	13	17	13	17	13
15	14	16	14	16	14	16	14	16	14	15	14	16	14	16	14	16	14	16	14	18	14	18	14
16	15	17	15	17	15	17	15	17	15	16	15	17	15	17	15	17	15	17	15	19	15	19	15
17	16	18	16	18	16	18	16	18	16	17	16	18	16	18	16	18	16	18	16	20	16	20	16
18	17	19	17	19	17	19	17	19	17	18	17	19	17	19	17	19	17	19	17	21	17	21	17
19	18	20	18	20	18	20	18	20	18	19	18	20	18	20	18	20	18	20	18	22	18	22	18
20	19	21	19	21	19	21	19	21	19	20	19	21	19	21	19	21	19	21	19	23	19	23	19
21	20	22	20	22	20	22	20	22	20	21	20	22	20	22	20	22	20	22	20	24	20	24	20
22	21	23	21	23	21	23	21	23	21	22	21	23	21	23	21	23	21	23	21	25	21	25	21
23	22	24	22	24	22	24	22	24	22	23	22	24	22	24	22	24	22	24	22	26	22	26	22
24	23	25	23	25	23	25	23	25	23	24	23	25	23	25	23	25	23	25	23	27	23	27	23
25	24	26	24	26	24	26	24	26	24	25	24	26	24	26	24	26	24	26	24	28	24	28	24
26	25	27	25	27	25	27	25	27	25	26	25	27	25	27	25	27	25	27	25	29	25	29	25
27	26	28	26	28	26	28	26	28	26	27	26	28	26	28	26	28	26	28	26	30	26	30	26
28	27	29	27	29	27	29	27	29	27	28	27	29	27	29	27	29	27	29	27	1 (May)	27	31	27
1 (Mar)	28	30	28	30	28	30	28	30	28	29	28	30	28	30	28	30	28	30	28	2 (May)	28	1 (Apr)	28
2 (Mar)	29	31	29	31	29	1 (Dec)	29	31	29	30	29	31	29	31	29	1 (Jul)	29	31	29			2 (Apr)	29
3 (Mar)	30	1 (Feb)	30	1 (Jan)	30	2 (Dec)	30	1 (Nov)	30	1 (Oct)	30	1 (Sep)	30	1 (Aug)	30	2 (Jul)	30	1 (Jun)	30			3 (Apr)	30
4 (Mar)	31			2 (Jan)	31			2 (Nov)	31	2 (Oct)	31			2 (Aug)	31			2 (Jun)	31			4 (Apr)	31

174

Whelping chart. The first figure in each column indicates mating date, the second the expected whelping date.

and for about sixty days if she has 'missed' or not been mated. Consequently, a bitch that is not pregnant may, in some cases, show all the external signs of being in whelp. This is called a 'false pregnancy'. She may go off her food, produce milk, put on weight and indulge in frantic bed-making activity or a possessive preoccupation with toys. Extreme physical and mental reactions can be uncomfortable for dog and family and though these disappear naturally with time, your veterinary surgeon may be able to help alleviate the problem.

The Whelping

Although the gestation period is normally nine weeks, your bitch may whelp early so be ready to abandon all domestic pursuits from the fifty-ninth day onwards. Puppies born earlier are definitely premature and may not survive. Thankfully German Shepherd bitches are usually sensible mothers and whelping complications are rare. You will probably worry much more than she will, if it is your first experience of the whelping process but, provided you have made sensible preparation, all should go well.

Decide where your bitch will whelp and let her accustom herself to the place during the last fortnight of her pregnancy by ensuring she sleeps there. If she is to whelp in an outdoor kennel you will need somewhere for you to sit comfortably, and sufficient lighting to allow you to keep an eye on proceedings. Newborn puppies need warmth, and in the cold of autumn and winter a dull-emitter 300w heater lamp should be suspended over the whelping box. Have this in place some days before the litter is due so that the bitch can get used to it. Summer litters should not require artificial heat as the bitch is perfectly capable of generating warmth from her enveloping body.

A good whelping box is important. It must be big enough to allow the bitch room to stretch out comfortably with a few inches to spare. Three of the sides should be approximately 2ft (60cm) high, and the front should consist of removable boards, so that you can slide them out when the heavily pregnant bitch needs to step in sedately. They can be raised to full height when the pups become mobile at about three weeks, discouraging the more adventurous ones from climbing out. Some breeders fix broom-handles as guard rails around the lower part of the box to prevent the bitch from crushing a puppy against the box side. These can, however, be uncomfortable for a

Contented mother. Jayne Swan's Elka with day-old babies by Orno von Ohlenkopf.

nursing bitch. Most canine mothers are readily responsive to the alarms of a seriously trapped puppy anyway, and will take steps to help it. You should make sure that the box is made from good-quality, non-splinter plywood. If you need to scrub it before use, avoid strong disinfectants and make sure you do this well before the whelping date.

If the bitch is to whelp in an outdoor kennel with a wooden floor for warmth, you may dispense with a box and fill the complete kennel area with good-quality wood-wool. One bale will fluff out and provide a deep, warm bed in which the bitch will make her nest. If you use enough of the material she will be surrounded by enveloping swathes that will protect her and her babies from draughts and cold. Soiling will be hardly noticeable as you can thin out fresh wool daily. Wood-wool flattens less easily than commercially shredded paper and is therefore preferable for her nest. Both are better than straw, which is often dusty and spiky for newborn whelps.

Just before she is due to whelp, accustom your bitch to making use of the broad-sheet newspapers. Their generous-sized pages make excellent bedding material, absorbent and easily disposed of. Expect varying degrees of 'gunge' and fluid during the birth, so rugs or blankets are not recommended. Avoid glossy magazines, which lack absorbency, and beware of paper with staples, which can injure the puppies.

As the time for giving birth approaches, you will notice changes in your bitch's behaviour. Sometimes these are quite obvious: she will become increasingly restless and concern herself with finding a place she regards as suitable for the coming event. Her criteria may not match yours. A natural tendency to dig will become apparent, as you will soon find if she has free access to your garden. Nest-making activities will result in her tearing up the newspapers you have carefully smoothed flat for her comfort. She will probably go off her food.

During the first mild contractions of first-stage labour she will pant more regularly. Her temperature may fall from the normal 37.7–38°C (100–105°F) to about 36.6°C (98°F). Such temperature loss will probably fluctuate, however, and unless you take several measurements during the day, with the attendant risk of unsettling the bitch, the thermometer may be of no great help in estimating exactly when she will whelp. The first stage of labour varies in duration and may even last up to forty-eight hours, but most bitches will begin to get down to the business within twenty-four to forty-eight hours of the fall in temperature.

Before the major contractions necessary to expel the puppy begin, the bitch will pant rapidly and often shiver along the back. Most will lie flat but some produce puppies standing or even walking about. Calmly encourage her to lie still by gently talking to her, but if you can't control your own anxiety say nothing! She will begin to push at regular intervals and the first puppy should appear within half an hour. Each puppy will have been enclosed in the womb within an inner and outer foetal membrane or bag, both of which contain varying amounts of fluid. These 'water-bags' have to be broken during birth. In most cases the outer bag breaks inside the bitch before the puppy is born, but you may see it protruding before it ruptures and releases its fluid. The bitch will normally lick this up rapidly.

Some bitches have more forceful and urgent contractions, while others whelp with an apparent lack of effort. You will notice an arching of the back and a stiffening of the hindquarters before the tail moves at the root, the vulva distends and the first puppy begins to

177

emerge. You will probably see just the grey-green edge of the inner water-bag remain there for a while, waiting for the final contractions that will expel it. Avoid the temptation to interfere or do anything to distract the bitch at this stage. The puppy will be born inside the inner membrane which the bitch normally opens with her teeth, licking the puppy vigorously to dry it. The pup may be born head first or back legs first. If the bitch does not bite open the sac, gently ease it away from the puppy's head to allow air to reach its nose and mouth. The bitch should bite through the umbilical cord but if not, break it yourself about 1½ in (4cm) from the pup's stomach, using your nails or a pair of sterilized scissors. Be careful to avoid any pressure on the attachment at the stomach. The placenta and the remains of the outer water-bag (the afterbirth) are expelled by further uterine contractions. The bitch will eat these remains, which contain vitamins and nutrients believed to help stimulate the production of milk. Sometimes the placentas are passed during the actual expulsion of the puppy and immediately devoured so the number of afterbirths may not always seem to correspond to the number of pups.

Once the bitch has finished cleaning up, place the little steaming creature in the warmth of its mother's inner thighs and gently guide its mouth to the nearest nipple. If you tease out a little milk, the puppy's remarkable sense of smell will be activated. Hold its mouth to the teat, encouraging it to suckle. Don't be frustrated if it does not do so straightaway. Soon it will be quietly ingesting the precious colostrum, essential for the pup's resistance to infection, while its tiny paws knead its mother's breast.

The time gap between births varies considerably, but after two or three puppies have arrived it is best to place them in a roomy cardboard box on a hot-water bottle that has been wrapped in warm material. This will protect them from the repeated soaking they may have to endure during the birth of subsequent pups. As long as the box is near, the bitch will normally be unconcerned as she will be fully preoccupied in coping with each new whelp. This will also give you a chance to inspect the puppies for deformities, and to record their weight. A puppy experiencing difficulty in suckling or retaining milk may be afflicted with a cleft palate. Check the roof of the mouth for abnormalities and consult your vet. Very occasionally pups are born with a stumpy tail which will fail to grow to a normal length.

Some breeding lines will carry genes for non-standard colours such as whites, blues and livers. The gene for brindle, certainly present in the 1920s, seems to have disappeared. Whites are obvious at birth but it is not so easy to detect a blue. Some breeders confuse the colour with a grey-sable, but a sable puppy *must* have at least one sable parent. If two black and tan parents are responsible for a smoky-fawn puppy the chances are that it is a blue. Genuine sables normally have a black line down the back and are otherwise a uniform colour at birth. Some people are prepared to pay a high price for one of these so-called 'rare' colours, but responsible breeders will sell them only with a KC endorsement that their progeny cannot be registered, thus reducing their chances of being bred from and further perpetuating such colours.

If your bitch produces an exceptionally large litter you should think seriously about limiting the number you allow her to rear. A maximum of seven will certainly be enough for her to cope with: more will mean earlier weaning and less of the bitch's invaluable milk to go round.

There are few German Shepherds free from the gene that can produce a long coat but you will not be able to detect this at birth. Normal-coated puppies often have obvious waves down their neck and body, but only after four or five weeks will you be able to say with any certainty that there are probably long-coats in your litter.

A large litter can take several hours to deliver, and a tired bitch may decide to recuperate by going to sleep half-way through the procedure. Offer her a drink of milk with glucose or a little honey; food should not be given and will normally be refused anyway. If you employed ultrasonic scanning you will have a good idea of the probable number of puppies to expect. Scanning is not foolproof, however, and may underestimate the total. Otherwise you must use your intuition to sense when she has finished whelping. She should have been lying contentedly for two hours or so without any sign of further contractions and she will curve her body protectively around her babies as they suckle. Don't bother about soiled bedding at this stage. Simply allow her to rest undisturbed for the next few hours. You can clear up and put fresh papers down once she has rested.

Many bitches will be unwilling to leave their puppies to begin with but, after she has rested, she should be encouraged to leave the box to empty herself. You will need to wash her hindquarters and tail with warm water to remove the green staining. If you allow this discoloration to dry it will usually lead to unsightly loss of hair a few days later. Eating the afterbirth will probably result in a dark-coloured diarrhoea. This is quite natural and no cause for alarm. Once the bitch has settled down into her nursing rhythm and has been

179

Joan Sale's Natasha with her litter of four days.

This is all a bit much! Five weeks later.

gradually reintroduced to her normal food, her digestive system will stabilize itself, although you must expect a degree of looseness during the first few days after birth.

Complications

Most German Shepherd bitches whelp naturally and with a minimum of fuss but if you are concerned about your bitch's welfare you should always seek veterinary attention. Some of the minor problems, however, can respond to sensible steps taken by the careful owner.

A 'breech' birth occurs when the puppy is presented backwards, posterior first, and the legs are flexed at the hips so that the feet are pointing forwards. This is quite different from the normal

180

presentation of hind feet and tail together, which usually presents no problems for the bitch. A 'breech' will result in the bitch pushing in vain in an attempt to expel the puppy. Occasionally the head may be turned to one side, which also complicates delivery. Should the puppy be partly presented, allowing you to hold it gently between a well-soaped thumb and index finger, you can carefully collaborate with the bitch's contractions, easing it out in time with her pushing. If the bitch has been straining for more than half an hour without success, consult your vet.

Placentas that are not properly expelled, but retained inside the bitch, can lead to internal problems. It is sensible, therefore, to arrange for your vet to administer an injection the day after whelping to ensure that she is freed from such unhelpful detritus, which can lead to metritis (infection of the womb). Any foul-smelling discharge from the vulva must be a warning sign, though a little bleeding is quite natural as the womb contracts after the birth.

Some pups enter the world practically drowned, having taken too much fluid into their lungs. After the bitch has cleaned up and licked each pup, check that its airways are free. If it seems incapable of breathing freely, gently prise open its mouth and, keeping it open with the tip of your finger while you support the head firmly, shake the pup carefully with its head pointing downwards. If the congestion is more severe, you will need to gently rub and squeeze the little form from tail to head with a towel or even suspend him by his hind legs while you gently swing him from side to side.

A vigorous rubbing with a towel is sometimes effective if a puppy appears lifeless and his mother's solicitous tongue has not succeeded in mobilizing his circulation. Warmth and rough stimulation for up to four or five minutes can sometimes save a pup's life.

Occasionally a bitch will reject a particular pup in a litter, pushing it away to the perimeter of the box where it will distress you, if not her, by its weak, plaintive cry. There may be no apparent justification for her behaviour; the pup may not be the weakest or have any obvious defect. Once it is clear she is determined to reject it, however, there is little to be done. Bottle-feeding is a demanding and time-consuming option, and it may be better to allow the inscrutable maternal instinct to have its way. Some latent weakness may afflict the abandoned pup, and it may be wise to ask your vet to provide a painless end.

Eclampsia or milk fever is uncommon in German Shepherd bitches. The condition occurs when the bitch is apparently incapable of absorbing the natural reserves of calcium in her skeleton into the bloodstream. She is most vulnerable to an attack during the first two weeks of lactation (milk production) and the symptoms begin with panting, restlessness and whining. A considerable rise in temperature may be accompanied by a general unsteadiness and, in extreme cases, bouts of prostrate trembling resembling a fit. Consult your vet immediately as the condition can be fatal. Do not breed from the bitch again as she is likely to suffer in subsequent litters.

Occasionally the nursing bitch may develop an inflammation of the mammary glands or teats, usually called mastitis. One or more of the teats may become red, swollen and painful and she will be reluctant to allow the puppies to suckle. Like eclampsia, this condition is rare in bitches feeding a normal litter but may sometimes occur in those who lose litters. Seek veterinary attention.

Rearing the Litter

For the first two or three weeks you will have little to do other than to make sure the bedding in the whelping box is kept clean. The bitch will assist you in this by cleaning up after the pups have emptied themselves. Her solicitous licking sometimes stimulates their regular evacuations. You must make sure the bitch is lavishly fed and has free access to fresh clean water throughout the nursing period. A large litter will make considerable demands upon her physical condition, so try to ensure she does not lose too much weight at this time. Adding boiled rice, potatoes or brown bread to her food may help. Three or four small meals a day should be given in preference to one or two larger ones.

The puppies will spend most of their time sleeping and growing nicely rounded and fat. They should be weighed every day so that you can identify any that may need a little extra time at the teats. Greedy, forward pups delight not only in getting to the milk bar first but in monopolizing the fullest teats, even falling contentedly asleep with both mouth and stomach full.

Very occasionally puppies are born with what are termed 'dew-claws' on the hind legs. These form a little flap of skin with a tiny claw on the inside of the leg above the paw. They can be a nuisance in adulthood and, since they serve no useful purpose, it is best to ask your vet to remove them at four or five days of age. The corresponding dew-claws on the front legs should not be removed.

Not much room at the milk bar now! Elka's litter at twelve days.

From soon after birth puppies have a well-developed sense of smell which keeps them in contact with their dam. The puppies' eyes will begin to open at ten to fourteen days and they will slowly begin to accustom themselves to the light. By three weeks their tiny ears will react to sounds and they will begin to totter around on unsteady legs. Some puppies show, even at this early stage, a response to the human touch by tail-wagging. It is important that they have plenty of opportunity to get used to human contact through gentle handling and stroking. And, since their nose is the most important aid to exploring their new world, give them plenty of time to take the scent of your hands and clothing.

The size of the litter will determine when you should begin supplementary feeding. If the puppies are approximately doubling their weight each week and are fat, contented and sleeping well the indications are that they are gaining all they need from their mother's milk. You may begin offering them food at around three weeks of age, but make sure you worm them two days before you start. Several proprietary brands of puppy wormer effective against roundworm are

183

available, in a palatable liquid form which is easy to administer. Worms in a puppy will rob it of the full nutritional value of any supplementary food you offer. Throughout the weaning process you should aim at keeping the puppies well-rounded and plump without overfeeding. If you do your job conscientiously, they should never be thin or bony to the touch, though inevitably as they move around their body shape will alter.

There are no hard and fast rules about which food you should use at first. Specially prepared puppy food suitable for weaning is commercially available. Complete adult foods should never be offered as these are unlikely to be digestible at such an early stage. Puppies at about three weeks certainly do well if fed on the traditional diet of meat, milk and cereals. Good-quality raw beef should be scraped to remove all obstructive gristle and the resulting red paste should be rolled into convenient little balls and offered to the puppies. Take each puppy individually in your lap and offer it a tiny sliver of the pulped beef. You will soon find that it will wriggle with greedy enthusiasm to find more. About a dessertspoonful will suffice for each pup on the first day, and the same amount twice on the second day, increasing to four meals by the fourth day. Make sure the bitch is taken away while you feed, and try to offer the meat after the puppies have been sleeping for a time. When you have finished feeding each one, allow the mother back to the litter. Her milk will aid the puppies' digestion.

Fat and contented at thirteen days.

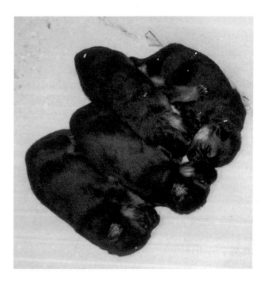

184

Three-and-a-half-week-old puppy, now sensitive to sound.

After four days on the scraped beef, the puppies should be introduced to lukewarm puppy milk. Cow's milk is unsuitable and will cause tummy upsets. Commercially prepared brands are specially formulated to match the bitch's milk. Again, your lap is essential: offer each pup the milk in a shallow saucer and gently encourage it to lap by dabbing a little milk on its nose and then very carefully dipping its little head on to the surface of the milk. After an initial splutter or sneeze it will soon be lapping. Make sure you keep the milk warm. By the time you reach the last pup in a large litter it may be too cold to offer.

Raw meat and milk alone will not keep weight on puppies, so you should add cereal or commercial puppy meal to the food from about four weeks. Gradually thicken the milk into a gruel-like consistency with a baby cereal or rusks which are nourishing and digestible. By four to five weeks each pup should be receiving two meat and two milk/cereal meals a day. Meat may be offered in finely chopped pieces now, as the puppies learn to chew. The bitch should be allowed access whenever she wishes but she must now have the opportunity to move to a place where she is free from the litter's insistent demands. You should have cut the puppies' nails, at the tip only, at about three weeks, as by this time they can cause considerable discomfort to the nursing mother.

If you cannot find a good supply of red meat at the right price, you can gradually introduce a complete meal or tinned puppy food. Avoid any rapid change in the diet, however.

Suggested Puppy Feeding

At two weeks　Scraped lean, good-quality beef. Avoid fat. A thumb-nail-sized pulped ball for each puppy, offered once on the first day then increased gradually to 2–3oz (60–80g) per puppy divided into three offerings each day.

At three-and-a-half weeks　Begin lukewarm milk (using puppy milk powder). Once puppies are lapping effectively, feed milk at 8am and 4pm with meat at 12 noon and 8pm.

At four weeks　Thicken milk feeds with baby cereal to a runny gruel consistency. Increase meat feeds to 4–5oz (120–140g) minced meat per puppy per day, offered in two meals. Add a little soaked, well-crumbled puppy meal to the meat.

At five weeks　Continue two milk-based and two meat feeds. Cow's milk can be gradually introduced if you began with powdered milk. Begin adding calcium/phosphorus powder to meat meal. Tablets may be crushed, according to the manufacturer's instructions.

At six to eight weeks　Four meals a day. Each puppy should be offered up to ½pint (250ml) of milk and ½lb (250g) of meat a day by eight weeks. The meat feed may be varied by adding minced tripe, tinned puppy food, chopped boiled egg or a little crumbled cheese. Crush a yeast tablet every other day into the meat feed. Fresh water must be available.

The Growing Pups

By five weeks the puppies should be practically independent of the dam, though she can be allowed in if she wishes to play, and to sleep with them at night. If she begins to lose weight rapidly at this stage, it is best to take her from the puppies completely. Give her plenty of nourishing food and the chance to rest and regain her strength. She should be wormed again on completion of her maternal duties.

The puppies need access to a covered run where they can play in the fresh air. They must not be allowed to sleep in the damp or in draughts. Given the opportunity, they will soon learn to empty themselves in a particular corner of the run on newspaper or sawdust, especially if you can put them there whenever you see that they are about to perform. Make sure your kennel and run doors have a lower inner-door or board which allows you, but not the pups, in or out. They will be expert escapees and will wriggle through any door given half a chance. Probably you will have your hands full, and a foot to ward off a milling little mob of pups never seems effective!

The puppies will benefit from a sizeable shin or marrow bone to exercise their jaws and strengthen their ear muscles. Fresh water should be available, but make sure it is in a container that cannot be tipped up.

Ideally each puppy should be regularly taken from the litter at five to six weeks and brought into the house by itself for a little individual attention. Talking to each pup and playing with it regularly will help to develop the puppy's temperament.

Parting with the Litter

Most breeders would like to plan a mating secure in the knowledge that all the resulting puppies have good homes waiting for them. Usually, however, it may be necessary to advertise at least some of the litter for sale – perhaps in the small-ads column of your local newspaper, when the litter is approximately six weeks old. If you advertise earlier than this you may attract time-wasters who order a pup only to fail to take it when it is old enough to go, at seven to eight weeks. You should not part with a puppy before this age. Although it may be fully weaned by five weeks, it must continue to have the security of the litter in which to develop further until it is old enough to have the physical resilience to cope with a change in environment. A puppy removed too soon from its litter-mates will not experience the rough and tumble of mock-fighting with other puppies that is necessary for it to learn the signals of social interaction with its own kind.

Watching the pups at play will reveal a great deal about their emerging characters. Some will dominate, while others may be quieter and more submissive. You need to keep such differences in mind when you consider homing each one. If a potential buyer seems the wrong kind of person for a dominant male puppy that may require quite firm physical control as an adult, you should politely suggest this to the prospective owner.

If you are a novice breeder it is unlikely that your litter will attract the attention of those seeking a puppy for the show ring. Nevertheless, if your bitch is of good quality and breeding, and if she has been noticed at a few breed shows, and if you have chosen a good sire that will suit her, you have every chance of producing an excellent puppy. Many a champion has been bred by beginners. But you cannot advertise your litter as of show quality, since no one can guarantee that even the best will develop into a winner. Hopefully you will be breeding from dogs with good hip scores, but do not claim that the puppies have good hips. If you have made a conscientious effort to breed from sound, healthy animals from good parentage you can justifiably maintain that the puppies are well-bred and promising, but no more. If the parents and immediate ancestors have done well in the show ring, the offspring should have every chance of being above-average representatives of their breed.

German Shepherd puppies attract a wide variety of potential purchasers but, in truth, the right owners, with time to devote to the growing dog and an understanding of the breed, are not easy to find. The ideal folk are those seeking a pup to replace a much-loved family pet which has been part of their lives for years. Perhaps the worst are the often well-heeled clients who want a dog to chain up to guard their business premises, or the show-ring fanatics who will simply discard a dog if he fails to win prizes. Regrettably many young couples buy a puppy only to experience later the break-up of their relationship, so that the pup is cast aside.

Before selling a puppy you should satisfy yourself that he will have a decent chance of a stable, secure life. He must not be left alone for long hours while his owners are at work. If he is destined to be a house-pet, there must be a place where the puppy can sleep undisturbed, especially if there are young children in the household. Growing puppies need plenty of sleep as much as they need food and fresh air. Problems may also arise if one member of a partnership does not share the other's enthusiasm for the dog. You will need a degree of psychological insight to place your puppies in the right hands!

Well before your litter is ready to go, you should have completed the KC litter-registration form which you will have received, signed and dated, from the stud-dog's owner. You will avoid any later administrative complications if you register all the puppies on the same form. Naming the pups can be quite tricky, especially if you do not possess your own kennel name, as you must avoid previously

His first photograph. Puppy dog at three weeks.

recognized names. Even if you breed from just one bitch, you can still apply for a protected kennel affix, which can be used only by yourself for puppy naming. On payment of the appropriate fees, the KC will send you a registration certificate for each puppy giving details of colour, date of birth, sire and dam and hip-scores if the parents have been through the BVA hip-scoring scheme. Since the puppies will be registered in your name, you will also need transfer of ownership forms to be given to the purchasers with each puppy. Some breeders have strong feeling about their stock being exported by middlemen to dubious destinations simply for commercial gain. You may ask the KC to endorse any registration certificate with the proviso 'not eligible for issue of an export pedigree'. Similarly, you may wish to discourage breeding from a particular dog or bitch because of some genetic failing he or she may transmit to progeny. In this case the KC will stipulate on the certificate that a puppy's offspring will not be eligible for registration. Unfortunately this will not deter the unscrupulous or indifferent person from breeding animals without KC papers, but it will make the sale of any resultant puppies more difficult, which may make people think twice about mating a bitch.

You must also provide each purchaser with a correct pedigree signed by yourself. A variety of forms are available commercially; most breed clubs can assist you in choosing one. Usually forms offer a five-generation format, which is all that is necessary for most breeding purposes. It is your responsibility to correctly transcribe the pedigrees of sire and dam on the new pedigree for each puppy. Typewritten or computerized forms are preferable, if only because handwriting can often be hard to decipher, especially when the spelling of unfamiliar foreign names is involved. If you are not conversant with the names and breeding of dogs on your pedigrees, it may be worth your while to consult a local expert to check for any errors. It is quite common for mistakes to be unwittingly perpetuated through several generations.

Traditional practice has been to present the names of champions in red, though there is no necessity for you to do so. If your pedigree contains German dogs, you will notice certain abbreviations often accompanying their names. 'V.A.' stands for *Vorzüglich Auslese* ('excellent select'). This is the top award given to any dog in Germany and is available only once a year at the Sieger Show. A number after the letter indicates the dog's position in the select group. Usually about twelve animals, from an average entry of three hundred, win this qualification. 'V' indicates an excellent grade at a breed show. 'Kkl.1.a' is sometimes found after names of dogs that have been placed in class one and recommended for breeding at a breed survey in Germany. The 'a' indicates that the animal has been X-rayed and has good hips. Since all 'V'-rated dogs must be surveyed such information is rather superfluous. Most German dogs on your pedigree will possess a training degree. The abbreviation Sch.H. is short for Schutzhund (protection dog) and will probably be followed by 1, 2, or 3 to indicate the level of achievement in the tests. Sometimes you will come across F.H. which stands for Fährtenhund or tracking dog. In addition to the abbreviation Ch. for Champion, British-bred dogs may have gained a Junior Warrant (J.W.) or Reserve Challenge Certificate (Reserve CC).

The new owner should also be given a diet sheet with directions for feeding the puppy. If he has been unable to obtain the puppy's usual food before purchase, you should be prepared to offer a day or two's supply. This will reduce the likelihood of digestive upsets as the puppy settles into his new home. Some breeders provide useful literature for the first-time owner in the form of small breed booklets or informative pamphlets. The GSD Breed Council has produced an attractive video on the breed, showing the German Shepherd in a variety of roles. A copy of this would make a useful present to accompany each puppy. Leaflets on insurance schemes to cover loss or sickness are also worthwhile, together with contact addresses of local breed and training clubs in your area. These will often provide you with a supply of membership forms to hand out.

Buying a puppy at eight weeks is quite different from buying a motor car or television set. With the latter you purchase a finished product designed to work properly from the moment you buy it. A puppy is simply the raw material, a furry bundle of potential, which the new owner is, in large part, responsible for rearing and shaping into the adult animal. Much can go wrong in the upbringing of the young puppy through neglect or ignorance so that he develops faults or weaknesses which would not occur in different hands. In these litigious times, it is not uncommon for breeders to be taken to court by a disgruntled owner whose pup has not fulfilled expectations. You must be careful, therefore, that you do not make unrealistic claims about your puppies' future development and that the purchaser knows exactly what he is buying at eight weeks. He is *not* taking home a future show-dog or obedience champion! All you can claim is that the puppy is healthy, without obvious faults, such as an overshot mouth or missing testicles and that you have taken steps to ensure that the sire and dam are free from hereditary health failings. A written contract to be signed by both breeder and buyer is well worth considering so that the terms of purchase are clear. It should require the new owner to arrange for an immediate veterinary health check to establish that the puppy is healthy on leaving your premises. You should specify, too, the grounds upon which you would replace the puppy or refund part or all of the purchase price. You cannot yourself be responsible for many developmental faults. Soft ears or missing teeth can occur in most lines, as can movement faults, whilst temperament failings can be as much the result of environmental factors as of breeding. But a new owner has the right to feel secure that his puppy will not be clinically affected by hip-dysplasia at an early age or suffer from ultimately fatal epileptic fits. In such cases, you must be prepared to replace the puppy. Some breeders sell every puppy with a 'not to be used for breeding' endorsement which they

191

then lift when the pup has reached adulthood and has been hip-scored. This is a commendable encouragement to responsible breeding. If you do finally decide to draw up a sales contract, consult your solicitor to ensure that it is legally binding.

If you are attracted by the idea of breeding on from the litter you have produced, but are unable to keep the best bitch puppy yourself, you may consider parting with her on what are called 'breeding terms'. Instead of a cash transaction, you agree with her new owner on an arrangement that will give you the opportunity to have one or more puppies from her in the future. Innumerable complications, however, can arise from such ventures and it is absolutely essential that you draw up a written agreement covering all the eventualities such as who pays for any veterinary attention needed during pregnancy and rearing, who chooses the stud-dog, who has the 'pick' of the litter, what happens if the bitch proves infertile and other complications. Don't rely on a verbal agreement: memories about what was said often prove to be highly unreliable and many a friendship has foundered on the rocks of disputatious breeding terms.

After the litter has gone and you have weighed up the cost, not only financially but in terms of the many hours of committed and often exhausting attention, you may feel that the experience is one you would not willingly repeat. Your real reward comes later: a visit from happy new owners with a healthy, bouncy puppy who is the apple of their eye.

10

Diseases, Ailments and First Aid

With the right combination of exercise, good food, regular grooming and intelligent management, your German Shepherd should enjoy a long and healthy life. However, emergencies do occur, and even the most well-cared-for dog is unfortunately not immune to the shocks to which canine flesh is heir. As a responsible owner you should develop a reliable relationship with your local veterinary surgeon and take a sensible interest in your dog's health. Avoid, however, the form of hypochondriacal anxiety that sends you off to the vet at the slightest indication your dog is unwell. Most minor illnesses respond to sensible domestic attention and the natural healing process.

Accidents and First Aid

Accidents demand immediate attention and you should have a first-aid kit handy. Since crises may occur away from the home, while your dog is exercising, it is useful to keep a kit in the car. A roll of bandage, a canine thermometer, a bottle of antiseptic, some sodium bicarbonate and vinegar (for stings), plaster, cotton wool and scissors should be included. Absorbent kitchen towel is also useful, as is a spare lead and material such as an old tie or tights for making a muzzle.

Traffic accidents are the cause of many canine deaths and severe injuries and your quick response may help maintain life until the vet arrives. No severely injured dog must be moved or manipulated but in other cases, if the dog has difficulty in breathing, it is essential that the airways are cleared. Any blockage at the back of the throat must be removed and the tongue pulled well forward. Lay the dog on his side and press gently down on the ribcage. Count five and repeat. You should then check that the heart is beating by placing a finger just underneath the left elbow against his ribs. Repeated pressure at five-second intervals should stimulate breathing. This must be maintained even if you are conveying him by vehicle to the vet's surgery. Opening a dog's mouth to give the 'kiss of life' is not likely to work. Instead, grasp his muzzle closed and blow down his nostrils, your lips enclosing his nose.

Shock

Major accidents and other forms of trauma can disturb the blood flow to the body tissues, leading to a serious lack of oxygen. The clinical state known as 'shock' sets in, characterized by weakness, near-collapse and a lack of response to stimulation. The breathing is rapid and the lips, gums and tongue are pale and cold. A lowering of temperature is accompanied by trembling or shivering. The heart beat will increase to more than eighty beats per minute and the dog's eyes will appear glazed and unseeing. The dog must be kept warm (but not overheated), dry and quiet. A loose blanket and hot-water bottle will help to sustain body-heat. Food should not be given, but a little warm thinned milk with glucose may be offered. Shock can have serious consequences so consult your vet immediately.

Bleeding

Minor cuts and abrasions normally stop bleeding after natural blood clotting occurs. You should not interfere with the clot formation or you will cause further bleeding.

Major external or internal haemorrhaging requires immediate veterinary attention. If a large blood vessel is severed or an artery damaged, the pressure of blood loss prevents clotting so the flow of blood must be stopped externally. A pressure pad of clean absorbent material, such as cotton wool, should be firmly and tightly bandaged in place over the blood vessel. A tourniquet may be made from a strip of cloth about 1–2in (2–5cm) wide, firmly tied around the affected limb or tail between the wound and the animal's body. A tourniquet is only a temporary emergency measure, to be used until your vet can attend to the patient. It must never be left in place for more than twenty minutes as it can cut off the blood supply and lead to gangrene. Severe bleeding is often accompanied by symptoms of clinical shock (*see* above).

194

Bites and Stings

Late summer and autumn often bring leisurely cruising wasps and bees around a dog-run, particularly if it is situated near garden plants. Unfortunately some dogs are unable to resist the temptation to snap at such tantalizing visitors. Bee stings may be eased with sodium bicarbonate, while a dab of vinegar should counteract a wasp sting. A bee sting may remain in the form of a black splinter which should be removed with tweezers.

Stings inside the mouth or throat will need veterinary attention, as will any dog unfortunate enough to swallow a bee or wasp, especially if he subsequently shows evidence of swelling on the head and tongue.

The venom from an adder bite can cause trembling and shock. Subsequent collapse may even prove fatal. The bite is indicated by severe swelling surrounding two small puncture wounds. Keep the dog quiet, avoiding activity, and if the vet is delayed clean out the wound with soap and water and apply an ice-pack. Bites from grass-snakes are usually not serious, but the wound should be cleaned to prevent bacterial infection.

You should also be on your guard against the common toad. It secretes a venom which, though usually not serious, can be a source of distress and irritation to a dog that picks one up in his mouth. Wash the dog's mouth with water or a weak sodium bicarbonate solution (one level teaspoonful to a tumbler of tepid water).

Poisoning

Though poisoning is not a common cause of death in dogs, there are so many potentially poisonous substances around that it is sensible to limit your dog's chances of coming into contact with them. Common disinfectants, weedkillers, pesticides, creosote, anti-freeze, substances containing lead (such as some paints, or old linoleum), together with most medicinal and addictive drugs are harmful to dogs. Many garden plants are toxic, such as some flower bulbs, holly and mistletoe berries, ivy, yew, laurel, delphiniums, lupins, and several others. Slug-pellets often attract an inquisitive or greedy puppy, and dogs out at exercise must be dissuaded from devouring carrion which may be contaminated.

Corrosive poisoning is caused by swallowing such substances as ammonia, de-greasing agents, dishwashing powder, creosote and certain disinfectants. Burning and blistering may occur around the mouth and the dog will suffer intense pain. Your immediate aim should be to wash out the mouth and neutralize the poison by diluting it in the stomach with plenty of water or diluted milk. On no account must you encourage the dog to vomit, which will simply cause more damage.

Non-corrosive poisons should be expelled if possible by making the dog vomit. A small crystal of washing soda (sodium carbonate) about thumb-nail size, should be given by pushing it well back into the throat. Hold the dog's mouth closed immediately and point his muzzle upwards, stroking the throat to encourage him to swallow. Don't release him until he has gulped. The soda will induce vomiting.

Consult your vet in all cases of suspected poisoning. Take with you a sample of the toxic substance to aid diagnosis.

Heatstroke

No dog should ever be exposed to unrelieved intense sunlight, either in an unshaded kennel or in a vehicle where the temperature can rapidly rise. At the onset of heatstroke the dog is incapable of regulating his body temperature. He will quickly become distressed, panting and drooling. His tongue and lips will appear bright red. You must act decisively to cool him down by applying cold water to the skin. Hosing or immersion in a bath will help lower his temperature and he should be dried and left quietly to rest in a cool, well-ventilated place with free access to drinking water. After sever heatstroke, take your dog to the vet.

When showing your dog in summer, make sure you park your car in a shady spot. A light blanket drenched in cold water can help reduce the build-up of heat if placed over the roof, and there must be maximum ventilation. Hold-ups on motorways in intense heat can also cause great distress to canine as well as human passengers. An ice-box will enable you to douse your dog's head with cold water to keep him cool, so carry a good supply of water and a large sponge.

Internal Parasites

Both internal and external parasites may affect your German Shepherd's well-being during some stage of his life.

Roundworms

The Roundworm (*Toxocara canis*) is found most commonly in young puppies and nursing bitches. A less common form, *Toxascaris leonina*, also occurs. The adult worm can grow to a length of 3–8in (75–200cm), inhabiting the small intestine of the host. Males and females develop, breed and produce eggs which are passed out in the dog's faeces. The eggs need a period on the ground to become infective and this may vary from a few weeks in summer to several months in winter. A dog swallowing such eggs will develop larvae in the small intestine which can then enter the bloodstream and migrate to various organs; in the case of very young puppies, they are coughed up and swallowed to mature into adult worms in the intestine.

A brood-bitch can carry larvae in the tissues which become active around the forty-second day of pregnancy and subsequently infect the unborn puppy. It is essential, therefore, that you make sure she is wormed before mating and, preferably, given a worming medicine under veterinary direction during the last weeks of her pregnancy.

As early as three weeks of age, puppies can be affected by roundworms. In severe cases they lose weight and their ribs become distended, giving a pot-bellied appearance. They may even choke on attempting to expel a heavy infestation.

The bitch's milk can be a source of infection. She may herself become re-infected as she cleans up the puppies' faeces.

Cleanliness in the whelping kennel and puppy run is important. Faeces should be promptly disposed of and a programme of regular worming followed. Since *Toxocara canis* can be ingested by humans, children should not be allowed to play in soil or grass which may have been contaminated by puppy or brood-bitch faeces.

Other animals may also act as host for the roundworm. Should a dog eat an infected host such as a mouse, rat, rabbit, chicken, pig or sheep the larvae will develop into adult worms within the dog who will then excrete eggs into the ground, thus perpetuating the infective cycle.

Tapeworms

Dipylidium caninum is the most common form of tapeworm in the adult dog. It is passed from an intermediate host, most commonly the flea, to the dog. The adult worm sheds small segments which resemble rice grains and contain the eggs. These are passed in the faeces and are usually found around the anus or tail. Flea larvae ingest the eggs, which then form cysts. If the dog swallows the mature flea while biting at irritation on the skin he will ingest the cyst, which will mature into the adult tapeworm. Remember you will probably notice nothing resembling your idea of a worm, though occasionally the grain-like segments are expelled in short chain-like formation. Since the flea is the common source of infection you should make sure that your dog's environment, particularly his bedding, is free from such parasites. Care should be exercised in the choice of anti-flea treatment and your veterinary surgeon should be consulted. The tapeworm cannot be passed from dog to dog, but the flea certainly can!

Most modern worm treatment is effective against both tapeworm and roundworm.

Other internal parasites

The parasite *Toxoplasma gondi* is more often found in warmer climates. Cat's faeces can carry the infective eggs, which may be swallowed by a dog. Sometimes cysts may enter the dog's food chain if he is fed on undercooked affected meat.

Hookworm and whipworm flourish in hot climates and occasionally appear in the UK during the summer. They may cause diarrhoea and loss of condition. The eggs can survive for up to five years in grass under the right conditions. Runs on grassed areas should be moved regularly to fresh, uncontaminated positions or replaced with concrete. Heartworm, a cause of heart disease in hot climates, and lungworm, which lives in the windpipe, blocking the airway, are other parasites affecting dogs, particularly in Australia, Africa, the USA and the West Indies.

Skin Complaints

Skin problems can arise from very many causes, including allergies, dietary intolerance or imbalance, and reaction to fleas or other external parasites. Often there is no simple remedy and diagnosis is rarely straightforward.

Flea-bites can set up itchiness (pruritus) which causes the dog to scratch and bite the skin, thus exacerbating the problem. A strict flea-eradication policy should be followed under veterinary guidance.

Sarcoptic Mange

Sometimes also known as scabies, this highly contagious condition manifests itself by intense itching and scratching. It particularly affects the ear-flaps and elbows. Caused by a microscopic mite that flourishes on or within the outer layer of the skin, it can be contracted directly or through grooming equipment. Veterinary treatment will be based on the identification and eradication of the mite, usually by means of an antiparasitic shampoo.

Demodectic Mange

This is the result of another skin mite, *Demodex canis*, living within the hair follicles. Unlike sarcoptic mange, it is not passed from dog to dog and cannot be transmitted to humans. Loss of hair, scaling and reddening of the skin is apparent, most commonly on the face and forelegs; it is very debilitating and can make a dog seriously ill. It is known to be hereditary. It is extremely difficult to treat and, in severe cases, euthanasia may be indicated.

Infectious Diseases

Distemper (Hardpad)

This major dog disease, once the scourge of localized canine populations, has practically disappeared thanks to effective vaccines. However, stray and unvaccinated dogs remain a possible infection source and vaccination is essential. You will need to provide evidence of vaccination if you wish your dog to be accepted by most boarding kennels and training schools, where strange dogs meet in close proximity.

Distemper is contracted through inhaling a virus which multiplies and attacks the immune system, damaging the alimentary, respiratory and nervous systems. Discharge from nose and eyes is followed by fever, vomiting and blood-stained diarrhoea. Fits and paralysis accompany severe stages of the disease, and 'hardpad' causes the skin of the pads and nose to become cracked, dry, and painful. So-called 'distemper teeth' – characteristic brown marks on the tooth enamel – used to be common in puppies who had contracted and overcome the disease.

Parvovirus Infection

Canine parvovirus infection caused considerable alarm in the late 1970s and early 1980s when it reached epidemic proportions around the world. It exacted a heavy toll amongst the canine population, particularly in dogs under twelve months of age. The virus attacks the intestinal lining so that eventually the dog is unable to absorb food and fluid. In severe cases dehydration and dysentery occur. Effective vaccines are available and may be administered as early as six weeks, but they are best delayed until the puppy has lost any maternal antibody from his dam. Sometimes a bitch may be unvaccinated and lack immunity, in which case her pups will be susceptible from birth. The virus can then weaken the heart and result in the sudden fatal collapse of an otherwise healthy-looking puppy.

Unfortunately, the virus is extremely resistant to disinfectant and should your premises ever become contaminated, you may have to adopt the draconian measure of destroying affected kennels, or leaving other buildings dog-free for at least six months. Any new dog brought on to premises where parvovirus has been present should first be blood-tested to ensure his immunity.

Hepatitis

Infectious Canine Hepatitis or Rubarth's disease is a serious disease of the liver, often proving fatal in young dogs. The virus is transmitted through contact with contaminated canine urine. Vaccines are highly effective and are usually given as part of a routine puppy vaccination programme together with those against distemper and parvovirus.

Severe cases are characterized by fever, inflammation of the liver and acute abdominal pain. Collapse and death may follow rapidly. In less severe cases the dog's natural immune system can eliminate the virus, leading to recovery. After initial convulsions, vomiting and diarrhoea may continue for several days, followed by jaundice. Occasionally a distinctive cloudiness of the front of the eye may develop about two weeks after infection. This 'blue-eye' is a temporary phenomenon, and a positive indication that the dog is on the way to recovery.

Strict hygiene and thorough disinfecting of kennels are essential if hepatitis has occurred, but dogs can excrete the virus in urine for up to nine months after recovery.

Leptospirosis

Leptospirae bacteria present in the urine of infected animals cause two forms of this disease, both often fatal for dogs and transmissible, with serious consequences, to human beings. The *icterohaemorrhagiae* form leads to liver and blood-vessel damage culminating in jaundice and widespread haemorrhage. Loss of appetite, dullness and fever characterize its onset, with blood in vomit and black diarrhoea. Severe abdominal pain can lead to dehydration and collapse.

Kidney failure is more marked in the *canicala* form, accompanied by thirst and arching of the back.

Since rats are the main source of the disease through infected urine, vermin control is essential in kennels. Water, uneaten food or bones must never be left in runs overnight. Rats may urinate on them and infect dogs that return to such leftovers the next day.

As with hepatitis, vaccinations against this disease are essential in puppyhood.

Kennel Cough

A number of different infections can affect the cells lining the nose and lung airways, leading to a characteristic harsh cough. In most cases the problem clears itself within two or three weeks. but occasionally severe cases can lead to sickness, pneumonia or chronic bronchitis, particularly harmful to puppies and elderly dogs. Kennel cough can be easily transmitted, like influenza in humans, in places where dogs congregate in confined spaces. Never take your dog to a show or training class if he has a persistent dry cough. Any kennel inhabited by an affected dog must be thoroughly disinfected and left empty for a week or so.

Rabies

Rabies is perhaps the most feared of all diseases. It affects all warm-blooded animals, including man, and is invariably fatal. Acquired when the saliva of a rabid animal enters a bite or scratch wound, the virus then spreads through nerve fibres to the spinal cord and brain. The incubation period varies from ten days to six months (even longer in rare cases). The affected dog initially behaves quite out of character: a friendly animal, for example, becomes inexplicably aggressive or vice versa. Soon he will begin to wander aimlessly, attacking anything that obstructs him. He will drop the lower jaw, salivate and adopt a glazed, stupefied expression.

Vaccinations against rabies are routinely administered in most countries where the disease is endemic. Regular boosters are necessary, certification to attest this being essential for entry at dog shows. Incidence amongst domestic dogs is very low, most outbreaks occurring in the fox population.

Britain's rabies-free status has, it is argued, been preserved by its rigorous quarantine regulations requiring that imported dogs be isolated from all canine and other animal contact for six months. Britain has, however, now negotiated an arrangement with its European Union partners that under the so-called Bali Agreement a dog may be imported from EU countries without quarantine provided that:

- it is an object of trade and not a pet
- it has never left the premises in which it was born in its country of origin before sale
- it has been vaccinated against rabies and blood-tested six months later
- it is blood-tested immediately on arrival in Britain.

At least one German Shepherd Dog has entered Britain under these regulations. If you ever decide to import a dog, consult the Ministry of Agriculture, Fisheries and Food for more information about the necessary procedures and paperwork.

Non-infectious Conditions

Anal Furunculosis

This chronic and distressing disease is limited to large breeds. Unfortunately the German Shepherd has proved to be susceptible. The illness begins with small ulcerations of the skin around the anus. Each ulceration is accompanied by a hole or sinus through the skin layers. The dog often suffers intense pain. Irritation and inflammation cause frequent straining. The sinuses may bleed and discharge a foul-smelling liquid. The affected animal will constantly lick or chew the inflamed area to soothe the pain. The condition can result in incontinence or constipation. The dog stops eating and loses weight.

The causes of this disease are not known. Treatment with antibiotics has had limited success. Sometimes surgery, involving cutting away diseased tissue or even, in extreme cases, tail-amputation, is used. A genetic factor has not been definitely identified, nor does diet seem to play a significant role.

Gastric Torsion (Bloat)

The distressing condition is regrettably not uncommon in the German Shepherd Dog. Its onset is often alarmingly unpredictable, its development rapid and, unless veterinary treatment is sought immediately, it can be fatal. An accumulation of fluid and gas builds up in the stomach, which may eventually rotate within the abdomen, twisting the entrance and exit. Trapped gas is unable to escape and the resulting distension interferes with the blood supply. Shock may rapidly lead to collapse and death.

At the commencement of an attack the dog may be restless, licking its lips and attempting to gulp. The abdomen swells and becomes tense, and gurgling may be heard. It is imperative that the dog be taken immediately to a vet. Treatment to release the trapped gas and return the stomach to its proper position can save the dog's life. If your dog lives in a kennel, you should develop a routine of checking an hour or so after his main meal. Unfortunately many kennelled dogs are fed in the evening, develop torsion and are discovered dead the next morning.

The causes of 'bloat' have yet to be definitely identified. The practice of feeding large meals, involving significant fermentation of carbohydrates during digestion, has been suggested as a contributory factor, as has swallowing large amounts of air by greedy dogs during feeding. A hereditary disposition has not been ruled out by some geneticists, who link it with a physiological inability to belch and release gas. Some point the finger at modern processed complete foods.

You should certainly make sure your dog is kept quiet before and after feeding. Never exercise him after he has finished a meal. You can discourage him from bolting down his food if you serve it up rather warmer than he would like!

Pancreatic Disorders

Exocrine pancreatic insufficiency is a condition in which the bulk of the cells producing the pancreatic enzymes necessary for the breakdown of food and its proper digestion have been destroyed. In spite of a voracious appetite, the dog loses weight markedly and produces large amounts of loose, very pale faeces often characterized by a greasy, film-like surface. Serious loss of condition occurs and you should take a sample of your dog's faeces for veterinary inspection. With a blood test, this may confirm the problem, which is quite common in the German Shepherd. Enzyme tablets may have to be given for the rest of the dog's life.

Epilepsy

Though there is no statistical evidence to establish the incidence of this condition in the German Shepherd Dog, it can occur and causes great distress to owners as well as dogs. A large dog, incontinent, convulsed in violent spasms, confused and potentially dangerous, presents a frightening spectacle. A hereditary form of epilepsy has been identified, though its exact mode of inheritance has not been established by geneticists. Certain bloodlines are known to be suspect, producing animals which, given the appropriate conditions and stimuli, will tend to have fits. Fitting usually begins between one and three years of age and may happen at any time, at irregular intervals. Between seizures the dog will lead a perfectly normal life; there is absolutely no connection between a dog's temperament and his susceptibility to the condition. No responsible breeder would use afflicted animals for breeding, and line-breeding to suspect families should also be avoided.

The non-hereditary form of epilepsy can be the result of injurious influences during puppyhood, such as illnesses, tumours or other causes of brain damage.

Mild occurrences can be controlled by drugs administered throughout the dog's life. There is, however, no cure, and euthanasia may be the most merciful response to severe or repeated attacks.

Haemophilia A

Though very few cases of this condition have occurred in the UK, it is taken seriously by responsible breeders, and the German Shepherd Dog Breed Council encourages owners to submit their animals for blood-testing under its own scheme.

Haemophilia arises through an inherited deficiency in the normal blood-clotting mechanisms. In mild cases, animals may bruise readily if knocked, while the more severely affected suffer spontaneous bleeding in joints and muscles.

A haemophiliac is usually male; female sufferers are extremely uncommon. An affected male inadvertently used at stud will transmit a defective chromosome to *all* of his daughters. These bitches, although perfectly healthy in themselves, are likely to transmit the problem to half of their sons. All the sons of a male haemophiliac will be unaffected and free of the condition, since a male can inherit it only from his dam. If your German Shepherd is to be used at stud, you should make sure he is blood-tested before mating his first bitch. The chances of his being affected may be remote, but it is better to be safe than sorry, for both your sake and that of the breed.

Elbow Dysplasia

This general expression is often used loosely to describe a number of specific problems that can affect the growth and development of the elbow joint. The somewhat circular bone at the end of the humerus (upper arm) should fit snugly into the notch at the top of the ulna (forearm) but abnormal development militates against this. Incorrect points of contact can lead to fracturing and splintering of the bone. Small, bony particles can find their way into surrounding cartilage, resulting in lameness and arthritis.

Osteochondritis (OCD) and fragmented coronoid process (FCP) are specific conditions that may affect growing dogs, particularly in the period of most rapid growth from four to eight months. The young animal will begin to limp intermittently or show a tendency to throw out his elbow while moving the foreleg in an irregular, rotating manner. The straight column of support from shoulder blade through the upper arm, foreleg and pastern to the foot will be broken.

The mode of transmission is not simple, though geneticists point to hereditary factors. Some researchers have identified a tendency for the bones of the forearm, the radius and ulna, to develop at an irregular and uncoordinated pace. Others indicate a significant influence by environmental factors such as too rapid growth. Dogs that develop mature body weight at too early an age place extra stress on growing joints. Some dogs support excessive weight on the forehand because their centre of gravity is pushed forward through structural imbalance. There may even be nutritional excesses, such as too much protein or unnecessary supplementation with vitamin D, which can affect skeletal growth. Such considerations underline the importance of sensibly controlled exercise during growth, of avoiding the temptation to force a dog into premature body development, and of sensible diet. The medium-sized, slow-maturing German Shepherd must remain the ideal.

The British Veterinary Association, in connection with the Kennel Club, operates an elbow-screening scheme so that dogs which are apparently sound but have joint abnormalities may be detected. Breeders then have the option of rejecting affected animals from their breeding stock. The minimum age for X-raying is twelve months, but there is no upper age limit. Your local vet will take three X-rays of each elbow and submit them to a BVA panel for grading.

Hip Dysplasia

Hippocrates is credited with the discovery of this condition in man before 300 BC, but its presence in dogs was not recorded until 1934 when it was diagnosed in an English Setter in America. The famous American breeder of German Shepherds, Marie Leary of the Cosalta kennels, investigated the condition in her own dogs through the use of X-ray examination and discovered that its incidence was widespread in both home-bred stock and dogs imported from Germany at that time. An American veterinarian, Gerry Schnells, using new X-ray equipment, discovered varying degrees of defective hip-joint in large breeds and published an account of his findings in 1935 and 1937. For some years the problem was regarded as essentially an American one, until the late 1950s, when Scandinavian workers alerted Europe to the existence of dysplasia in Swedish dogs. The Alsatian League and Club of Great Britain initiated an X-ray scheme in 1961 which was later replaced by a scheme set up by the British Veterinary Association (BVA) in 1965. In 1967 the SV in Germany and the Orthopaedic Foundation for Animals (OFA) in America set up their own screening processes. Radiographic examination is now generally established in most countries.

The word 'dysplasia' is of Greek origin and literally means 'abnormal development'. It should not be confused with the English word 'displacement'. Puppies are born with normal hip-joints and dysplasia develops during growth. The ideal joint is one in which the ball-shaped head on the upper end of the thigh bone or femur fits snugly into a cup-shaped socket called the acetabulum situated on the pelvis. In normal hips the acetabulum is deep, allowing a close,

206

firm fitting of the femoral head. Strong, stable hips are the result. Varying degrees of shallowness in the socket predispose the dog to looseness in the joint, in which case excessive movement of the femoral head may lead to further erosion of the socket and to the development of gristle-like cartilage and calcium deposits in an effort to stabilize the femur. These compensatory features often break down with age, leading to the onset of arthritis.

Geneticists have established that there exists a hereditary disposition to develop abnormal hips, though environmental factors play a significant role too. Unfortunately you cannot tell whether a dog has abnormal hips simply by looking at him. There are signs that might raise suspicions, such as a dog that moves in a characteristically 'bunny-hopping' manner, or one that shows a disinclination to jump, or one that walks rather than skips up stairs. Occasionally a slight click in the hip joint can be heard as the dog walks. Nevertheless, it must be emphasized that dysplasia can never be diagnosed without an X-ray.

Once your German Shepherd is twelve months old you can submit him for radiographic examination. The vet will anaesthetize him and place him on his back, with his pelvis symmetrical and both hind legs stretched perfectly parallel behind him. Some vets will X-ray a sedated, rather than anaesthetized, animal, but these are in a minority. The resultant plates, provided that they are of good quality, will then be submitted by your vet to the KC/BVA panel of scrutineers for assessment or 'scoring'. The plates must bear the dog's KC registration number for identification.

'Scoring' involves a careful examination of those features of the hip joint that deviate from the normal. A figure ranging from zero to fifty-three is given for each hip. The higher the score, the worse the hip. The average score for German Shepherd Dogs so far in the UK is around eighteen as a total for both hips. Ideally breeding animals should not exceed the average score by a significant amount, and preferably should be below it. The score of an individual dog may not be a reliable indication, however, of its chances of breeding good or bad hips. High-scoring parents can produce low-scoring progeny just as parents with very good hips can, regrettably, give poor-hipped offspring. Much depends on the family hip profile and often an individual dog is X-rayed in isolation from its litter-mates. Until whole litters are routinely X-rayed, individual scores are bound to be of only limited value as predictors of breeding performance.

Remember that scoring is not an exact science, since variations in positioning of the dog may have an effect. There is evidence that a certain degree of joint-laxity may occur when bitches are in season. Nevertheless, scoring does give you a reasonable indication of whether, in breeding, you must take a partner's hip-score into account. You should aim at mating to improve hips whilst remembering that there is more to a German Shepherd than good hips. Temperament, type and soundness matter too.

An above-average score does not automatically mean that your dog is destined to become a cripple. Very many dogs so affected live to a ripe old age and are capable of a perfectly normal life and activity. The development of strong muscle over the thighs and pelvis can compensate for hip weaknesses. Avoiding excess weight and pursuing a regular, controlled exercise regime will help too.

Chronic Degenerative Radiculomyelopathy

This disease, usually referred to as CDRM, involves a progressive degeneration in the muscles of the hindquarters, leading to a loss of mobility. The spinal column is affected and there is little hope of a positive response to treatment. This crippling affliction usually develops in the older dog and is often mistakenly regarded as evidence of hip dysplasia. It appears to be primarily, though not exclusively, confined to the German Shepherd Dog, which suggests that a genetic factor may be involved.

The German Shepherd Around the World

The Breed in its Homeland

'Shepherd-dog breeding is working-dog breeding, otherwise it is not shepherd-dog breeding.' From its very beginning, in April 1899, the Verein für Deutsche Schäferhunde (SV) or German Shepherd Dog Club placed this maxim at the centre of its concerns for the newly evolving breed. It developed a carefully structured organization committed to the controlled, directed breeding of a dog characterized by an extraordinary versatility, fulfilling many useful working functions in society. And it expected every member to be committed to that informing principle.

The SV: History and Structure

At the end of 1899 the SV had a mere sixty members and between then and 1902 registered just 250 dogs in its stud book. By 1923 the number of members had risen to a staggering 57,637 with a stud-book total of 50,000 dogs. The breed's popularity had rocketed world-wide and much indiscriminate breeding was practised by those wishing to profit financially from the boom. Realizing the dangers to the breed's future, the SV initiated a breed survey scheme in 1922, to select for breeding only those animals that were sound in mind and body. The combination of strict breeding controls and the economic deprivations of the recession certainly seemed to deter the get-rich-quick merchants. By 1939 membership had slumped to 11,118, fewer than a quarter of the 1923 total, and just 10,000 dogs were registered. In 1946, after the Second World War had left Germany devastated and divided, the SV's membership stood at 30,125 and an amazing 25,000 dogs were registered by the end of the first year of peace-time. By 1963 membership totalled 38,012 with a stud-book entry of 21,000. Since then the strength and influence of the SV have grown steadily. Its membership world-wide now exceeds one million making it the largest breed club in the canine world. Around 30,000 dogs a year are registered with the SV, which exercises control over all aspects of the breed, from overseeing breeding practices, registering and tattooing litters, issuing pedigrees, and organizing breed surveys, shows and working trials. All dogs destined for breeding must be X-rayed to determine hip status; they must possess a working qualification, and be free from major faults.

In 1974 the SV was instrumental in forming the WUSV (World Union of Shepherd Dog Clubs), which exists to encourage uniformity world-wide in the breeding, showing and training of the German Shepherd Dog. The British Association for German Shepherd Dogs and the German Shepherd Dog League represent Britain at the WUSV's annual conference, usually held the day after the SV's main breed show, the Sieger Show, in the same city.

One of the great strengths of the SV is its organization at grassroots level. For administrative purposes the country is divided into a number of Länder (states). Since unification there are now nineteen such Ländesgruppen (state groups), each with its own chairman and committee. Each state has a breed warden and a chief training administrator, both of whom represent their state at national committee level. The state breed wardens are responsible for co-ordinating the work of local breed wardens, who operate at local group level. Each member of the SV belongs to his local Ortsgruppe (local group), of which there are 2,200 throughout Germany. They provide training facilities for both working and showing, and offer the services of a breed warden to members intending to breed a litter. Advice will be given on the choice of a suitable stud-dog, although there is no obligation to follow the suggestions offered.

Breeding Regulations

The local breed warden is responsible for clarifying to group members all matters concerning breeding, rearing, registering and showing. He is entrusted with the task of officially inspecting every litter bred by club members no later than three days after the birth and regularly thereafter on at least three occasions. He has to check the tattoo identity of the dam and make sure that the conditions in which the puppies are reared satisfy requirements. He must report any infringement of regulations to his state warden.

The SV encourages breeders to limit the size of a litter to eight and organizes a foster-mother service to provide for puppies above that number. The foster-bitch is not allowed to nurse more than six puppies, including any of her own. All breeds are used for the service provided that they are at least 20in (50cm) tall and have an excellent temperament. The local warden has to record (officially) the fostering arrangements. If a bitch rears more than eight puppies, she is not allowed to be bred from again until at least six months after her previous whelping. No bitch may be mated before she is twenty months old. All puppies have to be tattooed on their ear before sale.

Stud-dog owners, too, have to observe strict regulations. A dog must be two years old before beginning his stud career and possess a working qualification together with either a breed-show grade of at least 'Good' or a survey pass. An 'A' stamp on his pedigree, indicating good hips, is also obligatory. He may mate a maximum of sixty bitches a year in Germany, and an extra thirty foreign bitches. Before mating his thirty-first bitch, the stud-dog must be X-rayed again to clearly establish the identity and reliability of the first screening. He must also be submitted for a DNA test under an SV-approved vet. Strict penalties are imposed upon owners who break these regulations.

The survey system to select and identify the best animals for breeding is well established throughout Germany. Every dog surveyed must pass an endurance test, trotting beside a bicycle for 10 miles (15km) without showing obvious weaknesses. Each dog must also possess a working qualification. Over 150 surveys are held each year in the nineteen areas, with over 3,000 dogs being newly surveyed and passed for breeding.

Future developments will involve extending compulsory DNA testing to all breeding animals; special programmes to combat elbow dysplasia; and the use of family profiling to identify dogs likely to produce good hips in their progeny. Updated breeding information will be communicated on the SV Internet site to all groups, so that breeders have the best possible guidance in planning their matings.

Showing

Apart from the many breed shows run by local groups throughout the year, each Ländesgruppe holds an annual state breed show where many of the current top-winning dogs compete. The main breed show, the Sieger Show, is held in a different city each year and

211

attracts thousands of visitors from around the world. It has established itself as a truly international event and the entry, often exceeding 1,200 dogs and bitches, includes many from other countries. Recent shows have attracted entries from North and South America and from Russia. As the Mecca for all German Shepherd enthusiasts, the Sieger Show is well worth a visit, if only once in a lifetime.

Dogs under two years old are shown in one of two classes: twelve to eighteen months (Junghund Klasse) or eighteen to twenty-four months (Jugend Klasse). All those over two years enter one class, the Gebrauchshund Klasse (Working Dog Class), in which every entrant must undergo a courage test to establish the dog's confidence and determination in responding to a threatened attack on his handler. Failure to acquit himself convincingly in this test will deny him the best grading in the judge's final assessment. The show extends over three days. By the time it draws to a close on Sunday afternoon, the judges of the adult classes will have placed the dogs in order of merit, graded them Excellent, Very Good or Good and selected around ten or twelve dogs at the top of the class for the highest show-ring award available in Germany: the coveted V.A. or Vorzüglich Auslese

Crowning of the Sieger Uran von Wildsteigerland and the Siegerin Tina von Grossen Sand at the 1984 Sieger Show. (Note the crowded football stadium.)

(Excellent Select). The dog at the head of the V.A. group is the Sieger for that year. The V.A. award in males is based not only on the dog's external appearance but on his pedigree and, most importantly, on his actual or predicted ability to produce good offspring. The Saturday morning of the show is devoted to the progeny parades in which all the top stud-dogs enter a huge football stadium followed by the best of their sons and daughters. This impressive display has a significant influence upon the awarding of the V.A. grade the following day.

The corresponding national event for working trials enthusiasts is the annual Bundesieger Prüfung, held in the autumn. Here the very best Schutzhund dogs that have qualified in their Ländesgruppe heats compete for the Leistung Sieger (Working Champion) title. They are thoroughly assessed in the three areas of protection work, obedience and tracking, based on the requirements of the Schutzhund III test. Dog after dog exemplifies the highest form of training: enthusiasm and spirit combined with outstanding control and precision in the execution of each exercise. A national agility competition is also held in conjunction with this event.

The huge popularity of dog-training among the German Shepherd Dog fraternity is reflected in the number of dogs passing working tests each year. Over 20,000 dogs annually are entered for Sch.H. I–III tests. In 1996, for example, 10,884 dogs passed Sch.H. III alone. In 1997 42,986 dogs were submitted for various SV working tests.

The third annual national event held by the SV is the Sheep-herding Championship, in which the Shepherd Dog is shown performing his original work with a flock. Qualifying heats are held during the year and some twenty dogs make it to the three-day final. The shepherd works two dogs, one sometimes on the lead and the second free. Only the latter is marked by the officiating judges. The work involved is quite different from that demonstrated by a Border Collie with a handful of skittish mountain sheep. A flock of over 200 sheep, usually stolid merinos, must be herded along a road while traffic approaches from in front and behind. The dog must make sure the flock does not obstruct any oncoming vehicle. If the vehicle is forced to stop, the dog will be penalized. In addition, the dog must assist in driving the sheep on to grazing land and make sure none of them strays on to neighbouring crops. Any that do must be disciplined by a firm clean bite on the neck or thigh and brought back to the flock. The dog must gait calmly but enduringly around the perimeter of the flock, acting as a kind of mobile fence yet never

A Shepherd Dog keeps the way clear for oncoming traffic – a scene at the SV Herding Trials.

disturbing the sheep as they graze. He must help his handler to drive the sheep across a narrow bridge and assist in penning them at the conclusion of the trial. Finally, he must be prepared to defend the flock against a suspicious character threatening its welfare. Such work with a flock demonstrates the essential characteristics of the German Shepherd Dog: physical resilience and endurance exemplified in a tireless trot; a willing responsiveness to his handler; the ability to work independently and use initiative; courage and fearlessness in defence, and a calm, self-possessed, unflappable nature.

Two Shepherds left in charge of the flock after penning.

214

The USA

The first German Shepherd to reach the United States was Mira von Offingen, imported in 1906 but shown in the miscellaneous classes at shows and never formally registered as a German Shepherd. That honour was reserved for a bitch known as Queen of Switzerland. By 1912 a small band of enthusiasts, in particular Benjamin H. Throop and Miss Anne Tracy, had registered their own dogs and begun to promote them at all- breed shows. In 1913 the German Shepherd Dog Club of America was formed. It held its first speciality show at Greenwich, Connecticut in June 1915, when forty dogs competed. In 1914, Ch. Apollo von Hunenstein, Champion in Germany, France, Austria and Belgium, was imported – the first of many top German show dogs to make the journey across the Atlantic.

The popularity of the breed after the First World War was advanced by the impact of the legendary canine film-star, Rin-Tin-Tin, the sole survivor of a litter of German Shepherd puppies discovered in a disused dug-out by Lee Duncan, a serviceman with the US forces in France. The 1920s saw the arrival of such famous dogs as the 1920 Sieger Erich von Grafenwerth, Gerri von

Eight American champions (1924). Left to right: Dolf von Dusternbrook, Erich von Grafenwerth, Anni von Humboldtpark, Cito von Bergerslust, Debore von Weimar, Schatz von Hohentann, Irma and Isa von Dornerhof, Freya von Humboldtpark.

215

Oberklamm and his Sieger son, Cito von Bergerslust. The 1925 grey Sieger Klodo von Boxberg and his son Utz vom Haus Schütting also influenced the breed. In 1936 John Gans imported Pfeffer von Bern, a dog destined to have a major impact on the breed's development for several years.

After the Second World War the American breeders continued to import German-bred dogs from the currently successful bloodlines. Combining the lines from the famous 'R' von Osnabrückerland litter and Axel von der Deininghauserheide, through such good animals as Troll von Richterbach and the excellent dark grey, Cito von Hermannschleuse, Lucy Woodard bred the outstanding 'F' Arbeywood litter, of which six obtained titles. A dog, Fortune, sired the dog of the era: 1967 Grand Victor Ch. Lance of Fran-Jo. In subsequent years considerable line-breeding was practised to Lance so that he dominated the pedigrees of the time.

Showing

American shows are organized on a points system. At any show with classes for the breed a number of points is offered to the best of each sex; the number of points depends upon the number of that sex shown. The American Kennel Club (AKC) varies the number of dogs necessary to qualify for a certain number of points according to the breed population of a particular area. The more Shepherds there are about, the greater the number of entries required to qualify for a one-, two-, three-, four- or five-point event. Shows offering three to five points are called 'Majors' and to gain the title of Champion a dog must achieve a minimum of two 'Major' wins. At the annual Specialty Show of the GSD Club of America the titles of Grand Victor and Victrix are awarded to the best male and female. In addition the judges place outstanding animals in order of merit in a 'select' group. Dogs and bitches who have proved to be excellent producers may qualify for the title of ROM (Register of Merit) after their name.

The Schutzhund sport has increased considerably in popularity in recent years. The GSD Club of America, through its affiliated Working Dog Association, has sponsored American teams in the WUSV International Working Trials in Europe and in 1998 the WUSV World Schutzhund Championship takes place in Boston, hosted by the United Schutzhund Clubs of America. A North American 'Sieger' show is now held annually, run on SV lines with

216

USA Grand Victor Lance of Fran-Jo.

courage testing, grading and Excellent Select awards. The USA is top of the international league outside Germany for the number of dogs tested in Schutzhund work. Of 7,500 assessed in twenty-six countries, the USA was responsible for 4,000 by the end of 1997.

The American show ring has always tended to place greater emphasis on glamour and presentation in all breeds, sometimes at the risk of sacrificing type to fashionable exaggeration. Judges who prefer extremes of angulation and height at wither have played their part in the evolution of an identifiable 'American type', strikingly dramatic in stance and side-gait but too often departing from the balanced construction of the genuine working Shepherd.

Australia and New Zealand

German Shepherd dogs were first imported into Australia during the 1920s, some sixty dogs forming the original foundation stock. The breed was soon to meet with hostile opposition from influential sheep farmers who, fearful that this 'wolf-dog' might mate with

217

An Australian champion (Almark Black Prince) before the lifting of the importation ban.

dingoes and produce hybrids dangerous to the flocks, lobbied to stop the importation of further animals. In time, they hoped, the breed would die out in Australia. An importation ban remained in place for forty-three years. Breeding was severely handicapped by the lack of fresh blood. Type and temperament suffered. In 1960 the German Shepherd Dog Council was formed to promote the interests of the breed and in March 1974 the ban was lifted. Many good animals were purchased from Great Britain and interest in the breed developed rapidly. Australian breeders wanted the best and lost no time in setting up an effective breed organization that is the envy of many countries outside Germany. In 1976 they introduced a nationwide breed survey scheme and no dog can be granted the show grade 'Excellent' unless he has been surveyed. A national tattoo register was launched in 1978 and a hip dysplasia scheme set up. In 1967 the Council organized its first National GSD Show and Obedience Trial. Although there was a remarkable entry of 398 animals, the SV judge, Herr Huffer, was candid about the generally poor quality of the Australian-bred dogs. Since that year the National has been held annually on a rotational basis in a different state. Exhibitors travel thousands of miles to compete at this splendid event, which often attracts an entry of up to 1,000 dogs.

In 1987 the concept of a main breed show was evolved, in which the breeding worth of animals is taken into account when awarding top honours in the Open classes. The concept reflects the SV Sieger Show practice of identifying animals of actual or predicted producing ability.

In the twenty-five years since the lifting of the ban, Australian breeders have made tremendous progress. Australia was the first country in the world to introduce blood-testing for haemophilia. A negative result is mandatory for any male presented at the breed survey. Furthermore, an elbow-screening scheme has been in existence since early 1993. The Quarterly National Review, the Council's official magazine, is a much-respected publication containing useful breed articles and news.

Similar progress has characterized the German Shepherd scene in New Zealand, where speciality breed shows attract excellent entries of first-class Shepherds. Visiting SV judges regularly compliment New Zealand breeders on the sound, correct type bred in the islands.

Sensible use is made of excellent imported dogs from Australia and Europe in combination with very good home-bred stock. A particular feature of the New Zealand show scene is the prevalence of outstanding grey and gold sables. Top dogs often compete at the Australia National and the GSD Advisory Council runs a breed survey scheme to guide the breed's development along the right lines.

Austral. Ch. Iniff Vagrant C. D. Ex, national Gold Medal winner and important sire.

Ireland

Originally two national breed clubs existed in Ireland. The German Shepherd Dog Club of Ireland was founded in 1927. In 1936 it amalgamated with Alsatian Club of Ireland to form one national club. The name 'Alsatian' was dropped and the breed was known in Ireland by its German name several years before the British KC agreed to recognize it.

For many years after the Second World War, Gwen Barrington's Brittas kennel dominated the German Shepherd scene in Ireland. No other kennel bred on the same scale and with the same remarkable consistency. In the early 1980s the All-Ireland German Shepherd Dog Club was formed, creating a second national club, which functions largely in the south of Eire.

Both clubs stage an annual championship show. The title of Champion is awarded to dogs winning a total of forty points at Green Star shows. The Green Star is awarded to the best of sex and may carry from one to ten points depending upon the number of exhibits present at a show. Four 'Major' Green Stars, carrying a minimum of five points, must be won as part of the total. The number of

Ir. Ch. Wenden Hannah.

220

Green Stars on offer at shows throughout the year is determined by the Irish KC on the basis of a 'breed index' taking into account the average number of each sex shown during the previous year.

The Irish KC is affiliated to the FCI and has already staged an all-breed show on FCI lines offering the Certificat d'Aptitude au Championat Internationale de Beauté (CACIB) – the FCI's International Champion award – Best of Sex winners.

The GSD Club of Ireland has always been forward-looking. It introduced breed surveys, age classes at its shows, and a compulsory gun-test.

The National GSD Working Dog Association, operating independently from the Irish KC, has done much to further the Schutzhund sport in Ireland. With the active support of the SV, it organizes trials judged by German experts and has a number of training clubs throughout the country. It seeks to promote the Shepherd as a versatile working dog with a reliable, dependable character.

The West Indies

Jamaica
(Edwin Besterman – Enkidu GSD)

Jamaican quarantine laws permit only dogs born in the UK to be imported. No imports can come from Germany or the USA. German Shepherd registrations make up the largest number of any breed registered at the Jamaica Kennel Club. The increasing popularity of the breed is shown by annual registration figures: 404 in 1993, 406 in 1994, 536 in 1995 and 626 in 1996. These are mostly locally bred puppies. Registered German Shepherd breeder affixes number fifty-nine over twenty-five years; today there are about twenty active breeders. In Jamaica there is no call for herding; guard-dog work is the main task. There is an active obedience club and of course German Shepherds are in demand as pets.

The Jamaica German Shepherd Club was founded in 1974 with help from Mr and Mrs Beech. It is affiliated to the German Shepherd Dog League of Great Britain and the National German Shepherd Dog Breed Council. UK kennels that provided Jamaica with dogs in the early days were Stranmillis, Aeroken, Kenya, Ramokan, Shootersway, Gayville, Chalkville, Glenteal, Rondens, Brinton, Oldway, Huesca,

Brinkmore, Goldencob, Balder, Iolanda, Gregrise, Greenveldt and Karenberg.

Breed shows were annual events, judged by Americans for reasons of economy. The Jamaica Kennel Club mounts three or four all-breed shows annually, which are still judged by Americans. CCs and Reserve CCs are awarded at all shows, and champions are recognized

Dericky's Verrus at Enkidu at six months.

Verrus at maturity: a fine champion male in Jamaica.

after obtaining fifteen points from three different judges. Forty-five German Shepherd champions have been registered since 1974.

Since the change towards conformity to the 'German' type of dog, there has been an increase in imports of the newer dogs. The English kennels supplying these include Kelnick, Bedwin, Jutone, Chanask and Dericky-Romainville. Fortunately this change coincided with the introduction to Jamaica of foreign processed dog foods. Now, internationally known petfood manufacturers provide sponsorship for Jamaican dog shows, enabling the German Shepherd Club to pay for European SV judges to visit for breed shows. Thus Jamaican shows are now teaching events as well as venues for dog evaluation. Two breed shows annually attract between fifty-five and sixty-five entries. The consistency in evaluation between SV judges is in contrast to the placings by American all-breed judges. This causes confusion among spectators and novices, who may see a dog awarded 'Excellent' and gaining first place in a breed show, only to see him relegated to last, on another occasion, by an all-breed judge unfamiliar with the modern Shepherd. The overall type of dog in today's breed shows in Jamaica is quite different from that seen a few years ago. The modern dog dominates the show, and our SV judges are often pleasantly surprised by the dogs they meet.

Trinidad and Barbados

The German Shepherd has made considerable progress in these islands also. Very good animals have been imported from the UK and Germany. Enthusiasts have spared no expense in promoting the German Shepherd through organized shows and seminars at which top British and Continental judges have officiated. Unfortunately the West Indies are dependent on visiting judges. With the proximity of the USA, inevitably many American judges are invited, whose interpretation of the Standard may differ from that of European experts. Perhaps, in the future, the islands may co-operate in their own training scheme for home-bred judges.

South Africa
(Janet Thompson – Janshar GSD)

South Africa's twenty-two member clubs operate various GSD trials throughout the year. These include an endurance test, where dogs

A seven-week-old puppy is prepared for identification tattooing in the right ear.

are run over 12 miles (20 km) in three stages with short breaks between, and trials for Begleithund (Companion Dog) and Schutzhund I, II and III, all carried out in accordance with SV rules and regulations. SV judges, who must be approved beforehand, preside at the one- or two-day breed shows.

All classes at these are age-related, i.e. six to nine months, nine to twelve months, twelve to eighteen months, eighteen to twenty-four months, and over twenty-four months. Gun tests in the ring are carried out for all classes over twelve months. The entries for these shows usually average 150. Provincial shows and trials, jointly organized by clubs in designated areas, operate along the same lines.

There is one main National Breed Show, held over two days with a breed survey the day before. Entries for the show currently average about 350. The titles of South African Sieger and Siegerin are awarded. The highest gradings are South African 'V.A.' followed by 'V.'. Dogs and bitches over three and a half years of age cannot be awarded 'V.' gradings without breed surveys. 'V.A.' awards are preferred to dogs with working qualifications but this is not essential. All dogs and bitches entered in the Open classes must go through a test of courage (manwork) over short and long distances before the final day, when the Open classes begin. The results count towards placings. Gun tests are again carried out in the ring for all classes involving dogs over a year old. Progeny groups and kennels groups are paraded and placed in order of merit.

Breed surveys are carried out either by SV-qualified judges or by qualified South African senior judges. Training seminars are held throughout the year for helpers, who must pass a written and practical test before being allowed to help officially at breed surveys or Schutzhund trials. Dogs must be hip-scored and have completed the endurance test before being subjected to a breed survey. The survey also requires a gun test and a test of courage (manwork) over short and long distances. Awards are Class 1 or Class 2 (or Fail, if the dog does not fit the Breed Standard or lacks courage in the manwork test).

The Begleithund (Companion Dog) test must be done before the Schutzhund I. The only departure from SV rules is that dogs do not have to pass Schutzhund before their breed survey, but this will change in time as more and more dogs are trained for working. All dogs and bitches must be tattooed as puppies before they can be registered.

The top South African kennel of recent years is von Grehenheim, owned by Frikkie and Sonia van Kraayenburge. The winner of the Sieger title for 1997 was the South African-bred dog Bovasz von Plato, owned by the National Training Supervisor, Mr Vie Theunissen.

Appendix

UK Breed Standard
(Reproduced by kind permission of the Kennel Club.)

General Appearance
Slightly long in comparison to height; of powerful, well-muscled build, with weather-resistant coat. Relation between height, length, position and structure of fore- and hindquarters (angulation) producing far-reaching, enduring gait. Clear definition of masculinity and femininity essential, and working ability never sacrificed for mere beauty.

Characteristics
Versatile working dog, balanced and free from exaggeration. Attentive, alert, resilient and tireless, with keen scenting ability.

Temperament
Steady of nerve, loyal, self-assured, courageous, and tractable. Never nervous, over-aggressive or shy.

Head and Skull
Proportionate in size to body, never coarse, too fine or long. Clean cut; fairly broad between ears. Forehead slightly domed; little or no trace of central furrow. Cheeks forming softly rounded curve, never protruding. Skull from ears to bridge of nose tapering gradually and evenly, blending without too pronounced a stop into wedge-shaped, powerful muzzle. Skull approximately 50 per cent of overall length of head. Width of skull corresponding approximately to length, in males slightly greater, in females slightly less. Muzzle strong, lips firm, clean and closing tightly. Top of muzzle straight, almost parallel to forehead. Short, blunt, weak, pointed, overlong muzzle undesirable.

Eyes
Medium-sized, almond-shaped, never protruding. Dark, brown preferred, lighter shade permissible provided expression good and general harmony of head not destroyed. Expression lively, intelligent and self-assured.

Ears

Medium-sized, firm in texture, broad at base, set high, carried erect, almost parallel, never pulled inwards or tipped, tapering to a point, open at front. Never hanging. Folding back during movement permissible.

Mouth

Jaws strongly developed. With a perfect, regular and complete scissor bite, i.e. upper teeth closely overlapping lower teeth and set square to the jaw. Teeth healthy and strong. Full dentition desirable.

Neck

Fairly long, strong, with well-developed muscles, free from throatiness. Carried at 45 degrees angle to horizontal, raised when excited, lowered at fast trot.

Forequarters

Shoulder blades long, set obliquely (45 degrees) laid flat to body. Upper arm strong, well muscled, joining shoulder blade at approximately 90 degrees. Forelegs straight from pasterns to elbows when viewed from any angle, bone oval rather than round. Pasterns firm, supple and slightly angulated. Elbows neither tucked in nor turned out. Length of foreleg exceeding depth of chest.

Body

Length measured from point of breast bone to rear edge of pelvis, exceeding height at withers. Correct ratio 10 to 9 or 8.5. Under-sized dogs, stunted growth, high-legged dogs, those too heavy or too light in build, over-loaded fronts, too short overall appearance, any feature detracting from reach or endurance of gait, undesirable. Chest deep (45–48 per cent) of height at shoulder, not too broad, brisket long, well developed. Ribs well formed and long; neither barrel shaped nor too flat; allowing free movement of elbows when gaiting. Relatively short loin. Belly firm, only slightly drawn up. Back, between withers and croup, straight, strongly developed, not too long. Overall length achieved by correct angle of well laid shoulders, correct length of croup and hindquarters. Withers long, of good height and well defined, joining back in a smooth line without disrupting flowing topline, slightly sloping from front to back. Weak, soft and roach backs undesirable and should be rejected. Loin broad, strong, well muscled. Croup long, gently curving downwards to tail without disrupting flowing topline. Short, steep or flat croup undesirable.

Hindquarters

Overall strong, broad and well muscled, enabling effortless forward propulsion of whole body. Upper thighbone, viewed from side, sloping to slightly longer lower thighbone. hind angulation sufficient if imaginary line dropped from point of buttocks cuts through lower thigh just in front of hock, continuing down slightly in front of hind feet. Angulation corresponding approximately with front angulation, without over-angulation; hock strong. Any tendency towards over-angulation of hindquarters reduces firmness and endurance.

227

Feet

Rounded toes, well closed and arched. Pads well cushioned and durable. Nails short, strong and dark in colour. Dew-claws removed from hind legs.

Tail

Bushy-haired, reaches at least to hock – ideal length reaching to middle of metatarsus. At rest tail hangs in sabre-like curve; when moving raised, and curve increased, ideally never above level of back. Short, rolled, curled, generally carried badly or stumpy from birth, undesirable.

Gait/Movement

Sequence of step follows diagonal pattern, moving foreleg and opposite hind leg forward simultaneously; hind foot thrust forward to mid-point of body and having equally long reach with forefeet without any noticeable change in backline.

Coat

Outer coat consisting of straight, hard, close-lying hair as dense as possible; thick under-coat. Hair on head ears, front of legs, paws and toes short; on back, longer and thicker; in some males forming slight ruff. Hair longer on back of legs as far down as pasterns and stifles and forming fairly thick trousers on hindquarters. No hard and fast rule for length of hair; mole-type coats undesirable.

Colour

Black or black saddle with tan, or gold to light grey markings. All black, all grey, or grey with lighter or brown markings referred to as sables. Nose black. Light markings on chest or very pale colour on inside of legs permissible but undesirable, as are whitish nails, red-tipped nails, or wishy-washy faded colours defined as lacking in pigmentation. Blues, livers, albinos, whites (i.e. almost pure white dogs with black noses) and near whites *highly undesirable.* Undercoat, except in all-black dogs, usually grey or fawn. Colour in itself is of secondary importance having no effect on character or fitness for work. Final colour of a young dog ascertained only when outer coat has developed.

Size

Ideal height (from withers and just touching elbows): dogs 62.5cm (25in); bitches 57.5cm (23in). 2.5cm (1in) either above or below ideal permissible.

Faults

Any departure from the foregoing points should be considered a fault, and the serious-ness with which the fault should be regarded should be in exact proportion to its degree.

Note

Male animals should have two apparently normal testicles fully descended into the scrotum.

Glossary

A.D.   Ausdauerprüfung (endurance test).

AKC   American Kennel Club.

ambling   moving both left and both right limbs simultaneously; a departure from the diagonal trot.

angulation   the angles at which the bones of the shoulder and upper arm meet at the shoulder-joint, and those of the upper and lower thigh meet at the knee-joint.

barrel-ribbed   having an excessively rounded ribcage rather than flattish, oval-shaped formation.

B.H.   Blindenfuhrhund – a dog qualified to lead a blind person.

bite   the relationship of upper and lower incisors when the jaw is closed.

bloodline   animals sharing a specific familial relationship over several generations.

bow-hocked   having the points of the hocks inclined outwards instead of parallel to each other.

Bp.D.H.   Bahnpolizei Diensthund – a dog trained to work with railway police.

brisket   the lower end of the ribcage (between forelegs).

CC   Challenge Certificate. Awarded at British championship shows to the dog and bitch which, in the judge's opinion, most merit the title of Champion on the day of the show. Three CCs under three different judges are needed to qualify for the title of Champion, which may be withheld if no dog merits it.

C.D.   Companion Dog. The first of five working qualifications, each of increasing difficulty, awarded to dogs gaining a certain percentage of the total marks at working trials in Britain (*see* page 113). C.D. Ex. = C.D. Excellent.

close-coated   having a shorter coat than is desirable.

couplings   the loin.

cow-hocked   the opposite of bow-hocked (*see* above). The dog stands and moves with the points of the hocks turned inwards.

crabbing   indirect line of progress in movement where the hindquarters are inclined at an angle to the forequarters, instead of in direct line with them.

croup   the pelvis together with its covering of muscle and coat.

cryptorchid   a male dog with only one testicle (unilateral), or neither testicle (bilateral) descended into the scrotum.

dew-claw   additional toe on the inside of the leg, above the foot and making no contact with the ground. Many puppies are born without them on the rear legs.

dewlap   loosely hanging skin under the throat.

D.H.   Diensthund (service dog).

D.P.H.   Dienstpolizeihund (serving police dog).

dry   of firm muscularity, without flabbiness or excess flesh.

drive   forceful thrust from hindquarters in trotting.

entire   having both testicles in the scrotum.

extended gait   the maximum length of trotting stride before breaking into a gallop.

F.H.   Fährtenhund – tracking qualification.

forehand   head, neck and front assembly; all that is in front of a line dropped vertically from the highest point of the withers to the ground when viewed from the side.

French-front   front feet turned outwards.

front   the view presented by the dog when seen from the front. 'Unclean front' occurs when the line dropped from shoulder joint through elbow joint to foot shows divergence from a clean vertical. Protruding elbows, curved forelegs and feet turned out may affect cleanness of front.

Gebrauchshundklasse   (working dog class) the only show class available for animals over two years old in Germany.

gene   the unit of heredity found on a chromosome, transmitting characteristics.

genotype   the genetic make-up of an animal.

gay   of tail carried high and curved above the back.

guard hairs   the harsh outer coat of the German Shepherd, overlapping the softer under-coat.

hackney gait   lifting the front feet high when trotting, thus wasting effort.

hare-foot   long, narrow foot, rather than well-knuckled, somewhat rounded foot.

H.G.H.   Herdengebrauchshund (herding dog) – a qualification of dogs working with flocks.

high-withered   when the area where the neck runs into the back is definite, long and well filled in with muscle over the vertebrae between the shoulder blades, and slopes into the back, rather than being horizontal with it (flat-withered).

hyena-type   excessively high at the withers, resulting in an exaggeratedly sloping back.

inbreeding   deliberate mating together of close relatives.

I.N.T.   Internationale Prüfungsklasse – international working qualification obtained on the Continent.

Jugendklasse-Ruden youth class at German shows for males of twelve to eighteen months. Jugendklasse-Hundinnen is the corresponding class for bitches.

Junghundklassen young animal classes for exhibits of eighteen to twenty-four months.

KC The Kennel Club (UK).

KK1 Körklasse (survey class).

Körung German breed survey to select animals for breeding (Class I – animal recommended; Class II – animal suitable).

lippy having loose, hanging lips rather than cleanly fitting ones.

loin the space between the last rib and the hip-bone.

L.W.H. Lawinenhund – a dog trained to find missing persons in avalanches.

(M) Mangelhaft (faulty) – an official German show grade.

mask dark, usually solid black, colour of part or all of the muzzle.

monorchid a dog possessing only one testicle in the body. Not to be confused with unilateral cryptorchid, where both are present but only one has descended.

muzzle the front part of the head from the nose to the stop.

occiput the bony protuberance at the top of the skull between the ears.

overbuilt moving or standing with croup higher than withers.

P.D. patrol dog – a British working trials qualification gained in stakes involving 'criminal' work and open to service and civilian handlers and dogs.

phenotype physical (and visible) characteristics of an animal.

pin-bones the crest of the ilium, or beginning of the pelvis, often protruding if the dog is thin.

prepotent having the ability to transmit consistently specific characteristics to offspring.

R.E.H. Rettungshund – a dog working with ambulance services in disaster zones.

Roman nose incorrect convex curving of the muzzle, emphasizing the bridge of the nose.

sable a grey, brown or fawn foundation colour with black-shaded guard hairs. The wolf-like colouring of the original Shepherd Dogs. It is incorrect to describe a Shepherd as black and sable.

Sch.H. Schutzhund (protection dog) – the most common German working qualification, obtainable in three grades.

S.G. Sehr gut (very good) – an official German show grade and the highest obtainable by dogs under two years old.

slab-sided of flat ribs, lacking in correct curving or spring.

snipey of a muzzle which is too long, sharp, narrow or pointed, often with a weak underjaw.

stop the depression between the eyes where the skull runs into the muzzle.

SV   Verein für Deutsche Schäferhunde – the GSD Club of Germany.

tail-set   the root of the tail at the end of the croup.

S.1.   Stud Book (Germany).

T.D.   Tracking Dog – the highest British working qualification for nose-work, where the track must be at least three hours old.

throaty   having an excess of loose skin under the neck.

true moving   direct forward movement of limbs without deviation at foot, hock, knee or elbow.

U.D.   Utility Dog, British working qualification obtained in the first of the tracking stakes, where the track is half an hour old.

V.A.   Vorzüglich Auslese (excellent select) – the highest award attainable by a German show dog and granted only at the annual Sieger Show. On average some twelve to fifteen animals of each sex are selected for this honour each year.

'washed out'   marked paling of colour and pigment in nose and nails.

W.D.   Working Dog – the second tracking qualification earned at British working trials, where the track is at least one and a half hours old.

weaving   faulty action in front, when forelegs appear to be crossing over each other.

Z.H.   Zollhund – a dog trained to work with customs police.

Useful Addresses

American Kennel Club Inc.
  51 Madison Avenue
New York
NY 10010
USA
Tel. (212) 696 8329

Australian National Kennel Council
PO Box 285
Red Hill South
Victoria 3937
Australia
Tel. 00–61/015 304 338

British Association for German
  Shepherd Dogs
Copper Beech
81 Park View Road
Sutton Coldfield
West Midlands
B74 4PS
Tel. 0121 353 9872

German Shepherd Dog Breed Council
  of Great Britain
94a Shepherd Hill
Harold Wood
Essex
RM3 ONJ
Tel. 01708 342194

The German Shepherd Dog Club
  of America Inc.
30 Far View Road
Chalfont
PA 18914
Tel. (215) 822-6159

The GSD 'Alsatian' Club of the UK
Field House
Newton Place
Lee on the Solent
Hampshire
PO13 9JL

GSD League and Club of Great Britain
Warrantwood Farmhouse
Tern Hill
Market Drayton
Shropshire
TF9 2JH
Tel. 01630 638540

The Irish Kennel Club
Fottrell House
Greenmount Office Park
Dublin 6
Republic of Ireland
Tel. 00 353 533 300

The Kennel Club
1-5 Clarges Street
Piccadilly
London
W1Y 8AB
Tel. 0171 493 6651

Verein für Deutsche Schäferhunde
(SV)
Steinerne Furt 71/71a
86167 Augsburg
Germany
Tel. 0821/740 02-0

National Dog Tattoo Register
Tel. 01206 397510

233

Our Dogs
5 Oxford Road
Station Approach
Manchester
M60 1SX
Tel. 0161 228 1984

Dog World
Somerfield House
Wotton Road
Ashford
Kent
TN23 6LW
Tel. 01233 621877

Bibliography

Allen, R. and C., *A Dog Owner's Guide to German Shepherd Dogs*, Salamander Books (1988).
   The Essential German Shepherd Dog, Ringpress (1996).

Bennett, J.G., Delinger, M.G., Paramoure A.F., and Umlauff, G.M., *The Complete German Shepherd Dog*, Howell, New York (1970).

Cree, J., *Training the German Shepherd Dog*, The Crowood Press (1996).

Elliott, N. and P., *The Complete German Shepherd Dog*, Kaye and Ward (1983).

Hart, E.H., *The Complete German Shepherd Dog*, TFH, Neptune City, New Jersey (1985).

Ixer, J.M., *The Alsatian (The German Shepherd Dog)*, Bartholomew (1977).

Lanting, F.L., *The Total German Shepherd Dog*, Alpine, Loveland, Colorado (1996).

Nicholas, A.K., *The Book of the German Shepherd Dog*, TFH, Neptune City, New Jersey (1983).

Pickup, M., *All About the German Shepherd Dog*, Pelham (1973).
   The Alsatian Owner's Encyclopaedia, Pelham (1964).
   German Shepherd Guide, Pet Library, New York (1969).

Pickup, M., Schwabacker, J. and Gray, T., *The German Shepherd Dog* (9th ed. of Schwabacker), Popular Dogs (1990).

Strickland, W.G., and Moses, J.A., *The German Shepherd Today*, Macmillan, New York (1974).

Tidbold, M.E., *The German Shepherd Dog*, K. and R. Leicester (1978).

Von Stephanitz, M.F.E., *The German Shepherd Dog in Word and Picture*, SV, Augsburg (1923; 8th ed. 1950).

Willis, M.B., *The German Shepherd Dog : A Genetic History of the Breed*, Witherby (1991).
   The German Shepherd Dog, its History, Development and Genetics, K. and R. Leicester (1976).
   Pet Owner's Guide to German Shepherd Dogs, Ringpress (1995).

Wootton, B.H., *The German Shepherd Dog*, David and Charles (1988).

Magazines and Handbooks

The Breed Council of Great Britain: *National Magazine* (monthly); *Annual Handbook*.

The GSD League of Great Britain: *Annual Handbook*.

The SV: *Zeitung* (monthly), available only in German with annual membership subscription.

The British Schutzhund Association: *BSA News* (quarterly).

The German Shepherd Dog Council of Australia: *Quarterly National Review (German Shepherd Dog)*.

The German Shepherd Dog Club of America Inc.: *The German Shepherd Dog Review* (monthly); *Annual Red Book* – breeding and showing information.

The GSD 'Alsatian' Club of the UK: *Year Book*

Working Trials Monthly.

Index

237